BE A REAL ESTATE
MILLIONAIRE

BE A REAL ESTATE MILLIONAIRE

SECRET STRATEGIES FOR LIFETIME WEALTH TODAY

Dean Graziosi

Vanguard Press
A Member of the Perseus Books Group

Vanguard Press books are available at special discounts for bulk purchases in the U.S.
by corporations, institutions, and other organizations. For more information,
please contact the Special Markets Department at the Perseus Books Group,
2300 Chestnut St., Philadelphia, PA 19103
or email special.markets@perseusbooks.com.

Cataloging-in-Publication Data for this book is available from the Library of Congress.
ISBN-13: 978-1-59315-446-2; ISBN-10: 1-59315-446-1
Author's Edition: ISBN-13: 978-1-59315-469-1; ISBN-10: 1-59315-469-0

DESIGN BY JANE RAESE
Set in 11-point Dante

20 19 18 17 16 15 14 13 12 11

To my daughter

BREANA JEWEL GRAZIOSI

whose birth coincided with the completion of this book.

Your birth was the greatest gift I could have ever received

and I now know that you will be the inspiration

for my greatest accomplishments.

CONTENTS

Introduction   ix

PART I: MAKING A FORTUNE IN REAL ESTATE   I

In this part, I demystify the process of how the real estate market works from an investing point of view. In addition, I talk about what you need to do to get started investing.

1 Why Real Estate?   3

2 Cashing In on Real Estate   16

3 Identifying National and Regional Factors   27

4 Identifying Local Factors   41

5 Knowing Your Real Estate Market   53

6 Getting Started Investing in Real Estate   66

PART II: BUILDING A FOUNDATION FOR SUCCESS   83

Even though you may understand the real estate market, that knowledge is useless if mental blocks are delaying action. In this part, I explain how you can overcome problems and mental blocks that stand in the way to success.

7 Putting Your Finances in Order   85

8 Removing Your Mental Blocks to Success   98

9 Eliminating the Fear of Failure   114

10 Finding the Time to Improve Your Life   124

11 Making Your Goals a Reality   136

PART III: CREATING REAL ESTATE WEALTH   149

In this part, I explain how to apply the knowledge of Part I with the mental tools of Part II to create wealth in real estate by understanding cycles, strategies, and when to apply the right strategy for maximum profit.

12 Understanding the Different Types of Real Estate Investments   151

13 Identifying Loans and Finding Sources of Money   162

14 Buying Real Estate with No Money Down   179

15 Profiting from Lease Options and Locking Up Deals   198

16 Making Money with Foreclosures   212

17 Buying Pre-Foreclosures, REOs, and Short Sales   223

18 Cashing in on Tax Sales and Tax Liens   240

19 Managing Rental Property   251

20 Starting Your First Deal Now   267

Glossary   275

Acknowledgments   281

Resources   282

INTRODUCTION

If you've ever dreamed that you and your family could become financially independent, investing in real estate could be your answer. Making money from real estate isn't just for other people; it's for you!

I'm Dean Graziosi, and after spending years investing in and generating millions of dollars from real estate, I've learned the single most important lesson that most real estate experts never tell you: You can make money in any real estate market. After you learn my easy techniques for understanding real estate cycles, you'll learn what thousands of other self-made real estate millionaires and I have learned—there is a fortune to be made whether the real estate market in your area is booming, flat, or falling. Even better, you don't need a lot of money or experience to get started.

Real estate investing is easier than you think, and this book will show you what to do, when to do it, and how to do it. Think about the real estate market in your own area. Prices might be skyrocketing, which means you could make a fortune buying a piece of property now, cleaning it up with new carpets, landscaping, or paint, and selling it a short time later at a huge profit (a technique known as a "fix and flip"). On the other hand, maybe the real estate market in your area is doing the opposite. Now might be the time to buy foreclosures and distressed properties for pennies on the dollar, rent them to cover your costs, and hold onto them until the market goes up again and you can sell them at a huge profit.

The point is that you can always make money in real estate by identifying the current real estate cycle and then applying the proper money-making strategy to maximize your profits within that cycle. I promise that this is a hundred times easier than you could ever imagine, and I'll be with you every step of the way to show you exactly what to do.

Everything I teach in this book comes from my own experience. I've been doing real estate transactions non-stop for more than twenty years and have generated millions of dollars because of it. To be honest, I've sometimes failed miserably, but most of the time I've made a fortune. If my methods can work for me, they can work for anyone, including you.

I never went past high school, I'm terrible at learning in a classroom setting, and I've read only a handful of books. Even though I was never the best student, I know I am good at two things: making money in real estate by thinking outside the box and teaching others how to make money in real estate by following my simple steps. Think of this book as your action plan for success and the tool for you to gain financial independence.

What does financial independence mean to you? Whatever your answer, I bet it means less about having a big stack of cash in your pocket and more about having control over your life. Maybe you want to provide better things for your family, have a nest egg for retirement, reduce stress, or have more time to explore your own creativity. Financial independence allows you to take charge of your destiny and become the person you were meant to be.

I wasn't born rich and I didn't get the best education. As a kid, I wore hand-me-downs, grew up in the only trailer park in town, and lived with my mom, who worked two jobs just to make about $90 a week. Kids made fun of my mom's car because it was so junky, and because of that I made her drop me off a few blocks from school just to avoid the teasing.

I hated watching my mom work so hard for other people and get nothing from it, but I was fortunate enough to discover something at an early age. If I wanted something, I had to take action. Not just talk about it, not just dream about it, but do something to get it.

What gave me financial independence was taking action in real estate. Real estate made me a millionaire in my twenties and a multimillionaire in my thirties. The amount of money I've made, however, is far less important than the freedom it has given me. I can afford to give my family the better things in life, travel all over the world, and never worry about retirement or being forced to work for anyone else. Financial independence can give you freedom, confidence, security, and so much more.

Take a look at just a few of the people who used my techniques to start making money in real estate and changed their financial future forever:

- Scott, a college student, closed his first real estate deal at the tender young age of twenty and netted more than $10,000 profit after just five hours of work. This one transaction made him more money than all of his past summer jobs.
- Paul from Maryland had never done anything with real estate before and on his very first foreclosure deal he profited over $106,000 in less than 4 days without using any of his own money.
- Nathan liked his job but his salary just barely covered his bills and it definitely did not leave him any money for saving or to invest. Yet after two short years, he had purchased almost a dozen properties worth more than $1.2 million dollars—without using a dollar of his own money. His

net worth has gone to more than $300,000, an amount he said he could never have saved in a lifetime if he didn't start investing in real estate.

- John and his wife, Vickie, earned more money on two real estate transactions than Vickie made in an entire year. That allowed Vickie to quit her job, buy their son a home, and take vacations they could only once dream about. They celebrated their twenty-fifth wedding anniversary by visiting Hawaii, paying cash for the trip with the money they made from real estate.
- Suzanna, a single schoolteacher from Denver, overcame her fears, ignored her skeptics, and made more than $20,000 with eighteen hours work on her first real estate investment. To save that same amount of money on her teacher's salary would have taken many years.
- Louie was a landscaper whose wife lost her job (and benefits) at the same time she got pregnant. By using my techniques, Louie not only paid his bills, but earned enough to live in a beautiful home. He currently has a net worth of more than $500,000—all without using a penny of his own money.

You'll learn more about these stories plus many of my own throughout the book. There is no better way to learn than from the experiences of others. My real estate methods have worked for construction workers, landscapers, teachers, stay-at-home moms, secretaries, state workers, computer technicians, hospital workers, janitors, and car mechanics. They all came from different backgrounds, but they all shared one thing in common: They decided they were sick of the rut they were in and gave my real estate investing techniques a try.

Right now, you may be where these people once were. Now is the time to take action. Let me show you how to use real estate investing to achieve the life you've always wanted. It doesn't matter where you live, what you do for a living, or what your background is. All that matters is your own desire to get more out of life.

This could be the first time in your life you have a chance to stop hoping for a new life and start creating it. Don't let old habits, fear, or criticism hold you back. Let go of your fear and take advantage of a proven and easy-to-understand wealth-building system.

What I'm going to show you are the two steps to minimizing your risk and maximizing your profits in real estate. First, you must understand the current real estate cycle. Second, you have to apply the proper strategy to make money in that cycle. It's that simple!

You owe it to yourself and your family to at least try. Now let's work as a team and show the world your real potential.

PART ONE

Making a Fortune in Real Estate

In this part, I demystify the process of how the real estate market works from an investing point of view. In addition, I talk about what you need to do to get started investing.

CHAPTER 1
WHY REAL ESTATE?

Every day, you'll have opportunities to take chances and to work out-side your safety net. Sure, it's a lot easier to stay in your comfort zone . . . but sometimes you have to take risks. When the risks pay off, that's when you reap the biggest rewards.

Are you rich? Do you have everything you want? A nice car? A great relationship? The house of your dreams? The freedom to go anywhere and do anything regardless of the time or cost? If you can answer yes to each of these questions, congratulations! You're living a totally fulfilled life with no limits on your potential.

But if you're like most Americans, you probably can't answer yes to all these questions. You may be working forty or more hours a week, earning just enough money to slowly keep sinking a little more into debt every month. Maybe you're relying on credit cards to keep paying your bills, but you know that can't last forever. Even worse, do you even know whether you'll have a job next month? Next year? With outsourcing, downsizing, and corporate bankruptcies, working a job is no longer a secure way of making a living.

What about your retirement? If you're having trouble paying your monthly bills, you can't set anything aside for retirement. By the time you reach retirement age, Social Security may be paying only a fraction of what you should be getting—if Social Security is even around to pay you anything at all. In a typical year, how much time do you spend working on a detailed, practical retirement plan that has a realistic chance of being implemented? Or are you like most people, who have a "someday" wish list. "Someday, I'm going to retire." "Someday, I'm going to pay off the mortgage." "Someday, I'll travel to Europe."

Maybe working a second job might help pay the bills, but at what cost to your physical well-being, emotional state, and the time you spend with your family and friends? Do you want to work so hard and for so long just to pay your bills? I don't think so, and that's why I'm here to tell you that there's another way to live. You may be thinking, "Well, this is a great book! You just reminded me of all the stressful things in my life." But I want you to remember what bothers you so you'll take action. I have a proven system that could change your life and your destiny.

My method isn't a form of gambling because you can implement many of my strategies and never risk losing any of your own money. Gambling is for wishers and dreamers, but the outcome is always out of your control. The odds always favor the house. So why not shift the odds in your favor? My method is for doers, which means the outcome is in your hands at all times.

My method doesn't need special training or education. I know this can work without an education because I never went past high school.

My method is like starting your own business, except it won't cost a lot of money, won't take up all your time, and won't burden you with upfront costs.

This bears repeating. My method allows you to start your own business! When you consider that close to 90% of all businesses fail in the first few years, you'll be glad that my method doesn't involve owning and running a traditional business. And most importantly, if you follow what I have been able to learn and what thousands of my students have already done all over the country, you could make a fortune and take control of your destiny.

You're probably ready to scream, "Okay, okay! What exactly is your method?"

Before I tell you about my method, let me tell you its advantages. First, you can get started right away at no cost. Second, you can get started in your spare time and then decide to go full-time later if you want. Third, you can get started where you live. Fourth, you can make a little money or a lot. The only person setting limits on how much you can make is you.

Now you're probably really screaming, "Okay, okay. Just what is your method that can lead to financial freedom?" Here it is: Real estate. I'm not talking about buying and selling exotic properties such as oil fields or gold mines, nor am I talking about buying and selling Donald Trump-like sky-scrapers or luxury hotels. I'm talking about buying and selling ordinary, everyday homes and property.

Before you tell yourself that you know nothing about real estate or that real estate is too complicated, let me ask you this: If you don't try something new, what do you think you'll have one year from now? Five years from now? Ten or twenty years from now? Real estate investing is for anyone who wants to make money and change his or her life.

If you don't change and try something new, chances are good that you'll have more of what you already have. But because you're reading this book, you probably want more out of life. That means you need to change —and the sooner the better.

If you don't change and try something new, chances are good that you'll just have more of what you already have. Because you're reading this book, however, you probably want more out of life. That means you have to change. But what exactly do you need to change to reach your goals? Here's another question: Do you believe that you could become a millionaire if you followed the same success principles that millionaires use? Of course! Success is like a recipe. If you use the same ingredients and follow the same step-by-step instructions, you'll create the same results like anyone else.

Millionaires make their money in different ways, but almost every one invests at least part of that money in a safe investment that's virtually guaranteed to increase in value. Guess what safe investment millionaires depend on? Real estate!

Now your first comment may be, "Millionaires can afford to invest in real estate but not someone like me." Let me show you why that type of thinking is wrong:

- Real estate is everywhere. Somebody is selling real estate and somebody is buying real estate no matter the location, the weather, or the time of year. Ordinary people buy and sell houses all the time. Why can't that person be you?
- Anyone can do it. Doctors and lawyers can make a lot of money but look how many years of education they need before they can even get started. Real estate is different. You don't need a license, special education, or long years of training. You can get started right now, and I'll show you how.
- Real estate can generate huge profits. One real estate transaction can earn as much profit as most people make in a year. Think about that. Would you rather work all year for the same amount of money you could make in a fraction of that time?
- You can get started with no money down. What other type of investment enables you to potentially earn thousands, hundreds of thousands, or even millions of dollars without risking a penny of your own money? If this sounds impossible or unbelievable, read on and I'll tell you exactly how to do it.

Real estate is one of the fastest, easiest, and safest paths to financial freedom if you know the real estate market you're in and apply the proper strategy. Here's just one of the many secrets that make real estate investing so profitable.

Almost every millionaire invests in real estate. Real estate is one of the fastest, easiest, and safest paths to financial freedom.

Suppose someone gave you $10,000 to invest. What would you do? Put the money in the bank? If you earned 5% interest, your investment would be worth $12,762.82 after five years. Not bad, but with the current rate of inflation of 3% per year, your investment may not make you much in the long run after you pay Federal income taxes. In other words, you are barely keeping up with inflation.

What about investing your $10,000 in the stock market? A good mutual fund can earn 10% to 15% a year. Not bad, but not all mutual funds will earn that amount. Some go up and down just like stocks do.

Maybe you can get a much higher rate of return by buying stocks, but which stock do you choose? Even stock analysts can't agree on which stock will increase in value, and guessing proves nearly as accurate as relying on the advice of so-called stock experts. Stock values can go up tremendously, but many more go down or increase slowly. Although you can make money in the stock market, even the best knowledge can't guarantee a profit. Do you want to hedge your future on something as unpredictable as the stock market?

What about starting a traditional brick-and-mortar type business? Your $10,000 may not even get you in the front door. Maybe a restaurant? Only about 10% of new restaurants nationwide ever make it.

If you invest $10,000 in the stock market, a bank account, or a business, what do you have? A $10,000 investment. But look at what happens if you invest $10,000 in real estate using a principle known as *cash on cash returns*. Even with a traditional loan and a down payment of $10,000, you can purchase a $100,000 property. So your $10,000 investment is actually worth $100,000. Where else can you buy a $100,000 investment for a fraction of its actual value? And unlike any other investment, you can buy all types of real estate without using any of your own money. Imagine the type of return that can yield!

Suppose your real estate property increases in value from $100,000 to $110,000. You've just earned back your $10,000 investment, for a 100% return. How many other types of investments can give you a potential 100% return in such a short time? It's as simple as this: If you got 5% interest on your $10,000 in the bank, you would make $500 in one year. If you used that same $10,000 for a down payment on a $100,000 home and it went up in value the same 5%, you would earn $5,000 on your money because you are making a profit on the entire worth of the property, not just your investment.

Real estate is the only type of investment that allows you to invest with little or no money down but still gain 100% of the appreciation from the entire value of the property. You get 100% ownership, 100% of any rental income the property generates, 100% of all appreciation, and best of all, 100% of the tax advantages. And you're not using all your money to buy the property, which essentially lets you get rich on somebody else's (the bank's) money.

Now let me improve the return on your investment even further. We will get into the details of rents and expenses in later chapters, but assume for a moment that after collecting rent and paying the taxes, insurance, and mortgage, you net an additional $100 per month, or $1200 per year. If you divide the $1200 net positive cash flow per year by your $10,000 initial investment in this property, your cash on cash return on investment is an additional 12% per year. And I haven't even touched on the increase in your return as a result of the income tax benefits.

Real estate isn't just an investment; it's a wealth-building strategy that lets you leverage your money—or lack thereof—to gain the advantages of a higher-priced investment at a fraction of its actual cost.

If this little secret to leveraging your money in real estate hasn't opened your eyes to the possibilities available to you, keep reading. I'm going to tell you every secret I know because I sincerely hope you will take action to improve your financial future. Even if you decide not to invest in real estate, I urge you to write down your goals, develop a plan, and take action now for achieving financial freedom in any way you choose.

I believe that real estate is the best investment option available. It allowed me—a regular guy with only a high school education, from a small town, starting with no money—to live a life I once only dreamed of. I've seen it work for hundreds of people who have followed my step-by-step real estate investing plans. It changed their lives from ones of despair and pessimism to ones of hope and optimism.

I know my real estate plan will work because I've tested it over and over. These techniques aren't something I dreamed up on the beach one day. They are proven techniques I learned through trial and error by studying other successful people. These are the techniques I'm going to share with you.

What you're getting is the best advice I know, but it's up to you to use my plan and take action to turn your life around. My plan is a roadmap, but you are the catalyst. Take action now! You owe it to yourself to live the best life possible.

WHAT IF I DON'T HAVE $10,000?

Maybe you are like most people and don't have $10,000 to start your real estate investing career. If so, you are probably a little frustrated right now and are asking yourself, "Where am I going to get my initial down payment money?" I have dozens of creative methods, developed over twenty years of investing, to get you started with little or no money of your own.

Now you might be thinking this isn't for real—that you can't invest in real estate without money. You will soon learn about locking up deals and assigning them to other buyers for huge profits, lease options, seller financing, foreclosures in which you get paid to take ownership of the property, tax sales, and much more.

A million dollars in property with no money down

Throughout this book, I share real-life stories in which I or one of my students used the strategies explained in this book to achieve massive success. Did it happen on its own or magically? Of course not. Armed with the knowledge of what to do and how to do it, successful students then took action to make it happen.

Real-Life Story

Nathan and his family live on the outskirts of Kansas City, Missouri. Before ordering my "Think a Little Different" real estate course, he had never invested in real estate. He thought that the only way to purchase property was if you had money saved for the purpose. Then he tried my no-money-down investing techniques.

In the two years since Nathan started, he bought eleven houses with a combined value of well over a million dollars, using none of his own money. He rents all his properties, earns a positive cash flow each month, and has increased his net worth by $300,000.

This is how Nathan bought his first foreclosure: He told his realtor that he wanted to look for some properties that were in foreclosure or that had already gone through foreclosure. His realtor called him a few days later with ten foreclosures to look at, one of which was a bank REO (you learn about REOs in Chapter 17).

When he saw the property, he was shocked. It was a beautiful five-bedroom, three-bathroom house on a one-acre, fenced lot. Nathan felt that the price was about $40,000 less than the market value. He told the realtor to start the paperwork because he wanted it. Nathan asked for a concession to pay for minor repairs and carpet. (The *concession* meant that the bank had to give back some of the purchase price to cover repairs.) The bank agreed and gave him $1200. He did the repairs for half that amount. Plus he used 100% financing for the property. (You will learn how to do this in Part III.) He wound up purchasing the house without a dime of his own money and ended up with $600 in his pocket.

He rents the house, and the tenants pay all his expenses plus give him an additional profit of a few hundred dollars every month—all while his equity in the property continues to grow. What a great deal for his first foreclosure!

Now if you're thinking that it seems like Nathan knew what he was doing, you're right. But he only put into practice the same principles I will be sharing with you in this book. So get ready for a life-changing experience.

It doesn't take money to make money

When I tell people about the incredible opportunities available in real estate, the first question most ask is, "Does it take a lot of money?" I've found that you can reword this question into another one that most people are too afraid to ask, "If I make a mistake investing in real estate, could I lose everything I own?"

As I explain in Chapter 14, you can invest in real estate without risking a single penny of your own money. I know this may sound too good to be true, but it's not.

Even if you invest your own money in real estate, can you really lose it all? If you put $10,000 in the stock market and the company goes out of business, you could lose your entire $10,000 investment. If you put $10,000 to start your own business and it fails, you could lose all $10,000.

If you invest $10,000 in real estate, you actually own more than a $10,000 piece of property. Depending on the real estate market, your property could be worth $100,000 or more. Historically, real estate appreciation has always increased faster than inflation.

If property values go up, your $100,000 property could conceivably be worth $120,000 or more, netting you a profit. If property values go down, you can still make money by renting your property and using the rent money to pay off the mortgage, essentially giving you the property for free. When the real estate market eventually increases, you can sell the property at a profit. And this is only one strategy of many that you are about to learn on making money in a booming or falling real estate market.

It is possible to lose money investing in real estate, and I've made plenty of mistakes. The main reason people lose money in real estate is by using the wrong strategy at the wrong time. For example, between 2001 and early 2006, home prices in Phoenix, Arizona rose at unprecedented rates. It was almost impossible not to make money by simply buying a property, cleaning it up, and putting it back on the market. I bought the house across the street from mine with 100% financing for $493,000. I then painted it, cleaned the carpets, and put in new appliances. Six weeks later, I sold the house for

$639,000. After paying the realtor's commission and the cost for the repairs, I pocketed more than $100,000.

What would have happened if I had bought that same house, fixed it up, and tried to sell it when the Phoenix real estate market was experiencing a downturn? If you guessed that I'd lose money, you're right! This is the way too many people invest in real estate, buying property and hoping that prices will rise. But as I'll show you, you can make money in any real estate market if you follow appropriate strategies.

I bought my first piece of property more than twenty years ago. Starting without a mentor, money, or experience, I made plenty of mistakes. But out of the millions of dollars in real estate transactions I've made over the years, I've lost money on only one piece of property, mainly because I was not experienced enough to read the real estate cycle I was in. Investing in real estate is more about how much you can make rather than how much you could lose. By following my methods, you'll avoid the mistakes that took me decades to learn, and you'll learn the techniques that can make you money the fastest, easiest way possible.

The best way to avoid losing a lot of money investing in real estate is to start with as little money of your own as possible. Ultimately, success in real estate investing depends less on the amount of money you invest and more on the amount of knowledge you apply.

REAL ESTATE INVESTING IS NOT DIFFICULT

Investing in real estate may seem confusing and complicated with all those contracts, property titles, and legal forms, but it's not. The main reason real estate investing seems so confusing is because it's new to most people.

What are you really good at? Are you good at your job? Your hobby? Being a parent? Being good at something gives you the confidence to make decisions that less experienced people might shy away from. If you are a parent, you probably go about your daily routine as if it were nothing. But to someone who isn't a parent, your tasks might seem overwhelming, difficult, or even impossible

If you tried to teach me how to do a skill that you excel at, do you think I could? Yes! Maybe not as well as you at first—or ever—but I can learn from you and you can teach me.

In my case, I know real estate! I've made millions in real estate where others could not see the profit, and I've taught thousands of people all over the country how to make money in real estate. So I know how to personally profit from real estate as well as how to teach others to make money from real estate. By reading this book and following my step-by-step approach, you'll gradually gain confidence and learn how to do everything that I've done. If I can do it, you can too!

Learning how to invest in real estate requires time. The good news is that I'll tell you exactly what to do and how to do it. Even better, I'll show you shortcuts to help you get started investing like a real estate pro. Remember, you don't have to learn everything from scratch like I did. You'll be using my proven, time-tested methods, and I'll walk you through every step.

All the knowledge you need to get started is right here. The only way you can fail is by not taking action.

FEAR OF CHANGE

The one permanent emotion of the inferior man is fear—
fear of the unknown, the complex, the inexplicable.
What he wants above everything else is safety.
—HENRY LOUIS MENCKEN

For most people, perhaps the biggest obstacle to realizing their dreams is the fear of change. Oftentimes it's easier to face the misery that we know rather than taking a chance to face the unknown.

When people first go to prison, they hate it. The longer they stay there, the more they start to tolerate it. If they stay too long, they start embracing it until finally the thought of leaving is more painful than the problems of staying. When people can no longer function outside prison, they're said to be institutionalized. If they were set free tomorrow, they would be so terrified at the thought of freedom that they would do anything to return to the known miseries of prison, where they feel comfortable and safe.

Don't let yourself become institutionalized. If your job isn't the best it could be, it's time to change. If your relationship isn't the greatest it could be, it's time to change the way you behave or it's time to find a new relationship. If you're not happy with your house or car, it's time to make a change.

Here's a secret when it comes to change. Everyone is afraid of change. Courage comes from going through with change, accepting it, and adapting to it.

You can't stop change, so you might as well learn to embrace it. If you do absolutely nothing, guess what? The world around you changes anyway and ultimately forces you to change.

Later in the book, I share with you the same proven techniques that I shared with people in my bestselling book, *Totally Fulfilled*. I'll show you how to embrace change and make it something you look forward to instead of fear. You will love the new outlook you can gain from these simple techniques, and they will help eliminate the fear of change in your life forever.

FEAR OF THE UNKNOWN

You block your dream when you allow your fear
to grow bigger than your faith.
—MARY MANIN MORRISSEY

Combined with the fear of change is the fear of the unknown. Starting anything new can be frightening. Remember your first day of school? You may have been going to that school for the past few years, but starting a new school year always created anxiety until you settled into a routine.

One student told me that he watched my TV show for years, contemplating whether he should get my program. He had plenty of discussions with his wife about whether or not they should take the chance. Now remember, this isn't the fear of buying his first property but the fear of just getting the course. He was brought up in such a structured home that anything out of the ordinary—in this case, investing in real estate without using your own money—was fearful.

Eventually, he purchased my course, my book, and some advanced training. He is now on his eleventh property, his net worth is $300,000, he has a positive cash flow from the properties he bought with no money down, and his outlook on life has changed. I'll tell you more about him later in the book.

Doing anything new causes that same feeling of anxiety. When I bought my first property, I was nervous and frightened. I didn't have anyone to guide me or any books to help me. I felt anxious and fearful. Fear is natural.

People who succeed face their fears and take action despite them. People who succeed have an undying passion to accomplish and achieve their dreams and goals. People who succeed believe in themselves, are highly focused, are driven, and use fear as a motivator to find a way to achieve.

Now if you're saying, "Maybe I'm not that kind of person," I say you're wrong. We are all that person on the inside, but in many cases an unsatisfied life has beaten us down. Or we looked for an opportunity for a better way for so long with poor results that we gave up. You have the ingredients to overcome anything, to embrace the unknown, and to accomplish your dreams—you just may need to wipe away those cobwebs and find the inner you that deserves to come back in view.

You can never eliminate fear, but you can use your fear and turn it into your strength. If your fear tells you that you might lose a lot of money, great! Take some extra time to thoroughly study the situation and do whatever you can to protect yourself. If your fear tells you that real estate is too complicated or hard to understand, great! Use the examples of other people in this book and on my web site at www.deangraziosi.com to build confidence. Any time your fear tells you that you can't do something, use that as motivation to learn more so that the reason behind your fear melts away. Your fear is doing nothing more than trying to protect you. Use it!

Your fear might be telling you that you can't make money investing in real estate, but put your fear aside for a moment and I'll show you exactly how you can succeed. I'll give you real-life examples so you can learn what other people did right (and wrong). I'll guide you through real estate investing so you'll know exactly what to expect, what to do, and what to look for. I'll show you how to find, evaluate, and analyze properties. I'll lead you through a process that will allow you to understand real estate as a whole. By the time you finish this book, you'll know more about real estate transactions than most people out there already making money.

Your fear may come from a lack of resources. I'll show you everything I know, but if there's anything you don't understand, ask questions from other people and keep searching for answers so you can keep moving forward. Don't let fear paralyze you. Let fear motivate you!

Preparation and knowledge can calm your fears and increase your confidence, so when it comes time to take action, you'll feel comfortable. Like any skill, the more you learn and take action investing in real estate, the easier it will get. Remember, knowledge without action is just good reading but knowledge combined with action equals results.

I will show you how to establish a team of professionals who can act as advisors in real estate transactions: real estate agents, attorneys, insurance agents, home inspectors and appraisers, accountants and CPAs, bankers, property managers, and contractors. Although we are all responsible for our own decisions, I will show you how to best utilize the strengths of your network of professionals and how to avoid overreliance on them as well. I will show you the qualities I look for when I am selecting my team.

After you overcome your initial fear of real estate investing, it's only natural for new fears to pop up. Maybe you're afraid of paying too much for a property. Maybe you're afraid of buying property at the "wrong" time. Relax! I'll show you how to minimize those fears by teaching you how to evaluate properties and make money regardless of the real estate cycle. I want you to develop the confidence to analyze property and determine whether to purchase it, how much to pay for it, and how to turn a losing property into a winner. There is rarely a wrong time to buy property because I'll show you how to make money whether the real estate market is shooting up, falling down, or doing nothing. The secret to my real estate techniques isn't timing but applying the proper strategy to maximize your profits no matter what the real estate market is doing.

You can build on my foundation. I'm confident that if you follow my techniques, you can be successful at real estate investing too! If you study successful people, you'll find one common thread to their success. They have a passionate commitment to achieving their goals. When you combine passion with goals and a solid program to guide you, fear takes a back seat to your passion and desire to achieve. You provide the passion and dream and I'll provide the plan to show you how to get there. So let's get started!

ONE OF MY FIRST REAL ESTATE DEALS

I think that as we get older, trying something new becomes harder because we get stuck in our ways. I ask that you read this book with a childlike enthusiasm and think of no option except that it can work for you if you apply my proven principles and strategies.

Taking action always outweighs overanalyzing. But the right combination of knowledge and action is even better, and that's what you're going to learn in this book.

One reason my first real estate deal worked was because I never thought that it wasn't going to work. My youth and inexperience kept me focused on winning and nothing else. If I had been older and overanalyzed the situation, I may have never have done it.

In my late teens, I was flat broke. An apartment house in town had once been a decent place, but the owners had let the wrong tenants in and the place began to deteriorate. Soon there were broken-down cars in the yard, garbage piled in the hallways, a broken front door, and some busted windows.

This apartment house was for sale, but its horrible appearance meant that no bank was going to give anyone a loan to buy it. It wouldn't have been able to get a certificate of occupancy, and in most cases, you can't close on a piece of property unless a certificate of occupancy exists. A *certificate of occupancy* means the property is livable—and this place wasn't, especially with the front porch ready to fall down with an eight-foot drop underneath it.

After some negotiations with the sellers on the price, I told them, "I'd like forty-five days to clean that place up, but then you have to sell it to me. To keep you from selling it to anybody else, I'm going to give you a tiny down payment. But in forty-five days, I will start pursuing a bank loan. Then I have sixty days from that point to close on the property."

The seller agreed. Now here is the scary part that I would not suggest anyone else do. Once the seller and I had a deal, I immediately went to work on the place before I even knew whether I could get a bank loan. I thought if the bank were to look at this place before I made it look pretty, I would never get the loan.

So I blindly put my heart, soul, and sweat equity into cleaning up the place. First, I got rid of the junk in the front yard by calling a junk dealer, who took everything away for free so he could sell it for scrap. Then I got together with some friends and hired the cheapest laborers I could find. Together, we fixed all the broken windows, the front door, and the porch. My contract with the owners allowed me to evict some of the worst tenants, so I got rid of the ones who were unwilling to be part of the massive cleanup.

We planted flowers across the front, mowed the lawn, trimmed the hedges, and painted the front of the building. Then we went inside and painted the hallway and cleaned up a couple of the apartments that we had evicted people from. They were nice apartments; they just needed to be cleaned.

In forty-five days, the building looked gorgeous. I then went to the bank and was fortunate enough to get a loan. In fact, I got a loan for 100% of the money I needed because the property appraised for much more money than I was buying it for. I kept that apartment house for many years, and each month I enjoyed great positive cash flow from it. Then I sold it during a peak cycle and made a wonderful profit.

What a great learning experience and what a great sense of accomplishment. To this day, I can remember standing on the front lawn, looking at the house after I purchased the property, and feeling the sense of accomplishment that came from knowing I did everything I said I was going to do.

CONCLUSION

Now I don't suggest that you rush into your first deal like I did. But looking back, I was so aggressive because I knew what I wanted and I wasn't going to let anything stand in my way. There was no "what if" option—only "when."

If a naive kid—who came from no money, had no mentors, and never went to college—can do it, you can too. This book will give you the tools you need to get started. You just have to promise me that you'll take action. Your first deal could be just weeks away.

CHAPTER 2

CASHING IN ON REAL ESTATE

*What is important is to keep learning, to enjoy challenge, and
to tolerate ambiguity. In the end there are no certain answers.*
—MARTINA HORNER,
PRESIDENT OF RADCLIFFE COLLEGE

In early 2005, real estate prices in Phoenix were skyrocketing. I bought a house in my neighborhood for $525,000, cleaned it up, and sold it thirteen months later for $710,000. Some people work a lifetime to save up the kind of money I made on this one real estate transaction.

Now you might be saying, "Anyone can make money in real estate when the market is hot." That's true in many cases, but everyone also knows that hot markets last only so long and then they become cold again—and that's exactly what happened a few months later. By the middle of 2006, the Phoenix real estate market completely changed when the supply of houses far outstripped the demand. Not only were houses selling much more slowly than before, but their prices were dropping. This is the time when un-informed investors can lose money. In the current Phoenix market, if you tried buying a house, fixing it up, and selling it right away for a profit, you would likely lose money. That's the time when too many people throw up their hands in disgust and mutter to themselves, "Real estate investing just isn't for me."

The problem isn't the market or real estate investing in general. The problem is using the wrong strategy and not understanding market cycles and adjusting to them accordingly.

Let's say you're playing baseball and pitching against the other team's best hitter. For your first pitch, you throw a fastball right down the middle and the batter swings and misses. You might be thinking that the batter can't hit your fastball, so for your second pitch, you throw the same fastball right down the middle and the batter swings and misses again.

Now you're starting to think you can do nothing wrong, so for your third pitch, you throw the same fastball right down the middle—and the batter knocks it out of the ballpark for a home run.

What did you do wrong? You kept applying the same strategy even though outside circumstances were changing. The first and second time you threw a fastball, you might have surprised the batter. But the third time you threw the same fastball, the batter was ready and waiting. When outside circumstances change, make sure your strategy changes too.

A common definition of insanity is doing the same thing over and over and expecting a different result. I'd like to modify that and say that doing the same thing over and over and expecting the same result even under different circumstances is also a form of insanity. That's why I urge you to think outside the box. Don't just look at what everyone else is doing. Look at the same situation from different points of view.

When the real estate market falls, most people are ready to think like Chicken Little and proclaim that the sky is falling. That's not the time to flee the real estate market. That's the time to switch gears and adopt a different strategy. And that is exactly what I do. Instead of looking for properties to buy, fix, and quickly sell (flip) for a profit, I look for foreclosures and distressed properties that I can buy for a major discount, rent to pay expenses, and sell when the market goes back up. For example, a few weeks before I wrote this, I purchased a two-family home in foreclosure for less than $60,000. I immediately refinanced the property for $192,000 and walked away with a check for well over $100,000 after all expenses were paid, and I still owned the property! Now I can rent this property to cover the mortgage and when the home market takes off again (and it will eventually), I'll be able to sell it for a profit or hold it through the next up cycle.

Could I buy a house during a hot real estate market and rent it out? Of course! But if you don't sell the property at a profit during a hot market, the market will change and you'll miss out on your opportunity to walk away with a good chunk of cash. Notice that as long as you understand the up and down cycles of real estate, you can't lose; you just might not walk away with the maximum amount of profit.

That's what makes the secret of my book so simple. First, you have to understand what real estate market or cycle you are in. Then you have to apply the proper strategy to make money in that cycle. In this way, you can minimize your risk and maximize your profits.

TIMING IS EVERYTHING—WRONG!

You cannot afford to wait for perfect conditions. Goal setting is
often a matter of balancing timing against valuable resources.
Opportunities are easily lost while waiting for perfect conditions.
—GARY RYAN BLAIR

Most people only know and use one strategy. Then they try to time the market so their strategy provides the maximum payout. But timing is difficult and chances are good that you'll never get it right. My method is different because it doesn't rely on timing.

I'm not saying that timing isn't important. I'm saying that what's more important is correctly identifying the current market conditions and then applying the right strategy. Once you can predict the real estate market you're in, you'll know exactly what the market is going to do and you'll know exactly how to profit from it. And unlike the stock market, which can change or crash overnight, the real estate market takes months and in most cases years to change, so it is easier to forecast changes and plan.

When most people talk about timing, they're usually talking about buying properties when the real estate market has hit rock bottom and then trying to sell those same properties when the real estate market has reached its peak. The problem with this strategy is that you have to guess correctly when the real estate market has hit rock bottom and then guess correctly a second time when it has climbed back to its peak. Unfortunately, by the time you identify the rock bottom cycle of the real estate market, prices will have already started climbing. Then by the time you identify the peak of a real estate cycle, prices will have already begun falling. Most of the time, you're going to guess too early or too late.

Basically, all you need to know are four terms:

- An *up market* is when prices are rising. An up market is also called a *seller's market* because there are more buyers than sellers. The sellers can raise their prices to the maximum the market will allow due to multiple buyers scrambling to buy before the market goes even higher.

> *Real estate prices always rise and fall in a cycle. An* **up market** *is when prices are rising, a* **down market** *is when prices are dropping, a* **peak market** *is when prices are at their maximum, and a* **bottom market** *is when prices hit their lowest point.*

- A *down market* is when prices are dropping. A down market is also called a *buyer's market* because more people are selling properties than buying them. During this time, buyers can name their price and sellers will often accept less money just to get rid of their property.
- A *peak market* is when prices are at their maximum. A peak market is also called a *bubble market* because that's when prices reach the highest they're going to go before they start sinking back down. During a bubble market, the number of buyers and sellers is starting to equal out, so prices start falling.

- A *bottom market* is when prices hit their lowest point. A bottom market is when prices reach their absolute lowest level. This is when the number of buyers once again nearly equals the number of sellers, which starts the up and down cycle of the real estate market all over again.

Figure 2.1 identifies the different cycles of the real estate market. Sometimes prices are rising, sometimes they're falling, and sometimes they've reached their peak or bottom before changing directions. Think about your own area. You've probably seen or heard about prices rising or falling, but everyone knows that nothing lasts forever. Every time prices fall, they'll eventually rise again, and when prices rise, they'll eventually slow down and fall.

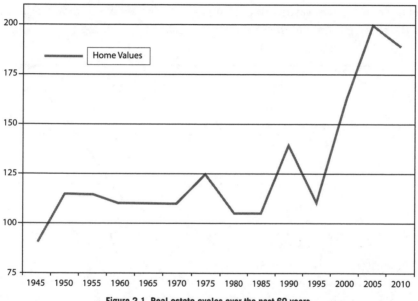

Figure 2.1 Real estate cycles over the past 60 years

Sometimes prices are falling or stagnant for long periods of time, and sometimes prices rise quickly and then taper off just as fast. No matter how long a cycle lasts or how high (and low) it goes, real estate always rises and falls in a cycle. The key to success is identifying what part of the cycle your real estate market is in. In this chapter, I'll show you exactly how to do it.

By understanding the predictable, cyclical nature of real estate prices, you'll never have to worry about whether you're in a booming market or a "bubble is about to burst" market. You can make money in any market as long as you use the proper strategy.

The highs and lows of real estate cycles may not be easy to predict, but overall real estate prices always increase over time. You've probably heard your grandparents telling you how they could have bought land decades ago for a small amount of cash, and now that same property is worth hundreds of thousands or even millions of dollars. But have you ever heard anyone complaining that they bought land decades ago and now that same land is worth less?

Furthermore, whatever a piece of property is selling for now, someday someone will say, "I remember when I could have bought that piece of property for $2000 an acre and now it is worth $100,000 an acre." Some day someone will wish they bought that property at $100,000 an acre when it is worth $150,000 or maybe $200,000. Historically, the average real estate price has always increased. As Figure 2.2 shows, real estate prices may go up and down, but the overall trend is for prices to increase in the long term. What makes real estate investing so exciting is that it's possible to make money in both the long term and the short term.

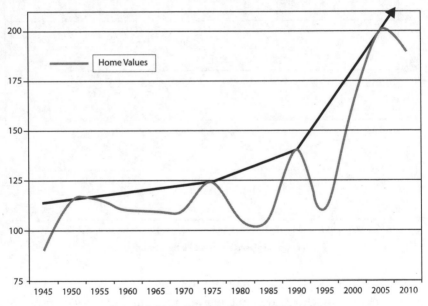

Figure 2.2 Real estate prices may go up and down but
average real estate prices increase over time

WHAT TYPE OF REAL ESTATE SHOULD I INVEST IN?

Before we go any further, you may be wondering what type of real estate you should invest in. Should you specialize in family homes or condominiums, or should you buy anything if it looks like a good deal? Before you decide what you should do, let me describe the two main types of real estate available.

The two main types of real estate are residential and commercial. Residential properties are considered anything that people can live in, such as single-family homes, duplexes, condominiums, and apartment buildings— basically anything that puts a roof over someone's head while he or she sleeps at night. Commercial properties consist of places where people do business, such as office buildings, retail space, and warehouses.

So given the choice between residential and commercial properties, which one should you choose? Although you can make money in both types of properties, I prefer and recommend residential properties for one simple reason: Everyone needs to live somewhere, so residential properties are much easier to buy and sell. In addition, residential properties are usually priced lower than commercial properties, thus making them more accessible to the average investor. Depending on your area, typical residential properties can range from $50,000 to $500,000 while commercial properties may start at $500,000 and increase to several million dollars or more.

Understanding the residential market is also much easier than understanding commercial real estate. For most people, their first experience with real estate is buying or selling a home, so lenders and agents are accustomed to helping novices understand and get started in buying and selling residential properties. Few people start out in real estate by buying or selling commercial properties, so these properties tend to be bought and sold by experienced real estate investors.

Residential properties are easier to purchase with little or no money down because banks and other lenders are more willing to extend credit to home buyers. In the unfortunate event that someone can no longer afford to make mortgage payments on their home (known as a *foreclosure,* which I'll tell you more about in Chapter 16), banks know that they can quickly get their money back by selling the foreclosed property. Commercial properties usually require more money upfront because banks know that commercial properties are typically more difficult to sell than residential properties.

Best of all, residential properties can be not only an investment but also a place for you to live. If you buy a duplex or an apartment building, you could live for free in your own property while letting your tenants pay your mortgage with their rent money.

When I was in my early twenties, I lived in one of my own multiunit apartment houses. It was run-down when I purchased it, but I slowly renovated it, one apartment at a time. I ended up living in one apartment and worked at night to finish the rest. Eventually I got all of them rented, had a great positive cash flow each month, and lived for free the entire time. Instead of spending money on my own home, I was able to use that money to buy and fix up more property. I lived in that apartment until I moved into a new, custom-built, four-thousand-square-foot home. That strategy of living for free really paid off. In Chapter 19, I describe rental units and all the benefits you can receive with the proper strategy and management.

Residential properties are also more flexible as an investment tool. Most commercial real estate investors make their money by leasing retail space to businesses such as restaurants, shops, or offices. If you can't find a business to lease your space, you don't make any money but you still have to pay your property taxes and meet your mortgage payments every month.

Everyone needs a place to live, but not everyone needs a retail storefront. As a result, commercial properties tend to be harder to sell and rent compared to residential properties.

Residential properties are just the opposite. Because everyone needs to live somewhere, residential properties are much easier to rent during slow real estate markets when people aren't buying homes. Residential properties are also easy to sell, especially when the real estate market is hot. These two advantages—easy to rent and easy to sell—make residential properties much more attractive, especially for the first-time or novice real estate investor.

Throughout this book, when I talk about investing in real estate, I'm talking exclusively about residential real estate: not only single-family homes, but also multiple units, such as duplexes, triplexes, or even apartment buildings. The advantage of an apartment building is that all your rental units are in one place, which makes them easier to manage. In addition, the combined rental income from all your units can produce a steady cash flow. The disadvantage is that you may have a high tenant turnover rate along with greater maintenance problems.

One type of residential property that most people don't think about is vacant land. In general, vacant properties aren't a good investment because you can't rent it out to generate income. To make money on vacant land, you have to sell it, and how many people want to buy vacant land compared to buying a house? You can make money on vacant land, but you have to be aware of costs, turnaround time, and other factors. The general rule with vacant land is that you need to sell it for more than twice what you paid for it within two years to justify the expense in owning the land in the first place. In Chapter 15, I'll show you how to lock up a piece of property for a certain amount of time and reassign the contract to another developer or buyer to make a profit as the middleman. This may be a great way for you to profit from vacant land with little or no risk.

Another category of residential property that many people overlook is distressed properties. A *distressed property* is usually in poor condition, in need of major repairs, or just owned by someone who wants to get rid of it as soon as possible due to a divorce, a job loss, a death in the family, or a mortgage that had a variable interest rate that the current owner can no longer afford to pay. Distressed properties can often be a great opportunity to purchase property inexpensively. I'll tell you more about them in Chapters 16 and 17.

WHERE TO BUY REAL ESTATE

Many people also wonder where they should buy residential real estate. Although you can buy property anywhere in the country, I recommend that you start buying property in your local area for several reasons.

First, by buying property locally, you know the area in a way that no outsider could know first-hand. You probably already know which parts of town are growing, which parts are sinking, which parts to avoid, and which parts have always been desirable. As a local resident, you may already know about changes that could increase or decrease real estate prices in your area. Is a new shopping mall, freeway, or office building being built nearby? Are factories and businesses laying off people, or is a new company coming to town? By living in your neighborhood, you already know about the trends and patterns of your local real estate market without even trying.

A second advantage to buying and selling real estate locally is that if your property is nearby, you can keep your eye on it. If minor problems occur, such as storm damage, graffiti, or routine wear and tear, you can spot and fix them right away.

Knowing the real estate market is a key to recognizing opportunities when they appear. Even if you focus locally, you might find that area too large to understand and monitor easily. In a small town of four thousand people, it might be easy to know the entire area. But in a large metropolitan area such as Phoenix, with more than five million people, it's impossible for even long-time residents to monitor, let alone understand, such a vast area. That's one reason why individuals can enter the real estate market quickly. Even multimillionaire, experienced real estate investors can't track all the changes in a single city, let alone in your neighborhood, which means you have an advantage over them just by virtue of living and investing right where you live.

I recommend that you initially focus on a handful of areas that you can monitor and understand, such as those within a ten-mile radius of your own home. If you're buying rental property, for example, it's much easier to manage five rental properties in the same area than five rental properties in five different parts of town, where real estate and economic conditions can vary dramatically.

Become an expert in your area. It's easier to research and become an expert in an area that you drive by every day. If you don't like the area around you, take the time to research an area that you do like (perhaps a place where you would like to live one day). If you can become an expert on a handful of areas in your neighborhood, you'll know more about the real estate conditions in those areas than any so-called experts.

Finally, I also suggest that you start out by investing in single-family homes because they're more plentiful and easier to sell than apartment buildings. You—and potential buyers—can get a wider range of financing plans for a single-family home than for any other type of real estate.

By sticking with single-family homes in your own area, you can ease into real estate investing and further minimize your risks. The main reason why most people think about investing in real estate elsewhere is because of the "grass is always greener on the other side of the fence" mentality; they want to chase a hot, booming real estate market somewhere else. The problem with this strategy is that a hot market will always cool down, which means you can chase hot markets all over the country and never get there in time. One day the hot market might be San Diego. Another time it might be Phoenix. Another time it could be Salt Lake City.

That's why my techniques emphasize making money in any real estate cycle rather than chasing hot markets in other parts of the country. After you understand how you can make money whether the real estate market is hot or cold, you'll know that you can make money right in your own neighborhood, right now.

SUCCEEDING IN ANY REAL ESTATE MARKET

The key to success in real estate is knowledge. Know the real estate cycle, know the area, and know the right strategy to use.

Is it possible to do everything right and still wind up losing? Of course. But your chances of making a mistake will drop dramatically because I already know what to avoid and what path to follow, and I will teach you to think a little differently. When confronted with a potential loss, too many people accept their situation and take their losses. I prefer to look

> *The key to success in real estate is knowledge. Know the real estate cycle, know the area, and know the right strategy to use.*

for ways to turn a potential money-losing real estate transaction into a sure-fire money-winning transaction!

Real-Life Story

A friend who is a real estate investor purchased a three-unit building at an incredible price in an area that seemed to be growing. Unfortunately, my friend didn't do all his homework. Although he studied the area during the day, he didn't realize that the neighborhood was crime-infested at night. In such a neighborhood, it was no surprise that he had trouble renting the units. After dealing with constant vacancies, he wanted out of this property, but how could he sell it without taking a loss? This was a classic mistake of buying property without understanding the area first.

That's where thinking differently came in. While looking for additional properties in a much better part of town, he found a single-family home advertised in the paper by the owner. The seller had purchased the home to renovate it, but he ran out of money and couldn't complete the remodel. Now he was stuck with a mortgage payment on a house he couldn't rent or sell. He didn't want his property and my friend didn't want his.

So my friend offered to trade the triplex for his half-completed house. The home-owner wanted rental property and was willing to deal with the problems of the triplex, and my friend wanted his house and was willing to deal with the problems of finishing the remodeling. The man advertising in the paper got a rental property, and my friend got a "fixer" that he was able to remodel and sell for a $45,000 profit. By using creative thinking, it was a win-win situation.

I know these were unique circumstances, but by allowing yourself to always focus on a positive solution, unique circumstances seem to pop up. By understanding the techniques I have learned over the past twenty years, focusing on always having a winning outcome can become an easy and normal task.

Real-Life Story

Here's an example where one of my students made more than $250,000 by knowing the real estate market and taking action when an opportunity presented itself. After visiting Hawaii and falling in love with the island, he decided to watch real estate prices on the Hawaiian island of Maui. He and his wife dreamed of someday investing in an oceanfront condominium in an area that they could see was increasing in value.

After the tragedy of September 11, 2001, when the World Trade Centers in New York City were hit by terrorists, air travel around the country dropped significantly. This was especially true for vacation spots that relied on air travel, such as Hawaii. Just a few months after the 9/11 disaster, most property prices in Hawaii remained the same, but the number of sales declined. Suddenly, one anxious seller dropped the price of an oceanfront condominium from $640,000 to $440,000. Most people would gladly pay $440,000 for a $640,000 condominium, but the seller had one condition. He wanted to spend three weeks in the condominium the following summer because he had already made plans to visit Maui with his family.

My student purchased the property for $415,000. The seller accepted the lower price because my student was the only one willing to accommodate the seller's desire to use the condo. This is an example of knowing the seller's "magic buttons" to structure a deal.

In addition to reducing the price by $200,000, the seller was willing to provide an additional $25,000 discount so he could have three weeks' use of the condo! My student was more than willing to agree to this. Since he knew the area so well from his research, he knew this was a distressed seller in a stable market. These condos were rented as vacation units, but because air travel had declined, the rental income had temporarily decreased. Instead of waiting for the temporary decline in travel to rebound, the seller got anxious and panicked. My student simply held onto the property until vacation air travel improved, and then he sold it for $660,000.

I've relayed these two stories as examples of how you can make money by being creative. You could find yourself a great deal in a great area and make a lot of money. Or you can find a bad property in an even worse area and still come out ahead and make money. Anything is possible!

My methods try to minimize your risks, but no method can be 100% foolproof. That's when you have to think differently. By now I hope you understand that it's possible to make money in any real estate market without ever having to risk it all. The next step is to identify the factors that can determine what type of real estate cycle your area may be in.

CONCLUSION

You can buy the best house at the wrong time and make little money, or you can buy the worst house at the right time and make a lot of money. Successful real estate investing is knowing the best strategies to use at different times. After you understand what your local real estate market is doing, you're halfway to making a tremendous profit. The next few chapters show you how to identify the real estate market in your area.

CHAPTER 3

IDENTIFYING NATIONAL AND REGIONAL FACTORS

Everything is connected . . . no one thing can change by itself.
—PAUL HAWKEN

By now you are starting to realize that real estate investing can be lucrative if you minimize your risks and maximize your profits. If you implement solid strategies, I have no doubt that you can dramatically improve your life and lift yourself out of the American rut.

I've spoken about how you need to "know the real estate cycle you are in," so now it's time to learn how easy that can be. In this chapter, you learn how to understand national and regional factors that may influence your real estate market and the area that you plan to invest in. Although some national and regional factors (such as interest rates) may have more of a direct effect on a particular area you might be interested in, it's important to stay current on a broad range of issues.

Even though newspapers and magazines may claim that the real estate market is going one way or another, you can't rely on them when investing in your neighborhood. Instead, I'll go through strategic questions to ask and steps to follow to define the real estate market on a national level. Then in Chapter 4, I'll show you how to define your local real estate market.

As I write this, most of the country just came off a five-year upward cycle with increasing (and in some cases, skyrocketing) prices. Now the real estate market has either peaked, leveled out, or is headed down. But that's what most of the country is doing. While the national real estate market as a whole may be rising or falling, you can always find areas where real estate prices are doing the opposite.

Real-Life Story

For example, Fabio, a good friend of mine from Brooklyn, New York, and his wife, Cathy, recently came to ask my advice about buying property as first-time real estate investors. Understandably, they were nervous and scared because they were in uncharted waters. So I decided to take them through the process I've outlined in this book.

First, I wanted to understand their reason for investing in real estate and how real estate could help them reach their goals. I believe that there is no better way than real estate for the average person to gain tremendous wealth, but you can't expect to become a millionaire overnight. You must develop your knowledge of real estate investing and then take action.

So when my friend asked me for advice about investing in real estate, I asked him if we could take a step back and determine in what area he wanted to buy properties and evaluate that area's real estate cycle. So we went through the questions and steps you're about to go through in the next several chapters.

Real estate can be a great way to make a lot of money, but don't consider it a get-rich-quick scheme. Thousands of investors have created an abundance of wealth, but they first developed a knowledge of real estate investing and then took action.

I asked him what the market conditions in that area were, and he said, "All I know is that the market is bad." I asked him how he knew that the market was bad, and he said that's what people were saying and it was on the news. I told him that the real estate market had slowed down in many markets across America, and in some areas, real estate prices were even falling. The good news was that if the market was also falling around Brooklyn, it really didn't matter. He could still make a ton of money in that market cycle just as if it was booming by applying the right strategy.

After getting a puzzled stare from him, I repeated, "If we take the time to understand your market, we'll know the right strategy to use."

Once we got started using the questions that you'll be answering later in this chapter and in the following chapter, I saw right away that my friend had been right that the real estate market was slow and falling in his area. Based on a downward trend, I told my friend about lease options and foreclosures as just two of the many ways he could profit from a downward real estate market. Then my friend's wife said, "But we're planning on investing about fifteen minutes away in Coney Island." And that fifteen minutes made all the difference in the world.

If the national real estate market is going up, I guarantee you'll find areas around the country where the real estate market is going down. Likewise, if the national real estate market is going down, I guarantee you'll find areas where real estate prices are going up, and that's exactly what we found about Coney Island.

Coney Island, which had been getting progressively run-down the last twenty years, was going through a rebirth, with new construction that may eventually include a casino. It was suddenly the hot spot where people wanted to live again. My friend even knew about several developers who were already in the early stages of major construction in the area.

Although Brooklyn was in a downward trend, the pocket area of Coney Island was in an upward trend, so I suggested several strategies: buying property with no money down, buying property and renting with a positive cash flow until prices in the area rose, and looking for residential homes in an area that was currently zoned or would in the future be zoned for commercial development so that way he would have a choice of either renting or selling the property to a home buyer or a business owner.

I explain each of these strategies in more detail in Part III, but for now I want you to understand that it doesn't matter whether your real estate market is booming, peaking, falling, or hitting bottom. Just as I did with my friend, I want to help you identify your real estate cycle and then apply the proper strategy so you can make a fortune any time in any market.

So the next time you hear people in the news talking about a buyer's market, a seller's market, a bubble market, or a market where the bubble is going to burst, you'll be able to determine what your true real estate market is doing regardless of what prices may be doing anywhere else.

NATIONAL FACTORS INFLUENCING REAL ESTATE

I'm going to guide you through five national factors that are a big part of defining the real estate market as a whole. In Chapter 4, I'll go over the local factors that can determine what cycle your local real estate market may be in. The five national factors to consider are

- Interest rate
- Inflation
- Flow of investment funds
- Business cycle
- Cataclysmic event

Remember, there are basically only four types of real estate cycles: up (seller's market), down (bubble has burst and buyer's market), top (bubble market), and bottom (buyer's market). I'll help you determine which of these cycles fits the area where you're planning to invest. The names in parentheses after the cycle are what people call those cycles, but you can buy and sell real estate, and make a hefty profit, in any cycle.

Taking these national factors into consideration and identifying developing trends can turn an average real estate investment into an exceptional one. Take the time to study how each national factor can affect your local market. Over time, you'll improve your ability to recognize changes in those factors, to identify trends that may occur as a result of those changes, and to take action to move ahead of the pack.

I made money for years in real estate by going with my instinct. Use these factors to optimize your profits and minimize your risk, but don't overanalyze so much that you don't do anything at all.

NATIONAL FACTOR #1: INTEREST RATES

Most people don't have a million dollars sitting in the bank to buy and sell homes for personal or investment reasons. Therefore, they have to borrow money to buy a house. This loan is known as a *mortgage* or *deed of trust*. In this book, I always refer to the loan as a mortgage. Naturally, the bank won't loan you several hundred thousand dollars without wanting something in return, so banks charge a specific percentage of the total amount due for the use of their money. The percentage that banks charge is known as the *interest rate*.

Although banks can charge any interest rate they want within the legal limits established in the U.S. banking system in each state, they generally base their interest rate on something called the *federal funds rate,* which is the interest rate that banks charge each other for overnight loans of federal funds, which are held by the Federal Reserve (also known as the Fed). Whatever interest rate the Federal Reserve establishes, banks usually charge a prime rate, which is always slightly higher than the federal funds rate. The *prime rate* is the interest rate banks charge their largest and best customers. When the federal funds rate goes up, the prime rate goes up. When the federal funds rate goes down, the prime rate goes down.

Without going into too much detail, it is worth mentioning that Fed policy on interest rates influences Wall Street, particularly the bond market. Bonds are interest-sensitive financial investments traded daily on Wall Street. Certain bonds, known as Treasury bonds (or Treasuries), form the basis for lenders to determine the interest rates that banks and mortgage brokers charge for residential mortgage loans.

So when the Federal Reserve increases or decreases the federal funds rate to manage inflation or boost (or dampen) the economy, banks adjust their prime lending rates and mortgage rates up or down at the same time, which ultimately boils down to increasing or decreasing the cost of money when buying real estate. For this reason, interest rates are an extremely important factor in the real estate market.

Now you may be asking yourself, "Is it better to invest in real estate when interest rates are high or low?" The answer is both! You apply different strategies depending on the circumstances. When interest rates are high, fewer people can afford to buy homes, so that's when it's easier to find tenants for your rental properties. High interest rates also cause many people to default on loans with adjustable rates, increasing the number of foreclosures. When interest rates are low, it's easier for you to buy new properties and leverage more funds.

Here is an example of the effect that a change in interest rates has on real estate investment purchasing power. Let's assume you want to get a traditional mortgage loan to buy a house. You contact a banker or mortgage banker and ask to borrow $100,000.

The banker will pull out his financial calculator and input some numbers. Assuming a thirty-year, fixed-rate mortgage with an interest rate of 5.5%, the banker would tell you that your monthly payment would be $568. (A *fixed rate* means that the interest rate won't change over the life of the loan, as opposed to a *variable or adjustable rate,* which can go up or down at agreed-upon intervals. A thirty-year mortgage means you have thirty years to pay off your loan.) Now if the interest rate increases to 6.5%, taking out that same thirty-year mortgage means your monthly loan payment would now be $632. As you can see, the higher the interest rate (in this example, an increase of 1%), the less purchasing power you have (in this case, $64 per month—$632 minus $568).

Back in the 1980s, interest rates were 12% or higher, which meant that the same payment would have been $1029! That is a reduction in purchasing power of $461 per month compared to 5.5% loan ($1029 minus $568)— quite an impact on how much you can purchase, wouldn't you say?

So should you care about interest rates? Absolutely! Interest rates directly affect your real estate purchasing power and the cycle the market may be heading towards. Rather than try to compute mortgage payments or mortgage loans based on current interest rates manually, you can use a special tool called a financial calculator, which you can find on the Internet or at my site, www.deangraziosi.com.

All-time-low interest rates were one factor that significantly helped create the real estate boom in the early 2000s. As interest rates kept dropping, mortgage debt payments were lower, allowing borrowers to take on larger loans and thus buy larger properties, increasing property values as potential buyers bid prices upward.

When interest rates are higher (typically when the Federal Reserve raises rates to reduce inflation or keep inflation level), banks follow by increasing their mortgage rates. With higher interest rates, lenders reduce the amount they are willing to loan on particular properties when the monthly income remains the same. Rarely do real estate prices fall too far below the original price. So while a $100,000 property might increase in value to $150,000 or more in a few years, it's much less likely to drop in value to $50,000. This is one key that makes real estate investing so lucrative with little risk.

After you determine what the current interest rate may be, you need to know how the interest rate has changed over the past few years. Have interest rates been low for a long time or have they been falling? Historically, interest rate cycles can last from five to ten years.

To fully understand the effect that interest rates can have on the real estate market, take some time to identify the following:

- Where are interest rates right now?
- Where were interest rates six months ago?
- Where were interest rates eighteen months ago?
- Do interest rates appear to be rising or falling or staying the same?
- What has been the trend of the Federal Reserve policy towards interest rates?

(For information history on past interest rates, ask a mortgage broker or go to www.google.com and search "historical interest rates.")

After you know this information, you can predict the real estate market fairly accurately. I describe the different types of loans in Chapter 13, but if you decide to use an adjustable-rate mortgage (known as an ARM), it is important to know how interest rates have changed and what trends have formed because your interest rate and loan payment will adjust over time. The real estate strategy that will work out best is significantly affected by the current and likely future interest rate and the type of loan you select.

If interest rates are currently near a five-year low, you can safely expect that they aren't likely to go down much further in the near future. Unfortunately, many people buy homes at these low interest rates using variable interest loans rather than fixed-rate loans, either because they can't qualify for a fixed-rate loan or because the variable interest loans offer much lower monthly payments initially. When interest rates inevitably start rising again, their mortgage payments go up too.

Rising interest rates create more distressed properties such as foreclosures, tax sales, and lease-to-own opportunities, which can create incredible opportunities to make a great deal of money. I expand on these real estate strategies in Chapters 15–18.

If interest rates just started going up after a five-year low, most likely they will continue to increase, and this would be an ingredient of a peak market. If they have been going up for six months to a year, this could be an ingredient for a downward market. If interest rates have been high for quite some time but are just starting to go down, you may have hit a bottom market. If they have been dropping for six months to a year or longer, that could be an ingredient an upward swing.

I use the word *ingredient* because although interest rates are a big factor in determining the current real estate cycle, no one factor alone can determine a cycle, especially when we also consider local factors. Interest rates could be going straight up and that would contribute to a downward market. But if Intel is building a new plant a mile from your home, rising interest really wouldn't affect the local real estate market nearly as much. So that is why we need to go through both national and local factors to identify your local real estate market.

So choose one of the following four symbols for interest rates, and in Chapter 4 you will do the same for all the local factors. Remember, you are deciding on the current state of each national factor and its effect on the real estate market:

↑ Top
↘ Down
↓ Bottom
↗ Up
N/A Not applicable at this time

NATIONAL FACTOR #2: INFLATION

At the simplest level, inflation is what causes prices to rise. The higher and faster inflation rises, the less your money will buy. For example, if your income is $1000 a month today, ten years from now, at a 3% annual inflation rate, you'd need to earn $1304 just to buy the same things.

Real estate acts as a hedge against inflation because real estate prices historically rise just as much (or more) than inflation. Although you may not be able to increase rents to keep pace with inflation (renters typically lock in fixed rental rates for one- or two-year periods), the value of your rental property will increase. Even better, if you have a fixed-rate loan, your expenses will stay the same, so inflation can make money for you through real estate. Can you think of a better way to create wealth and financial independence?

If inflation rises too rapidly, which is what happened back in the mid-1970s, expenses can rise faster than property owners can raise rents, wreaking financial havoc on the rental market. By contrast, when building costs go down, property prices usually follow, causing surrounding property values to go down as well.

Inflation occurs based on a variety of factors, such as the Consumer Price Index, the Wholesale Price Index, and the Producer Price Index. Don't worry if you don't know what these terms mean. The important point to re-member is that inflation isn't directly affected by a single factor.

Because so many factors influence inflation, it's nearly impossible to pin-point accurately the current inflation rate. You can, however, use newspa-pers and magazines to identify what inflation rates were like one, five, and ten years ago. Based on historical data, you can identify whether inflation is rising, steady, or even dropping.

As long as inflation changes moderately up or down, real estate is always a great investment. The time to worry is when inflation skyrockets, known as *hyperinflation,* or drops, known as *deflation.*

Under hyperinflation, rental properties cost more money to maintain than the rents you can collect. Under deflation, real estate prices dip or even drop dramatically. During hyperinflation, the best real estate strategy could be staying out of real estate altogether until the inflation rate moderates one way or another.

The easiest way to determine the inflation rate is to go to www.inflation-data.com and look at the history of where the rate has been and where you think it is going. Most of the time, inflation won't be applicable when deter-mining the cycle you are in. But you must know the general inflation rate in case there is an extreme swing one way or the other. So choose one of the following:

↑ Top
↘ Down
↓ Bottom
↗ Up
N/A Not applicable at this time

NATIONAL FACTOR #3: FLOW OF INVESTMENT FUNDS

The *flow of investment funds* refers to the number of people involved in real estate. When money flows into real estate, more people are buying and sell-ing. When money flows out of real estate, fewer people are buying and sell-ing. The more people involved in buying and selling real estate, the more prices fluctuate.

That's why sudden changes such as tax breaks on capital gains, new lend-ing laws, foreign investment in a local market (such as the increase of Japa-nese investment in California and Hawaii in the 1990s), and stock market crashes can cause sudden increases of investment funds, which can raise real estate prices. After those factors change, there can be a sudden outflow of funds, which can drop real estate prices.

For example, after the incredible surge in the stock market throughout the late 1990s, a massive wave of people rushed out of the stock market in 1999 and early 2000, as stocks started to drop, and poured their money into real estate. Because so many people were afraid of the stock market and felt more secure buying real estate, the flow of investment funds shifted from the stock market to the real estate market. This was a huge factor (in addition to the Federal Reserve starting to decrease interest rates) in kick-starting the real estate boom in the early 2000s.

The flow of funds can shift from real estate to the stock market just as quickly. When the Internet stock market boom took off in the middle to late 1990s, people were desperate to get in before the boom ended, so they often liquidated their real estate holdings to invest in the stock market. When people are shifting money from real estate to something else (such as the stock market), that's the time to buy real estate easily and inexpensively because people want money in a hurry.

Part of the key to real estate investing is to think differently and avoid following the crowd. Just remember that the stock market can crash at any time while the real estate market often takes months, or even years, to change. By just studying the flow of funds to and from real estate, you can roughly determine the best time to buy real estate and the best time to sell.

How is the flow of funds working at the time you are reading this? Is the stock market skyrocketing or dragging its feet? Are novice investors scared of where the real estate market is heading and desperate to pull out for safety reasons because they don't understand cycles? Did a lot of uninformed investors buy at the top of the market and now want the security of having their money in the bank rather than tied up in real estate? Maybe the stock market is dropping and a new wave of funds will flow into the real estate sector. Take the time to research the current flow of investment funds to see how it could affect your current market:

↑ Top
↘ Down
↓ Bottom
↗ Up
N/A Not applicable at this time

NATIONAL FACTOR #4: BUSINESS CYCLE

Just as the real estate market rises and falls in cycles, so does the national economy. As we cycle from economic prosperity to economic recession and back again, all forms of investments are influenced in various ways. When the economy is strong, incomes are high, unemployment is low, and people tend to have more discretionary income to invest in the real estate market. This is also the time that household incomes are high and more people can afford to buy their own homes (as opposed to renting) or purchase a more expensive home.

When the country is in an economic recession, incomes are lower and unemployment is higher. This can result in fewer real estate purchases, higher foreclosure rates, more renters, and lower property values. This could be the perfect time to use the strategic buying techniques outlined in Chapters 16–18 to buy tax properties and foreclosures.

Remember, I am just talking about national factors. In Chapter 4, I talk about local factors that could override national factors. For example, in Miami and San Diego, real estate prices have been steadily climbing for years as more businesses, people, and jobs flow into those areas. However, in places such as Detroit and Cleveland, factories are shutting down and people are losing jobs, so the local downward trend is overriding the national upward trend.

That can work both ways. Maybe a certain area could be experiencing a downward business cycle where companies are leaving and businesses are shutting down. Yet a new factory or shopping mall may be built nearby and real estate prices in that surrounding area could be skyrocketing tomorrow.

Identifying national business cycles is more a matter of reading the news than defining a specific number or value. Browse through several national magazines and newspapers such as *Fortune, Money, USA Today,* and the *Wall Street Journal.* You can find them online as well. Are most stories about different cities or businesses positive or negative?

A negative story might be one that talks about a decline of profits and falling market share for a major company such as General Motors. A positive story might be one talking about a new biotech research center opening near a major university. By tracking trends in business-related stories in national publications, you can get a fairly accurate feel for the mood and condition of the national economy as a whole.

The stock market also follows business cycles closely and can be a good indicator of national trends. If the stock market is dropping, the national economy tends to be dropping. If the stock market is rising, the national economy tends to be rising.

Again, after taking the time to get a feel for the current national business cycle, how does that ingredient affect the current market as a whole?

↑ Top
↘ Down
↓ Bottom

↗ Up

N/A Not applicable at this time

NATIONAL FACTOR #5: CATACLYSMIC EVENTS

Of all the factors affecting the national real estate market, none is more unpredictable than a cataclysmic event. For example, no one could have predicted what happened on September 11, 2001. Similarly, no one can predict when an earthquake in California, a flood in the Midwest, or a hurricane in the Southeast will affect not only the local real estate market but also the overall economy and real estate markets nationwide.

Obviously, predicting a cataclysmic event is impossible. However, by studying how such an event affects an area, you can predict which real estate strategy could work best in similar circumstances.

For example, the hurricanes that hit Florida, Louisiana, and Mississippi in 2005 wiped out entire neighborhoods. When people rebuilt those devastated areas, the price of building materials (wood, glass, concrete, sheetrock, and so on) rose quickly because demand outweighed supply. This had the indirect effect of increasing the price of building materials nationwide, which meant that prices of new homes in different parts of the country also increased rapidly.

When a cataclysmic event occurs, building material prices are likely to surge in the short-term, spiking real estate prices as well. Knowing this, you can either sell existing real estate for a higher price than you might have been able to do even days before the cataclysmic event, or you could avoid buying property until the price surge in building materials drops back to normal levels.

After Hurricane Katrina, many families moved to other parts of the country, such as Houston. A sudden influx of people raises real estate prices and rents as demand for housing outstrips the supply. However, once the supply of homes and rental properties catches up with the demand, prices level off or in some cases drop back down again.

Now I'm not telling you to capitalize from somebody else's misfortunes. Instead, I'm telling you to watch the trends and be aware of how they can affect the real estate market in your area in the short-term. After you know what to expect, you'll be in a much better position to protect your assets or take advantage of opportunities when they arise. You can also reduce your risks by making sure you have adequate flood and wind insurance. The key to real estate investing is to eliminate as much guesswork as possible and apply the right strategies at the right time.

I hope a cataclysmic event doesn't affect the nation or your area. But if one has occurred recently, consider what its impact may be in your real estate market.

↑ Top
↘ Down
↧ Bottom
↗ Up
N/A Not applicable at this time

CALCULATING NATIONAL FACTORS

Take the time to research each national factor. Remember, if interest rates are at an all-time low, the market might be on the upswing. If interest rates are at an all-time high, the market could soon be heading downward. If interest rates have been at an all-time high for many years, the real estate market is likely at the bottom and will soon start rising up. After you have this information, we'll put it together with local factors in Chapter 5.

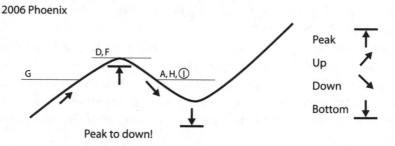

Peak to down!

For example, while writing this book in mid-2006, I would have rated the interest rate factor as follows. Interest rates had been at an all-time low for five years, then rose for several months in a row, and are continuing to creep up. I would guess that interest rates will level off or go just a bit higher. But based on history, I am confident that they will not be going down for quite some time. This would suggest a downward cycle may be upon us, so I would give the interest rate factor a ↘ symbol.

Don't worry about being exact. Just try to be as accurate as you can be. Remember, even the so-called economic experts are taking their best guesses, so you can too.

As I mentioned, not all factors have to relate to each other. Interest rates could be at an all-time low, and then we get hit with a cataclysmic event that slows the economy and the real estate market temporarily. But I promise that what you are learning puts you head and shoulders above many successful full-time investors and most novice investors.

Of course, understanding the national real estate market may be fine, but there will always be areas that don't follow a national trend. So to truly understand your current real estate market, you need to research local factors that may affect real estate, which is what you'll learn about in Chapter 4.

Most people understand how to make money in an upward cycle where prices are rising, but how do you know when the up cycle may end and leave you stuck with an expensive piece of property?

Many people are willing to cash out too quickly because they're afraid that they might hold on too long. For example, by analyzing the national factors listed in this chapter, combined with local factors in the following chapter, I could tell that the real estate market in Phoenix was in an upward cycle and likely to continue for at least another year. I took advantage of this extra time to make a fortune.

One day, I drove through a great neighborhood and saw a wonderful house where a woman had just started pounding a For Sale by Owner sign in her front yard. Curious, I stopped my car and struck up a conversation with the woman as her first potential buyer.

As soon as she showed me the house, I knew I had found a hidden gem. Not only was the house in an up-and-coming neighborhood, but it also sat on a flag lot off a cul-de-sac. A *flag lot* is a piece of property that looks like a flagpole. The flagpole is the driveway and the flag is the lot, which is stuck behind another piece of property. This type of property often tucks the house away from the road (and traffic noise) and neighbors for greater privacy. The house itself was only a few years old and had impressive sixteen-foot ceilings in the entryway.

At the time, I was selling my own house and was trying to figure out what to buy next. So I started the negotiations on the house that very day. The woman knew that the market in Phoenix had been hot for some time, but after living in the house for several years, she wanted to sell now to maximize her profits. Then she could use that money to buy and live in a smaller condominium.

Even though the Phoenix market was near the top, I calculated a variety of national and local factors and determined that the upward cycle would likely continue. By that afternoon, I agreed to buy the house for $525,000. I knew I was going to sell this house eventually, so I started some minor remodeling right away. Fortunately, this house was only a few years old, so it didn't need much. I painted the walls with warmer, traditional colors that weren't likely to date the house while giving it a fresh and more appealing look. Beyond new paint and fixing the busted motor in the backyard Jacuzzi, I spent a minimal amount of money to prepare the house for eventual sale.

I lived in the house for a year and then put it back on the market for $720,000. It sold for $710,000 in about forty-five days. Now remember, I had originally bought this house for $525,000, so after the realtor's commission and other closing costs, I still made around $150,000 in a little more than a year, and I got to live in the house the whole time too. As a kid, I never would have dreamed I could make that kind of money working a full-time job for three years, let alone on one house so quickly, but that's exactly the type of money you can make in real estate.

Before buying this house, I had noticed new restaurants and buildings being built in the area along with a steady flow of new jobs, so I felt that this particular area would continue climbing even if the rest of the country's real estate market peaked. (That same area is now in a downward trend. I sold just in time before we hit the top.)

I'm not saying you're going to make this kind of money on every transaction, but you can see the importance of studying real estate cycles and knowing approximately where you are in the cycle. Sell too soon and you make a small profit. Sell too late and you may not make any profit. But sell just when you believe the market is about to peak, and you can make a fortune.

CONCLUSION

By analyzing national conditions and how they affect the real estate market, you can take a lot of guesswork out of real estate investing. By predicting the real estate market, you can plan investment strategies one step ahead of others and make a profit quickly and easily.

If you could see into the future and know what was going to happen, wouldn't you be able to take advantage of this information? Of course, and that's what analyzing national factors can do for you. Now to help you further define your real estate market, you also need to analyze several local factors, and that's what I show you how to do in the next chapter.

CHAPTER 4

IDENTIFYING LOCAL FACTORS

A hidden connection is stronger than an obvious one.
—HERACLITUS OF EPHESUS

Your local real estate market may closely mirror national trends. But sometimes local factors can overshadow national ones and allow incredible opportunities for people who spot them in time. Remember, opportunities are always there—it's my job to help you clear away the smoke so you can see those right in front of you.

Local factors do one of two things. First, they may agree with national factors and help you make educated decisions based on the real estate cycle in your area. Second, local factors may be strong enough to override national factors and give your area, or your smaller pocket area, a unique cycle that's independent of the rest of the country.

By taking advantage of local factors, I have made a lot of money in my original hometown of Marlboro, New York, which lies about sixty-five miles north of New York City. Until recently, commuting from Marlboro to New York City took at least an hour and a half, when there wasn't traffic. Add rush-hour traffic into the mix and you could easily add another hour to a one-way commute.

But then a few things happened. Train service, just ten miles away, improved immensely, making the commute to New York City faster and more convenient. Then real estate prices in the neighboring suburbs of Westchester and Rockland counties skyrocketed, making homes in nearby Marlboro much more valuable as a result.

While moderate home prices in Westchester and Rockland were selling for approximately $500,000, similar homes in Marlboro, just forty-five minutes away, were selling for only $195,000. I suddenly realized that people working in New York City who couldn't afford homes in Westchester or Rockland would be willing to take a little extra time for their commute if they could buy a more affordable home in Marlboro.

One-acre vacant lots in Marlboro quickly jumped from $40,000 to $140,000. A typical home in Marlboro increased from $195,000 to $350,000 or more. People in Westchester started selling their thirty-year-old, 1800-square-foot home for $500,000 so they could move to Marlboro and buy a new, 3000-square-foot home for the same price.

This is an example of a local determining factor that could make you a fortune if you catch it in time. Many people who had sold their home at the first price increase netted a small profit, but if they had recognized how real estate cycles work and how long they take to change, they could have made a much larger profit. I even sold some properties much too soon, but I then did exactly what I am teaching you to do. I evaluated the local and national factors and realized that this was a long-term upswing for the Marlboro community.

Remember, you can always sell too soon and regret not waiting, or you can sell too late and regret not selling earlier. A wise investor once told me, "You can never fault a profit." You'll never know the exact best time to sell until afterwards. Follow national and local factors and make the most educated decision possible rather than getting caught up in the emotion of the market and making a hasty decision based on fear or a desire to make a quick buck.

"You can never fault a profit." You'll never know the exact best time to sell, so it's important to make an educated decision rather than a hasty decision based on fear or a desire to make a quick buck.

While local factors were driving the real estate market in Marlboro, I kept my eye on national factors too. At the time, interest rates were going down and the economy was improving. I realized that the real estate cycle was at the beginning of a much larger upswing, so I started buying more property and holding onto my existing ones. As soon as I determined that the real estate cycle had ended its upswing and was starting to slow, I started selling my properties at prices that would be near the peak of that particular real estate cycle.

You must always consider both local and national factors because one can affect or reverse the trends of the other. When home prices in Marlboro rose just 10%, the locals started telling people they were crazy paying those prices. I bought one parcel of land for $180,000, and a local businessman told me, "Son, you just made a big mistake." His limited thinking blinded him from seeing how real estate cycles work. I subdivided the property and pulled in more than $900,000 profit. I was able to do that only because I could see which direction real estate prices were going based on the current cycle.

I make mistakes, but I base my decisions on understanding what worked in the past, applying the right strategy during the right real estate cycle. In comparison, most people make decisions out of hope or by following the crowd, which rarely leads to an optimum result when buying or selling properties. By following the crowd, you'll generally be ten steps behind, making the "right" decision at the wrong time.

After a seven-year upswing in Marlboro, the real estate cycle started to slow, with homes taking longer to sell (a good indicator that the market is slowing) and prices dropping. To take advantage of this new cycle, I changed my strategy.

In just the few weeks before writing this section, I purchased a foreclosure for about 30% of its worth. I also bought a preforeclosure house in very distressed condition for $35,000. The lot alone is worth two times that figure. Plus I purchased a home that the owner had to sell immediately due to financial reasons for about $100,000 less than its value. Now I can rent my properties, and when the real estate cycle hits bottom and starts up again, I'll be able to sell these properties for a large profit or refinance them and pull out the equity to buy other properties. By understanding the cycle you are in, you can minimize your risks while maximizing your gains.

LOCAL FACTORS INFLUENCING REAL ESTATE

Here are the local factors we will be analyzing in this chapter:

- Migration and job growth
- Development plans
- New construction
- Supply and demand
- Neighborhood trends

As you did in determining national factors, you will decide how each local factor is affecting your market. As I mentioned, sometimes one or two local factors can outweigh all the national factors and the other local factors combined. If all the national factors point toward a downward trend but you are investing in a place that is booming or has become the new destination for upwardly mobile families, those factors can outweigh higher interest rates, inflation, and any other national factors. Remember the five symbols in Chapter 3: ↑, ↘, ↓, ↗, and N/A? Well, I'm adding a sixth symbol, MF (Major Factor), that identifies any factor that can have a dramatic effect on your local area.

LOCAL FACTOR #1: MIGRATION AND JOB GROWTH

Migration and job growth go together because if an area has a sudden increase of jobs, more people flood into that area, driving up real estate prices and apartment rentals. If an area suddenly loses jobs, more people will leave that area, depressing real estate prices and lowering rental demand. Each situation creates different but profitable opportunities.

The demographics of the people migrating into a certain area also play a role in determining how the real estate market will change. For example, if a large number of people with relatively high incomes move into a particular area, the demand for single-family homes will likely be higher than the demand for apartment rentals. Paying attention to these factors can help you determine the smartest types of real estate investment for your area.

It's no secret that the population had been steadily migrating from the northern states to the southern states. Given a choice between moving to a cold climate or a warmer one, many businesses are choosing the warmer climates. As a result, warmer climates tend to offer greater employment opportunities.

Now migration implies a trend and trends occur over time. To take advantage of any trend, you need to understand both the *macro* (grand) view and then drill down to how it affects the *micro* (local) view. For example, from 2000 to 2006, migration had a huge effect on real estate prices in Phoenix.

With all the national and local factors aligned for growth, California home prices doubled overnight, causing many people to cash out and walk away with huge profits from the sale of their homes. But when you cash out and sell your home, you may have trouble buying another home in that same area with that same money because the prices of all homes tend to increase at the same time. So people in California were stuck with a dilemma. Using the money from the sale of their first house, they could buy a similar, or smaller, house in the same area. Or they could simply move to an area where housing prices were much cheaper. In many cases, people from California migrated to the nearest area with similar job opportunities, such as Phoenix. One of the most successful realtors in Phoenix told me that at the time, nearly 40% of all new home sales were going to people moving to Phoenix from California.

As the real estate cycle in California peaked and started to turn downward, the real estate cycle in Phoenix kept climbing because people were still migrating from California. However, once I recognized the slowing cycle in California, I knew the Phoenix cycle would slow as well. This gave me enough time to buy properties, fix them up, and sell them before the Phoenix upswing cycle ended. As soon as the Phoenix cycle started downward, I switched strategies.

To understand how migration can affect your local area, you need to track migration trends nationally (which areas people are leaving) and locally (which areas people are moving into). One way to determine the flow of migration is to call your local U-Haul or other truck rental company. Normally, U-Haul lets you rent a moving truck in one city and return it in a different city with no penalty. However, if a certain area is seeing a high migration of people out, the U-Haul franchises in that area will often charge an extra fee for people taking one of their rented moving trucks out of the area, or they'll offer a discount if you return the moving truck to the same area instead.

Likewise, call U-Haul or a moving company and ask which part of the country most of their vehicles have been going to. During the big real estate boom in California, many trucks left California for less expensive places such as Las Vegas or Phoenix.

Real-Life Story

Sometimes migration to an area can occur from the strangest factors, as one of my friends found out in a way that made him a ton of money.

"We lived in a town with a small private university, where the enrollment had been stagnant for years. As a result, real estate surrounding the university had been flat for some time. Then the school hired a new head basketball coach who turned their average basketball program into one that made it to the NCAA tournament final 8, known as the Elite 8. The university gained national attention, and within a few years enrollment increased and student housing became scarce.

"By watching these local factors, we saw the demand start to increase, so we found a large home and remodeled it with five bedrooms for students. We normally could have rented the house for $695 per month, but by completing the remodel and renting to students, we were able to nearly double the rental income.

"This strategy worked even though the surrounding area away from the university was in a bottom real estate cycle. The lesson we learned was that by predicting the effect of increased migration into an area, we were able to profit from the soon-to-be-growing rental market."

So how is migration and job growth in your area? Are people coming or going? Are population and job growth in your area simply staying the same? Is there a lot of unemployment and minimal opportunity? Have companies shut down? Or are new commercial buildings going up? Do you see lots of new faces? Look in the local newspapers, go online, observe your surroundings, and make some calls—a little research will go a long way.

Either now or after you do some research, decide how migration is currently affecting your local market:

↑ Top
↘ Down
↓ Bottom
↗ Up

N/A Not applicable at this time
MF Major factor

LOCAL FACTOR #2: DEVELOPMENT PLANS

They say you can't judge a book by its cover. That's true for real estate too. If an area looks stagnant or run-down, it could be a gold mine waiting to be discovered.

Many areas are designated in the "path of development," which means that new construction is planned for that area, such as a shopping mall or a new or improved road. By checking with the city planning office or economic development committee (some towns and cities have a web site you can visit), you can learn about their long-term development plans and see which areas may be a good place to start looking for residential properties.

If a town doesn't have a planning office or an economic development committee web site, they will definitely have public meetings you can attend or public transcriptions from meetings. The trick is to learn about all planned development and how many years away each plan may be from getting started.

Real-Life Story

The following story tells how one of my students took advantage of development plans in his area and made a fortune.

"I found a nice, three-bedroom, brick home in a good rental area that I believed was in the path of commercial development. I purchased this home with 100% financing and rented it for a $100 per month positive net cash flow (after paying my mortgage, taxes, and insurance).

"I bought this home because I could see that the migration path of commercial development was headed right through the area where the home is located. I plan on holding onto this property until the path of commercial development drives my property value up and I can apply for rezoning to office/commercial and either sell or lease the property. I know that I need to hold onto the property for four to five years to maximize my profits, but because I bought it with 100% financing and the place makes me money every month, I am in no rush. This is the way smart people build wealth. At least that's how I feel now that I am a real estate investor."

Is a wave of development going on or planned for your area? Use the Internet to search past newspapers and current stories, and check your town or city's web sites for information about growth and zoning changes.

Decide which direction growth is heading in your area. I know this sounds like a little work, but the knowledge in this book combined with some effort and a desire on your part can produce millions. Take the time now and your life will change forever, I promise.

So, give development a symbol:

↑ Top
↘ Down
↓ Bottom
↗ Up
N/A Not applicable at this time
MF Major factor

LOCAL FACTOR #3: NEW CONSTRUCTION

Drive around any area and you can see whether any construction is taking place. In general, new construction of any type (including remodeling current buildings) means that the area has a positive future.

New construction affects the supply side of the real estate market. While market factors of job growth, migration, and future development increase the demand for real estate, too much or too little new construction can affect the supply of available real estate.

When you combine an oversupply of new construction with an undersupply of buyers, due to national factors (such as a recession), the result can be devastating to the market. On the other hand, combine an undersupply of new construction with a large pool of buyers, due to a strong economy, and other national or local factors, and the price of real estate can skyrocket.

New construction affects not only supply but also prices. Property owners will have a hard time increasing prices if new homes are built in the same area and sell for much less. Conversely, prices for homes in areas without new construction can rise much more rapidly because those homes are the only available options for people who want to move there.

Check with your local building department and see how many new building permits are being filed each month compared to a year and two years ago. When you see new construction in an area, that could signal either an upward or downward cycle. For example, during the hot real estate boom in California in early 2000, multiple new construction projects began to meet the rising demand for homes. However, by the time the real estate market cooled and began dropping, many of the later construction projects were just completed; this resulted in a sudden oversupply of homes, which helped push prices down even further.

Rate the construction in your area:

↑ Top
↘ Down
↓ Bottom
↗ Up
N/A Not applicable at this time
MF Major factor

LOCAL FACTOR #4: SUPPLY AND DEMAND

Supply and demand affects every real estate cycle. In an up cycle, demand is greater than supply. In a down cycle, supply is greater than demand. At the peak and the bottom, supply and demand briefly achieve equilibrium. The imbalances cause the shifts in the cycle from up to down and vice-versa.

It's important to monitor supply and demand for signs that the real estate cycle may be changing soon. I cannot stress the importance of this factor!

To understand the current demand in an area, keep track of the area's monthly home sales. I am referring to the number of homes sold, not the total number of homes on the market. By comparing the number of homes bought in the current month to those bought in previous months, you can see whether the market of buyers is increasing or decreasing. The number of homes sold has more to do with the number of buyers than the number of sellers. A higher number of homes sold indicates a higher demand by buyers.

To understand the current supply of real estate, watch the number of real estate listings in your particular market. You may be able to request a free report by filling out a form on your county assessor's web site, on sites such as www.dqnews.com, or by searching on Google (or any search engine) with the keywords "home sale statistics" followed by your state, city, or town. If you have a good relationship with a real estate agent, ask him or her to access this information through the Multiple Listing Service (MLS), which every real estate agent can use (but members of the public can not).

Keep in mind that real estate markets are often seasonal, depending on the area. Typically, more people buy and sell homes in the summer than the winter, so a straight month-to-month comparison of home sales can be misleading. Find the number of homes on the market and how long on average it takes a home to sell. Then write down those numbers for three time periods: a year ago, six months ago, and now.

If a year ago 1000 homes were on the market and it took an average of ten days to sell a house, six months ago 1500 homes were for sale and on average it took twenty days to sell a home, and now 2500 homes are for sale and the average time to sell a home is forty-five days, you know that supply far outweighs demand. Either too much building took place, the flow of funds into real estate has stopped, or migration and oversupply are driving down the market and prices. This signals a peak or downward cycle.

Visit or call new housing projects. During the big real estate boom in Phoenix, you had to put your name in a lottery just for a chance to buy a new home. Now new home buyers are doing the opposite. Supply far outweighs demand and developers who started too late are struggling to get rid of inventories by offering huge incentives.

As you should already know by now, there is never a better or worse time to invest in real estate. It's all about identifying the correct real estate cycle and applying the right money-making strategy.

So how is the supply and demand in your area?

⤒ Top
↘ Down
⤓ Bottom
↗ Up
N/A Not applicable at this time
MF Major factor

LOCAL FACTOR #5: NEIGHBORHOOD TRENDS

In any city or town, you can always find one area that's prosperous and another area nearby that's stagnant or declining. Drive around the neighborhood at different times of the day (morning, afternoon, night, weekends, and weekdays). Is the area run-down, with lots of broken-down cars on the streets and driveways and yards not maintained? Do just a few houses look like this or is the entire neighborhood run-down? Are some houses being fixed up? By looking for subtle signs about a neighborhood's condition, you can get a rough idea about the history and future of an area.

Beyond a visual study of a neighborhood, look into its background as well. What have the local employment statistics been over the last one to ten years? Has the city's population grown or declined over the same time period? What is the median income? You can get the median income by zip code from the local chamber of commerce or your local city or state web site.

What is the employment base of the area? Is it diversified or heavily reliant on a single industry or local employer? In the Midwest, the big three auto makers (Ford, General Motors, and Chrysler) are closing plants and lay-ing off workers. Even worse, many of these plants are the number one or two employers in town, so a single plant closing can have a major effect on the real estate market.

As a result, homes can often be purchased for the price of the land be-cause few people have the money or ability to finance properties. Because people still need a place to live, these types of areas can make excellent rental markets. You can oftentimes get 100% financing and still generate a positive cash flow. The key with rental property is property management. If you're not able or willing to manage the property yourself, you'll need to hire a good property manager. I'll discuss property management in Chapter 19.

A local factor, such as an economic condition, can change the strategy you use in purchasing properties. So the Midwest, for example, may not be the place to try the "fix and flip" strategy unless you can purchase the prop-erty at a deep discount. Instead, you'd be better off using a rental strategy.

When evaluating any area, you need to use a combination of objective data and your own instinct. Just be careful that you don't fall in love with the right house in the wrong neighborhood.

Real-Life Story

The following story of two of my friends shows the danger of relying too heavily on your instinct and not enough on objective information.

"We purchased a beautiful 1910 Victorian home that we fell in love with the mo-ment we stepped inside. Although the house was run-down, it still had beautiful leaded glass windows, natural woodwork, built-in hutches with glass doors, and hard-wood floors. We bought it, cleaned it up, and made it sparkle.

"We loved the house even though it was in a questionable neighborhood. As a re-sult, we violated the number one principle of real estate: Location, location, location. To make a long story short, the beautiful house we loved could be rented only to less than desirable tenants because the type of tenants we hoped to attract didn't want to live in that neighborhood.

"Although we later sold the house for a small profit, we would have been better off buying a different home in a much better neighborhood."

One neighborhood trend that can get overlooked is the commuting time to nearby jobs. People want the right balance of affordability and tolerable commuting time. In my neighborhood, home prices have been steadily in-creasing because of its central location to community events and businesses and its proximity to public transportation and the airport. The central location makes the commute time to work more tolerable, while the short drive to the airport makes business trips more convenient for regular business travelers. Best of all, the area is already built up, which means there is no room for expansion, making the existing homes more valuable and in limited supply.

So think about any neighborhood factors that affect the area where you want to invest and figure out what effect they have on your market:

↑ Top
↘ Down
↓ Bottom
↗ Up
N/A Not applicable at this time
MF Major factor

CALCULATING LOCAL FACTORS

A single local factor can outweigh multiple national factors, so it's important to understand your neighborhood thoroughly. That's why I emphasize that you should invest where you live, at least until you become familiar with real estate investment. After all, who knows more about a neighborhood than the people who live there?

For each local factor, circle one of the symbols (top, down, bottom, up, not applicable, or major factor). Because local factors can be so important, do your research carefully. You may just find a neighborhood that's ready to boom while the rest of the country is going bust.

In most of the country between 2000 and 2004, you could buy any house that needed a little work, clean it up, and sell it for a tidy profit. But no real estate market lasts forever. There's always going to be a time when the market starts coming down, and that's not the time to get scared. That's the time to become a switch-hitter. If a right-handed pitcher comes to the mound, bat right-handed. If a left-handed pitcher comes to the mound, bat left-handed.

That's exactly what you have to do with real estate. Use one set of strategies as the market goes up and a different set when the market comes down, and you can make just as much money going either way.

For example, my dad had a friend who wanted to buy a foreclosure. He asked my advice because I had done a lot of buying and selling in that area. Using both the national and local factors I've outlined in this chapter and in

Chapter 3, I determined that the local market was in a down cycle, so buying foreclosures and tax sales made the most sense.

My dad's friend soon found a foreclosure using my techniques, but he backed out at the last minute and asked whether I wanted to buy the property. The price was less than $60,000 for a two-family home. Now, I don't know where you can buy a two-family home for that kind of money anywhere in the country. I knew it had to be worth about four times that amount in that particular neighborhood. So I bought it sight unseen (not a strategy I recommend to novice investors).

Paying the past taxes, the attorney, and the purchase price cost me just under $60,000. I went to my mortgage broker and refinanced as fast as possible. Now remember, a good mortgage broker deals with a multitude of banks to help you find the best financing possible. I asked my mortgage broker to find a bank that didn't worry about seasoning. (*Seasoning* means that the bank wants you to own a piece of property for a certain period of time, such as six months or a year, before they'll approve you for refinancing based on the value of the property versus basing the financing on your purchase price.) You may have to pay an extra half a percent in interest for this privilege, though.

I told my mortgage broker that I had just bought a property for $60,000, but I thought it could be appraised for more than $200,000. Well, I refinanced that house and walked out of the closing with a check for $188,000. After paying back the $60,000, I still had $128,000 left.

My rental income from it pays the mortgage. Now I'm going to spend $30,000 to make improvements (with the bank's money) so I can rent it out for the maximum amount possible, and I'll still have $98,000 left. I'm going to hold the property until the market changes in a few years. Then I can decide to sell in an upward cycle and make even more money. Whether the real estate market goes up or down, I win, and these are the types of strategies I want to teach you.

CONCLUSION

By the time you are finished reading this book, I want you to know how to purchase properties just like I did in this real-life example. The key is to do your research up-front and buy properties at the right price. By using the right techniques, you will minimize your risk and maximize your profit. You will build a safety net (just like an insurance policy) so that you establish the right conditions before and when you purchase property. Read on, and the strategies and techniques will become clearer.

CHAPTER 5

KNOWING YOUR
REAL ESTATE MARKET

*Change is the law of life. And those who look only to
the past or present are certain to miss the future.*
—JOHN F. KENNEDY

In the last two chapters, I explained how to find and identify local and national factors that can influence the current real estate cycle in your area. Identifying all these factors may seem like a lot of work, but believe me, it's worth it. While others are guessing what the future may bring, you're moving forward with strategies that can equal a lifetime of abundance and wealth.

In this chapter, I want to make identifying the cycle of your real estate market so simple that anybody can do it. To help you understand how to use local and national factors to identify your real estate market, I use plenty of stories and examples from my own local area in Phoenix, Arizona.

Take the time to go through my examples and see how I came up with each decision. By the end of this chapter, you should be able to evaluate your own real estate market the same way. In Part III, I'll show you how to match your cycle with the best strategies for success.

If you're scared about getting involved in your first real estate transaction, relax. I'll be with you every step of the way.

THE PHOENIX REAL ESTATE CYCLE IN 2004

In 2004, the real estate market in much of this country was in an upward cycle due to affordable interest rates, flow of funds, job growth, and other upward cycle ingredients. Phoenix, however, became one of the hotter real estate markets in the country due to a number of local factors. By going though a quick analysis, I'll show why the Phoenix real estate market continued to boom for two years longer than most of the rest of the country's real estate market.

As we go through each local and national factor, I'm going to give each factor a symbol like the ones we used in the previous two chapters:

↑ Top
↘ Down
↓ Bottom
↗ Up
N/A Not applicable at this time
MF Major factor

Interest rates (2004)

During 2004, interest rates were at a record low, which encouraged more people to buy homes. People were using riskier forms of financing such as 100% financing, interest-only, adjustable-rate mortgages (ARMs), which allowed them to buy much more home than they could afford if they had to use a traditional thirty-year fixed mortgage with a 20% down payment. When interest rates stay low, adjustable-rate mortgages also stay low, but when interest rates rise, adjustable-rate mortgages become increasingly more expensive.

Because the market was appreciating much faster than interest rates, many people were buying homes as short-term, one- to three-year investments using ARMs. Then they would sell the house for a profit before the ARM interest rate could increase. Because so many people were buying homes, this contributed to the upward housing market cycle. In Phoenix during this time, you could buy a house, hold it for six months to a year, and sell it for a great profit.

So in 2004, interest rates were a definite ingredient for an upswing market:

Rating = ↗ and MF

Inflation (2004)

I think you can ignore inflation as a major factor in the real estate market unless it swings from one extreme (hyperinflation) to another (deflation). So in 2004, I would have rated inflation's effect on the Phoenix real estate market as not much of a factor:

Rating = N/A

Flow of investment funds (2004)

In 2004, the flow of investments funds was dominated by real estate. People still had no confidence in the stock market and were not ready to reinvest their money from the 2000 crash. The "buzz" of real estate profits made even more first-time investors flow into the real estate sector. So in my opinion this was a definite contribution to an upswing market:

Rating = ↗

Business cycle (2004)

The national business cycle during 2004 was stagnant. While there was some job growth in certain sectors, it was offset by many companies still recuperating from the stock market crash. Because of this, many businesses began looking for ways to increase profitability, such as through outsourcing to other countries. This ultimately took jobs away from Americans.

As a national factor, this contributed to a downward cycle. But remember that local factors can outweigh national ones. In Phoenix, the local business cycle was booming while in many midwestern and northern states, the local economy was much worse that the national average. Overall, let's rate the business cycle as an ingredient in 2004 for a down market:

Rating = ↘

Cataclysmic events (2004)

In 2004 no cataclysmic events had a direct affect on the real estate market so this factor is not applicable:

Rating = N/A

Migration and job growth (2004)

Local factors in 2004 made Phoenix one of the fastest growing cities in America. Approximately 110,000 people migrated to Phoenix in that year, which led to an increased need for housing.

Builders could not keep up and nearly every new construction project was selling out within hours.

Now remember, Phoenix was growing so fast because other places in the country were losing people that fast. For Phoenix in 2004, migration and job growth were strong and a definite ingredient to an up market:

Rating = ↗

Path of development (2004)

Phoenix is a growing city and has a lot of new development plans. Besides new housing developments, there have been plans for a new football stadium and a light-rail mass-transit system. While there were pockets of run-down areas, a little research from local government web sites and economic development committees could show you which run-down areas were right in the path of future development.

With so much new construction going on, the opportunities for flipping (buying and selling) properties was everywhere, so this was a definite ingredient towards an up cycle:

Rating = ↗

New construction (2004)

Builders could not build fast enough and were expanding further and further out of the city limits. Yet real estate prices in nearby areas such as Peoria, Glendale, Queen Creek, and Anthem remained extremely affordable, which drove many people to those outlying areas, even before the infrastructure (roads, sewage, shopping malls, and so on) in those cities could catch up.

With houses being sold just as fast as they were being built, this ingredient signaled a definite up market:

Rating = ↗

Supply and demand (2004)

The supply of homes could not keep up with the demand, which made Phoenix the second fastest-growing city in America behind Las Vegas. There are lots of ways to reinforce what was obviously happening in Phoenix. You could read about it in local papers, search online using search engines, check with title companies, and ask realtors.

I like getting the facts, so I asked my realtor to provide me with statistics showing how many more homes were being sold in a shorter period of time than before. Since homes were selling faster in 2004 than they had in the previous year (and even in the previous six months), the trend was heading straight up at this point, indicating an up market. I also rate this a major factor because home sales increased so rapidly:

Rating = ↗ and MF

Neighborhood trends (2004)

While overall real estate prices in Phoenix were climbing, in certain pockets prices were skyrocketing. In the older part of central Phoenix, homes were located on large parcels of land. This, along with its central location, made prices in the area jump practically every day. You could sell a house hours after putting it on the market, which allowed people to buy another house using the equity from their current home. Therefore neighborhood trends definitely pointed to an up cycle:

Rating = ↗

Analyzing the market in 2004

In 2004, the market was in such an incredible up cycle that you could buy a property, hold it for a short period of time, and then sell it in a bidding war for thousands more than even the inflated listing. Many people even started buying second and third homes so they could hold and flip (sell) them a short time later for a hefty profit. Such a frenzy fueled even greater demand as more people rushed into the real estate market before it was too late.

In such a frantic real estate climate, it's easy for people to scream "Bubble!" and warn everyone away. Although such skyrocketing prices couldn't last forever, here's where your research and homework can help.

Based on the national and local factors described in this section, it was obvious that the Phoenix up market would likely continue a few more years after the overall national real estate market had cooled. So while some people were jumping out of the real estate market, I felt that there was still time to take advantage of this up cycle.

Unfortunately, many people ignored the local factors that were making Phoenix an up market. If they had just held on from 2004 to early 2006, they would have made 50% to 100% gains on their property. So taking all national and local factors into consideration and plugging them into the graph in Figure 5.1, you can see that Phoenix in 2004 had an overabundance of up cycle ingredients. Therefore, we would use up market strategies (explained in Part III of this book) in our real estate transactions.

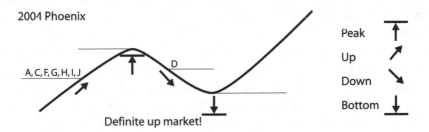

Figure 5.1 An evaluation of the Phoenix real estate market in 2004

National Factors
A = Interest rates
B = Inflation
C = Flow of investment funds
D = Business cycles
E = Cataclysmic events

Local Factors
F = Migration and job growth
G = Path of development
H = New construction
I = Supply and demand
J = Neighborhood factors

THE PHOENIX REAL ESTATE MARKET IN 2006

Now let's take a few minutes and compare the Phoenix real estate market in 2004 with the one in late 2006. By analyzing the local and national factors in 2004, I could see that the Phoenix market would continue its upward trend. How long was uncertain, but it definitely had a good amount of time left. By the beginning of 2006, the Phoenix market had peaked.

It's easy in hindsight to say what you should have done. But if you had analyzed local and national factors, you could predict with a fair degree of accuracy exactly what the Phoenix market would do. It's not rocket science. It's just doing your homework and understanding how the real estate market always moves in a gradual cycle. Unlike the stock market, which can crash in a single day, the real estate market is more predictable.

Understanding the current real estate cycle lets you make decisions based on solid information. Too many people ignore the facts, which everyone could study if they took the time, and either hope that the real estate up cycle continues forever (it won't) or panic too early and feel that any up cycle will suddenly drop overnight (it won't).

At the time that I'm writing this, it's late 2006, so let's go through the determining factors again and see where the Phoenix area as a whole seems to be heading.

Interest rates (2006)

After being at incredibly low rates for several years, interest rates are now rising to slow down inflation. This increase isn't significant all at once, but after so many years of all-time-low interest rates, these increases will most likely continue.

Low interest rates encouraged many people to finance new homes using adjustable-rate mortgages (ARMs) or interest-only mortgages. As interest rates slowly creep up, those people will need to pay more each month, possibly putting them in a financial bind. This will cause unprepared people to put their houses on the market, creating an overabundance of supply.

With interest rates climbing and showing no signs of dropping back down, banks are also more reluctant to lend money because of the slowing in the real estate market. Thus it's harder for people to qualify for a loan because banks are more selective, loaning money only to people whom they believe can afford the higher mortgage payments. At this time in late 2006, I would rate interest rates as a factor contributing to a downward cycle:

Rating = ↘

Inflation (2006)

A concern about the possibility of inflation is one of the reasons the federal government is raising interest rates. But at this time, inflation isn't a major factor:

Rating = NA

Flow of investment funds (2006)

Flow of funds from one investment sector to another is not much a factor at this time. Generally, the flow of funds is coming from first-time investors trying to pull out of the real estate market before it goes down any further.

People who used the wrong strategy towards the peak are now trying to make some of the funds flow back in their pocket. Flow of funds has some effect at this time, but I would say it is not applicable as a factor for determining the real estate cycle on a national level:

Rating = N/A

National business cycle (2006)

In 2006, the national business cycle was still uneven. While job growth continued in certain sectors, others continued to plummet, specifically manufacturing jobs. As a national factor, this continued to contribute to a downward cycle.

In Phoenix, the business cycle had slowed but still maintained a steady growth. Overall, I'd rate the national business cycle as pointing to a market that had peaked:

Rating = ↑

Cataclysmic events (2006)

Even though in late 2006 the threat of a terrorist attack is on everyone's mind, in my opinion it is not affecting the real estate market. We have become hardened as a nation since 9/11 and the confidence of getting through another possible attack is greater. So at this time I would consider this factor N/A:

Rating = N/A

Migration and job growth (2006)

Migration continued to increase in Phoenix at an even greater rate. In 2005, 137,000 people moved to the area, and that number is expected to increase for 2006. This has helped prolong a peak and downward market in Phoenix longer than in many areas of the country. This is a major plus for the Phoenix area, but soon you will learn how some determining factors can outweigh others and become a stronger ingredient in a peak and downward market. At this time, job growth and migration is still contributing to an up or peak market. I rate this factor as follows:

Rating = ↑

Path of development (2006)

With the huge wave of people continuing to migrate to Phoenix, lots of areas still need development. New construction is likely to continue, specifically in areas that grew faster than the infrastructure.

Because there are still pockets of growth throughout Phoenix, I'd rate this as contributing to an up market:

Rating = ↑

New construction (2006)

New construction of residential homes was one of the biggest local factors that caused the real estate market to peak in Phoenix in early 2006. Now in late 2006, new construction is down. Back in 2004 and even through the middle of 2005, people would line up outside a developer's office early in the morning just for the chance of putting their name on a list to buy a home in that community. As a result, builders overspeculated. Growth was so fast and furious that everyone overestimated what the area could handle. Many builders are in the middle of enormous projects, even though there is now more supply than demand for houses. For late 2006, new construction is contributing to a down market:

Rating = ↘

Supply and demand (2006)

To determine supply and demand, I asked a realtor for statistics about home prices. Not surprisingly, prices are declining and the number of days a house stays on the market is rising. The average home has dropped approximately $55,000 while staying on the market almost three times as long as the same date the preceding year.

To show you how far supply has exceeded demand, many developers are offering incentives (such as free vacations or appliances) just to get potential home buyers to look at their properties. What's crazy is that people are still moving into the area, but oversupply makes an excessive supply of housing not only a factor to promote a down market, but a major factor:

Rating = ↘ and MF

Analyzing the market in 2006

Overall, I'd say Phoenix in late 2006 completed a peak formation and is on a downward trend in most areas. But, as I will explain on the following page, due to unique circumstances in larger cities, each pocket or area could take on its own characteristics (trending up or down) based on the external factors that we have discussed. So always make sure to take that in to consideration. Figure 5.2 shows how I would chart Phoenix in late 2006.

Figure 5.1 represents exactly where the Phoenix area was in 2004, and Figure 5.2 shows where it was in late 2006, but there are always exceptions. Let me explain. The Phoenix light-rail mass-transit system is still being constructed, so properties near this path of development are increasing in price. Properties within walking distance of the light-rail transit stations have dramatically increased over the past two to three years and continue to do so. In addition, the value of property in the South Scottsdale area has increased because there is demand to be close to a new project: the Scottsdale Technology Park, a joint venture with Arizona State University.

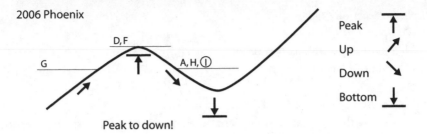

Figure 5.2 An evaluation of the Phoenix real estate market in 2006

National Factors
A = Interest rates
B = Inflation
C = Flow of investment funds
D = Business cycles
E = Cataclysmic events

Local Factors
F = Migration and job growth
G = Path of development
H = New construction
I = Supply and demand
J = Neighborhood factors

The real estate market in central Phoenix, known as Arcadia, has stayed strong as well. My guess is that this is due to its central location plus the fact that this older part of Phoenix offers large, green lots that can't be found anywhere else in the area. Because there are only so many lots available in this area, supply will always be limited and demand will always be high. So after considering all factors in an area, look for pockets that may be moving in the opposite direction.

At the time of this writing, based on the local and national factors in late 2006, I would tend to take a more conservative approach and say that Phoenix is in a downward cycle, which means your investing strategies should include more deeply discounted properties where you have greater opportunities for profit by purchasing properties below market value including: foreclosures, distressed properties, tax sale properties, and lease-to-buy options with no money down and no downside risk.

Within the hot pockets of Phoenix that are still in an upward cycle, I'd suggest 100% financing to buy a property with no money down and then flip it for profit as well as locking up a property on contract so you can buy it cheap before prices go up.

NOW IT'S YOUR TURN

Now let's talk about your area. Use the symbols that you selected from the previous chapters. Remember they are

 Top
↘ Down

↓ Bottom
↗ Up
N/A Not applicable at this time
MF Major factor

Interest rates

We'll start with national factors. What are the current interest rates? From your research, where were interest rates a year ago and six months ago? Do you think interest rates will climb or drop? Remember that interest rates usually have an opposite effect, so if they're rising it could be a sign of a down market, and if they're falling it could be an ingredient of an up market.

Rating = _____

Inflation

Now rate inflation. Take a quick look at inflation to make sure that it is normal. Remember that inflation is probably not applicable most of the time.

Rating = _____

Flow of funds

Have you seen any news regarding the flow of investment funds into or out of the real estate market?

Rating = _____

National business cycle

What is the economy doing? How is job growth nationally? Is the unemployment rate rising or falling? Is there an election coming up, helping swing things one way or another?

Rating = _____

Cataclysmic events

I hope the rating for cataclysmic events is N/A.

Rating = _____

Migration and job growth

Are people leaving your area for more prosperous parts of the country or are they coming into your community? Is a new company opening a plant or closing an existing one? Has your area been stagnant for a while and ready to explode or are there no signs of change?

Rating = _____

Path of development

Any new areas or communities ready to explode? Look for new drug stores, large department stores, and shopping centers where there are few houses. Is the city or town expanding your water or sewer districts? Are there new elected officials who want to promote or hinder growth?

Rating = _____

New construction

Check with the building department either online or in person. Is new construction on the rise? If so, are they selling or is there an overabundance of new homes? Is it hard to find a good new home in your area?

Rating = _____

Supply and demand

Remember to ask your current realtor or a prospective realtor to check today's statistics compared to a year ago at the same time and maybe six months earlier. Are more houses on the market and taking longer to sell? Are new home developments offering incentives to buy or do you have to wait in line to get a house? Are prices falling, staying the same, or rising?

Rating = _____

Neighborhood factors

Neighborhood trends are more personal to you than even the rest of the local factors. Is there any one thing or a few things that stand out in the area? A limited amount of homes? Convenience to airports, mass transit, or highways? A new company or mall coming into the area? Or is the area on the decline with an overabundance of homes for sale?

Rating = _____

Analyzing the market

Now that you have taken the time to give your best analysis of each national and local factor, let's chart it so you can see where your area is and where it may be heading. Place the letter representing each factor on the proper place on the chart shown in Figure 5.3 on the following page. If it is not applicable, just write N/A. If it is a major factor, write MF.

Now that you better understand how to evaluate your real estate market, you can use the same techniques for the rest of your real estate investing career. So revisit this as often as necessary.

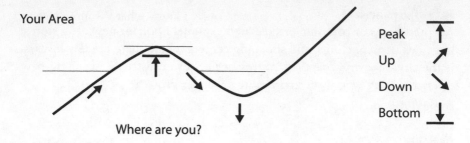

Figure 5.3 A blank chart for you to evaluate your own real estate market

National Factors
A = Interest Rates
B = Inflation
C = Flow of investment funds
D = Business cycles
E = Cataclysmic events

Local Factors
F = Migration and job growth
G = Path of development
H = New construction
I = Supply and demand
J = Neighborhood factors

CONCLUSION

Understanding real estate cycles can give you confidence to act even when things are changing. When I don't follow my own advice, I inevitably make mistakes. When I use all the factors covered in the last three chapters, I feel confident in my investing decisions, and my profits show I'm often right.

Recently, I found out that a home I had built and sold about six years ago was for sale. The house had been for sale through the up market but the owners had held out for too much money. They held out so long that they missed the up market, went through the peak, and still owned it as the area started a downward cycle.

When they put the home up for sale about two years ago, they were asking $675,000. Someone offered them $650,000 but they declined. After some time, they reduced the price, but they were still asking about $25,000 more than it was worth. Finally, when they got desperate, they rented the home with a lease option; that didn't work out and they had to evict the tenants.

To make this long story short, after not living in the house for two years and paying a mortgage, they needed to close on the home fast. That was about the time I found out that the home was back for sale. You can imagine their desperation and lack of confidence. They knew they had a great house but it would not sell and they had no idea why. There were several factors, but one was a cooling market. Now this house is in a small town in upstate New York where I do a lot of investing, so I know the area well. When I spoke to them on the phone about the house, I knew what I wanted to pay, yet I let them set the price. They had already been through a lot and I did not want to seem as if I was coming in to steal their property because they were desperate. They set a price of $455,000 and I agreed.

Now here is where confidence came in. This home was for sale for quite some time, and in this small town, a $500,000 home is among the top 5% of the most expensive homes. When a market takes a downward turn, this type of home is usually the first to be affected. I knew that the downward trend was going to last for probably a few more years. But buying a home worth probably $650,000 in a decent market for $455,000 is a good deal in any market, and I knew that with confidence.

In a downward market, I would typically say that buy, fix, and flip is not a strong strategy. But when you get such a discount on a home, it is a strategy in any market. In a down market, you will need to sell at a much lower price to move a home, but if you buy at a crazy low price, you can still make a profit in the middle, which is exactly what I did.

I had the place painted, installed new carpet, did some light landscaping, put sealer on the driveway, and put it on the market. After owning the home for about two months, it was under contract for $575,000.

And here is the best part: I did a 103% loan on that home. You will learn more about loans in Chapter 13, but for now I'll say that I borrowed enough money to buy the home plus cover all the closing expenses. I literally bought the home without using a penny of my own money. I made one payment on it, and it is set to close about a month from now.

How was I able to make money on a big home, in a small town, in a down market, with a flip strategy? Because I did my homework, I knew what I was facing, and I had the confidence to go for it.

> *Learn the cycle that your area is in and you will own something most people don't have—the confidence to make money investing in real estate in any market in any cycle.*

Learn the cycle in your area and you will own something most people don't—the confidence to make money in real estate in any market in any cycle.

CHAPTER 6

GETTING STARTED INVESTING IN REAL ESTATE

It's tangible, it's solid, it's beautiful. It's artistic,
from my standpoint, and I just love real estate.
—DONALD TRUMP

That wasn't painful now, was it? After going through Chapters 3 through 5 to identify national and local factors that could affect the real estate market, you probably know more about identifying and understanding real estate cycles than many full-time investors.

If someone had given me this information twenty years ago, I might have avoided major mistakes and made a lot more money. In all my years of real estate investing, I've been lucky enough to lose money on only one or two real estate deals, but until I learned about real estate cycles, I often bought and sold at the wrong time. With the information in this book, and the additional support you can get by going to www.deangraziosi.com, I have no doubt you can become wealthy investing in real estate.

To succeed in life, use a contrarian's approach: Think differently and do things that other people don't do.

From an early age, I learned to not follow the crowd. I worked hard when most kids were messing around. I got up early when others were sleeping in. I started investing in real estate long before it was cool or trendy. So much of what I teach is not the latest sexy glitz you see splashed across the Internet, but these tried-and-true methods and techniques have worked for me and thousands of my students.

So in keeping with the contrarian's theory, I try not to follow the crowd in real estate investing either. I try to make my money before I sign a contract to buy a property. Now you may be asking, "How does anyone make money before they buy property?" It's easy.

Make sure you get to know as much as you can before you commit your time and money to any investment. Think of this preparation as an insurance policy for your financial future.

To succeed in life, think differently and do things that other people don't do.

To make money before investing, I analyze a property's pros and cons. Most importantly, I analyze how I'm going to make my money on the property before I buy it. I want to clearly identify when I will sell the property and what I need to do to the property before I can sell it.

Furthermore, I like to have a backup in case my original plan doesn't work the way I intended. With more expensive properties, I create a backup to my backup for the worst case scenario.

Generally, if you do your homework and don't necessarily follow the crowd, you will achieve more success in real estate investing than you ever thought possible.

THE BASIC STEPS OF BUYING AND SELLING REAL ESTATE

For most people, the only time they buy or sell real estate is when they move to a new house, which happens so rarely that each time it happens, the entire experience can seem like they're going through it for the first time.

Basically, there are three steps to buying real estate. First, you need to find property to buy. Second, you need to negotiate a price with the seller. Third, you need to find the cash to pay the seller so you can legally take over the property.

To sell real estate, you follow similar steps. First, you put your property on the market to make it available to buyers. Second, you negotiate with a buyer for the price you want. Third, you wait for the buyer to give you the money.

Fairly simple, right? When you think about it, buying and selling real estate is really no different than buying and selling anything. The main differences are the details, and that's where buying and selling real estate can seem confusing. However, if you understand the basic idea of buying and selling anything, you already know most of what you need to buy and sell real estate.

Finding property to buy

Most people buy real estate by talking to a real estate agent, who then shows you different properties based on what you want to pay and the areas you want to buy. There's nothing wrong with buying real estate through an agent, but don't forget that you can find property to buy in many other ways as well, each with its own advantages and disadvantages.

For example, when you buy property through a real estate agent, he or she takes a commission that can range from 6% to 10%, depending on the property and the agent. In return for the commission, the agent can give you advice on good and bad things to look for in property, which might not be readily obvious if you know nothing about real estate.

Buying real estate through an agent is often the simplest and most convenient route for people who want help in buying property. Even if you're an experienced real estate investor, you might still want to buy property through an agent just because the agent spends his or her time constantly monitoring the real estate market.

A real estate agent can tell you the trends of a given area and let you know how long homes have been on the market and whether prices seem to be climbing or falling. A competent, trusted real estate agent can be a valuable ally no matter how much experience you might have in real estate. I still use agents on a lot of my deals. But one thing to remember is that agents are paid on commission and have a financial interest in getting you to buy or sell.

You don't have to use an agent. You can just as easily search for property to buy by reading the classified ads in your local newspaper. Or drive around and find For Sale signs planted in front yards. Your friends or relatives might even know of someone who's selling.

All these methods can take time, but they give you the advantage of finding property that real estate agents may not even know about. If you can find property before anyone else hears about it, you can buy it before anyone else can, thereby avoiding a possible bidding war.

Here's another way you can buy property. Ask. Just because you don't see a For Sale sign on the front lawn or an advertisement in the newspaper, that doesn't mean you can't buy that property. Go to the web site or office of your town or city's tax assessor, and you can find the name, address, and phone number of the property's owner. Then contact the owner directly and politely ask whether the property is for sale.

This approach is most successful when looking at distressed properties, such as an abandoned home, because the property might be a liability to the owner, who would be only too glad to get rid of it. Remember, it never hurts to ask. This is just a teaser of the techniques on finding and buying properties that you will learn about in Part III.

Analyzing the property

> *A successful man continues to look for work after he has found a job.*
> —UNKNOWN

Analyzing property means getting as much information as possible to help you decide whether this is the right property for you. Some important aspects of a thorough property analysis follow:

- *Location:* Look at the curb appeal, access, surrounding area, and future potential. Is the property location an asset or a liability? Make sure that the type of property fits the real estate cycle you are in.
- *Condition:* Consider eye appeal, needed repairs, and functionality. How much will it cost to bring the property up to your standards?
- *Value:* Consider the asking price, your offer price, the potential for future appreciation. Are you paying market price or below market price? This can be determined by having your title company run a sales comparison of similar properties that have recently sold in the area. (Remember that in some cases, full price can be your friend.)
- *Amenities:* What comes with the property that adds value? Appliances, a water conditioner, a newer air conditioning unit, a new roof, landscaping, a security system (leased or owned)?
- *Income potential:* Is the property currently leased at, below, or above market rates, and what improvements will be necessary to maximize income potential?
- *Functional obsolescence:* How is the property laid out? Does it work for your intended purposes, and would a prospective tenant or purchaser like what they see?
- *Extras:* Does anything else come as part of the purchase price, such as additional lots? (Always keep your mind open to thinking a little differently. You may be purchasing a single-family home, but the property may be large enough or laid out in a way that will allow you to subdivide another buildable lot or two that could put big cash in your pocket.)
- *Existing financing:* Is the mortgage assumable? *Assumable* basically means that the lien holder will allow the loan to be transferred to a new owner. If not, what are your chances of working with the current lender to restructure the debt in your name or of securing a new first mortgage?
- *New financing:* Know all the available options for financing and purchasing the property.
- *Liens and encumbrances:* What liabilities come along with the property in the form of unpaid taxes, special assessments, or other liens? Your title agent will deliver that information in the title report after you have a contract on the property. Read this document carefully. Better yet, if you have a real estate agent or mortgage broker working with you, have them review the report and outline any areas of concern.
- *Environmental issues:* Is the property located close to power lines, a waste disposal facility, traffic noise, a previous landfill? Does it have any other issues that would detract from its future sales price and the price you are offering? Has the property been tested for radon gas, formaldehyde, and lead paint?

Negotiating a price to pay

Real estate prices aren't fixed. You can always negotiate a price, but just ask-ing for a lower price is rarely going to work unless you can either justify a reason for your lower price or offer the seller something in return for the lower price.

For example, if you know that a home's chimney is damaged or the wiring needs to be replaced, you can offer a lower price and use these condi-tions to justify your reason. The seller might not agree with your price, but at least he or she can see that you have a reason for asking for a lower price. If you just ask for a lower price without giving a reason why, it tends to in-sult the seller and makes it harder to close the deal no matter how much you may really want the property.

If you can't find any faults with a property, try offering the seller a lower price plus something else besides money. For example, suppose the property has cars in the backyard that must be hauled to the junkyard. Offer the seller a lower price for the property, but say you'll take care of the junk in the backyard. This saves the seller the hassle and cost of doing this himself, which can justify your lower asking price.

Negotiating a price is the time to get creative. I once bought a house that several other people also wanted to buy, but the seller refused to budge from her asking price, which was about $10,000 more than it was really worth. I knew she would never lower her price, so I got creative and offered her the full asking price.

Of course, giving her full price made her happy, so I also asked her to do something to make me happy. Rather than accept full payment up front, I offered to pay her full price within two years at no interest, just monthly payments that came directly off the purchase amount. She would get her full asking price, and I would get the property with no money down and no interest fees. She agreed, and I bought her home.

So you see, when negotiating a price, find out what the seller really wants, identify what you're willing to give, and negotiate your price from there. Too many people just offer a price without explaining their reason why, so given a choice between selling to those people or to you, which would you rather do?

The oldest adage in real estate investing is that "if one person sets the price and the other person sets the terms, you can always come to an agree-ment for sale." It all comes down to benefits. Who gets what benefit, when do they get it, and what is it going to cost them to receive it? This simple "benefits" philosophy has been the basis for negotiating and creative financ-ing for ages, and I have used it often in my real estate purchases.

Every property is different, and each seller and each seller's motivation for disposing of an asset (or liability, as the case may be) is different as well. An essential part of making a property deal work for both you and the seller is the financing involved. The only way to know the right financing approach is to fully understand the who, what, when, where, why, and how much of the property in question. Then you can decide just how creative you need to be in your negotiations and financing proposal to the seller. In Chapters 13–15 you will learn a variety of financing techniques you can mix and match to make your deals become a reality.

Just remember that information is the key to your success! The more you have, the more likely it is that you will succeed in any situation.

Getting the money to pay the price

Here comes the part that seems tricky to many people. After you find a property to buy and negotiate a fair price, you need to come up with the money to buy that property. Unless you happen to have hundreds of thousands of dollars spilling out of your bank account, you'll probably have to buy real estate using a loan.

Typically, you go to a bank and ask for a loan. The bank determines how much money they think you can safely borrow and then they give you that money. You take that money, give it all to the seller, and the seller walks away with all the cash and you walk away with the property.

Naturally, banks don't make a profit by lending money unless they also collect interest. The simplest loan is a fixed-rate loan. The bank loans you money and you have a fixed amount of time, typically thirty or fifteen years, to pay back the loan at a fixed rate of interest.

A fixed-rate, thirty-year loan with a 20% down payment is what most people think you need to use when buying real estate. But in Chapters 13–15, you will learn that you can purchase property in many ways, such as private lenders, seller financing, and lease options.

Although I've simplified the steps involved in buying real estate, the basic ideas remain the same: Find property, negotiate a price, and pay for it.

Selling property

Selling real estate is basically as simple as buying. First you put your property on the market. This can be as simple as pounding a For Sale sign in your front yard, or it can include listing your property with a real estate agent. The purpose of putting your property on the market is to attract buyers.

When you sell your property can determine how much you can get for it and how long you may have to wait until someone buys it. In an up cycle, prices can rise every day and you might even have a bidding war, with two or more people increasing their offers to buy your property.

If you sell during a down cycle, you may need to leave your property on the market for a long time; even then, you may get much less than you want. In a down cycle, it's generally best to hold onto property, rent it, and wait for an up cycle before trying to sell.

As the property owner, you can determine the selling price. If nobody meets your price, you can hold onto the property. Many people sell property without waiting for the optimum time because they have to move (such as a job relocation) or they want to cash out now and not wait. As long as you don't need the money and you don't need to get rid of the property, it's best to hold on until you get the price you want.

When you sell property, the buyer basically writes you a check. This money is usually the bank's money (that the bank loaned to the buyer).

REAL ESTATE PEOPLE YOU MAY NEED

Although it's possible to buy and sell property yourself, even experienced real estate investors won't necessarily do that. Instead, most people use the services of one or more professionals who can give them advice and help them through the process of closing a real estate transaction.

Banker or mortgage broker
Probably the most important person you will need is a banker or mortgage broker. A banker is a loan officer for a single bank; a mortgage broker has access to a multitude of banks. For simplicity, I'll use the term *banker* for both bankers and mortgages brokers. A banker's job is to loan money to people whom the bank believes will pay back their loans on time.

A good relationship with a banker can give you the confidence to enter into real estate transactions. After you establish a record of borrowing and paying back loans on a regular basis, your banker can speed the process in the future and even loan you more money than the bank might normally do. This can come in especially handy when you spot a great opportunity that you need to act on right away.

The longer you work with the same banker, the better the banker will understand your needs and goals. A great relationship with a banker can make real estate investing so much easier.

Real estate agent
A real estate agent can help you find or market property and guide you through the process of buying and selling real estate. Because real estate agents often specialize in certain areas, they can often tell you average housing prices and how long homes have been on the market before selling.

Although not as crucial as your relationship with a banker, a relationship with a real estate agent can prove invaluable. After an agent knows the types of properties that you buy and sell, he or she can call you the moment a property becomes available that you might be interested in. By doing this, the agent can help you find bargains and give you a chance to buy the property before anyone else can. I still buy and sell property in the little town where I grew up, and I have used the same agent for almost twenty years. She is always in my corner and looking for the next best deal.

Attorney

Let's face it, when you purchase real estate, in most cases you will need a good attorney. In many states, one is not required and you can use a title company. But if there are any unique circumstances or you do not feel totally comfortable, get an attorney you can trust. Most people who buy and sell real estate infrequently may not need an attorney, but if you buy and sell many properties, including rental properties, an attorney can protect you from possible problems as well as help you draw up agreements to use when you buy and sell properties.

Handyman or general contractor

If you plan on using a fix and flip strategy, especially with properties that need minor or even major remodeling (often called "handyman specials"), you will want a trustworthy handyman or general contractor who can assist you and give you honest estimates before you purchase a property. The fix and flip strategy basically means buying a house, fixing and improving it, and then selling it for a profit.

Real-Life Story

Knowing the right handyman or general contractor can help you make money in real estate, as one of my students learned.

Suzanna works as a school teacher in Denver. After studying different types of investment strategies, she was particularly excited about the fix and flip strategy. But she didn't know how to do repairs herself and, being a school teacher, didn't have the time to learn. By asking around and checking references, she found a great general contractor who could help her every step of the way.

When she found a house that she thought was perfect, she brought in her general contractor and he gave her an exact price to get the house in the shape she wanted. After adding the purchase price, closing costs, holding costs (a few month's payments while it sold), and the contractor's price for the repairs, she realized she would still make a good profit.

So Suzanna used her own financing techniques to purchase the home and let the contractor go to work. All she did was stop by a few times to check on the repairs and improvements. This contractor handled everything for her and got the place ready for resale. As soon as the house was finished, Suzanna put it on the market and sold it within a few months. At the closing, she paid off the loan, paid herself back the money she spent on the contractor, and walked away with more than a $20,000 profit on her first real estate investment.

She could not stop bragging about her contractor, which just goes to show how priceless the right people in your network can be. Suzanna is now investing in her second property and planning on a profit of about $50,000 using the same strategy and contractor.

Like I said before, you don't absolutely need any or all of these people. But their services can be worth paying for so you can concentrate on buying and selling property without worrying about the legal or technical details.

UNDERSTANDING THE STAGES IN THE REAL ESTATE MARKET

Now that you have a rough understanding of how buying and selling real estate works and the types of people you may need, let's review the four major markets (there is a fifth one as well, but it's rare), so you can pinpoint where your local real estate market may be.

A real estate cycle has four stages. Think of a cycle as a roller coaster ride. In the beginning, there's the slow tick on the tracks as you gradually climb upwards. This is the time when most people get so excited that they think the climb will never end.

Then you reach the top. This is when you stop going up but you haven't started to go down yet. It's as if you're hanging in midair for a split second and nothing seems to have changed. Unfortunately, this is the time when most people don't see the new direction of the market.

Suddenly, you start going down. The higher you are, the faster you can go down. This is the time when people scream and panic while others throw their hands in the air and enjoy the ride down. In real estate, the people who didn't see the inevitable downward cycle are the ones screaming and panicking. The people who saw the downward cycle and planned for it are the ones throwing their hands in the air and enjoying the ride down.

Finally, the roller coaster levels off and you think, "Whew!" Just when your head stops spinning, you start going back up again. What makes the real estate roller coaster especially exciting is that you can make money any time—going up, going down, at the top, or at the bottom.

Where people run into problems investing in real estate is when they find one strategy that works and then keep trying to use that same strategy no matter how conditions around them may change.

Let's do a quick review of the different real estate cycles.

Up cycle

In an up cycle, demand for homes is higher than the supply, which increases property values. To tell whether the real estate market is in an up cycle, check how fast (or slow) properties are selling. In a hot market, homes often sell the same day they're listed.

Before investing in an area, pay close attention to how long it took for the latest property to sell. Also, try to find out how many offers each property received before selling. A bidding war on a property can drive the price up very quickly.

Although talking to real estate agents and brokers should give you a good idea if the market is in an up cycle, keep in mind that their commission-based pay structure leaves them little incentive to openly admit when the market is down. Check the real estate section of your local newspaper for articles that indicate whether or not the market is hot. In an up cycle, a great strategy is fixing and flipping (buying a house, fixing it up, and then selling it later for a greater profit as prices continue to climb).

Top cycle

At the top, or peak, supply is close or equal to demand and prices start stabilizing. Because cycles change directions slowly and there can be many small fluctuations within a cycle in any given real estate market, the actual peak isn't always obvious until after it's already passed.

When properties start taking longer to sell, that could indicate a peak market. Unless the seller is asking for an unreasonable amount and is in no hurry to sell, longer periods of time between the listing date and the sale date may indicate that the pool of buyers has dwindled.

Typically, the longer a property is on the market, the more likely the seller will accept a lower bid. After properties start selling at lower prices, the downward trend can snowball because the final sales prices on those properties will then be the comparisons (*comps*) in that area for other real estate.

The peak can be a great place to find motivated or desperate sellers and get a great deal on property. There is typically an excess of new construction, of investment properties for sale with investors looking for the "one last buyer," and of rental properties due both to overbuilding and an increased number of residential properties purchased by investors as rentals.

This oversupply brings about the market downturn, and not only the drop in property prices but also the drop in rents to compete for the available renters.

Down cycle

During a down cycle, supply is far greater than demand. Prices can fall fairly quickly, but history has shown that in most cases, prices just stop increasing or fall slightly and stick. After buyers realize real estate prices are dropping, they are less likely to want to buy out of fear that they will lose value. As a result, properties stay on the market even longer.

A down cycle can last for years, until the national and local factors described in Chapters 3 through 5 change and cause the cycle to go back up. At the start of the down cycle, there is a "fire sale" of unsold new construction units. Developers can't afford to let the property sit, so they start cutting prices. Just like retail stores, developers make their profit from all the properties they were able to sell at full price during the boom. The ones that go on the clearance rack, after demand has been met, are already calculated into the bottom line as an expense. Keep in mind that these are not foreclosures or fixer-uppers. They are new homes sold at extreme discounts.

Bottom and prolonged bottom

At the bottom of the cycle, supply is once again much closer to demand. Prices stabilize and buyers start to come back into the market, starting the cycle all over again.

In a normal bottom market, prices have fallen as far as they can but eventually start to rise again within a few years. In rare cases, a bottom market can stay in a prolonged bottom for many years, even decades. This is the rare but possible fifth cycle that happens most often in towns or small cities that rely on a single source for employment, such as a factory.

Many cities in the country's rust belt region, which depended on the steel or automobile industries, have been in a prolonged bottom market for decades. I have visited Buffalo, New York, for the past twenty years and have yet to see any signs of growth. Even in such a prolonged bottom market, however, it's still possible to make money with the right strategy.

One of my students is looking into buying houses in Buffalo because he can get them so cheap with no money down and still make money by renting them out for positive cash flow. Then when Buffalo's real estate market starts to rise again, he'll be able to sell his properties for a profit or continue holding them for the monthly rental income.

STRATEGIZING WITH DIFFERENT TYPES
OF PROPERTY INVESTMENTS

From what you've learned about real estate cycles so far, it would seem obviously that you need to use different strategies during each cycle. So why don't more people do this? Unfortunately, many so-called real estate experts have convinced inexperienced investors that the only way to make money in real estate is to buy and hold properties for the long term.

The prevailing theory is that if you purchase, say, ten properties and hold them long until the mortgages are paid off, you will receive monthly rental income from several million dollars worth of property owned free and clear. Many people have lost a lot of money trying to follow this formula because they weren't also told about the dynamics of cycle fluctuations. I'm not saying this strategy won't work. I'm saying it won't work all the time, and this is where people miss tremendous opportunities because they were either too busy losing money or thinking they had to wait twenty or thirty years to cash out and make a profit.

Basically, you just have to know the proper cycle and use the right strategy. For example, back in 2004, I remember the newspapers were all warning that the real estate bubble was about to burst. Yet between 2004 and 2006, many places around the country had gains from 20% to 100%.

Besides being aware of real estate cycles, you should have an exit strategy for every property you buy. By defining an exit strategy beforehand, you won't run the risk of falling in love with a piece of property and then kicking yourself for holding on too long and losing the maximum amount of profit.

Although every property you buy will be different, there are basically three types:

- The keeper
- The temporary hold
- The flip

Property type #1: *The keeper*
The keeper property is found in nice neighborhoods that are unlikely to suffer from any decline. Because of their location in a more affluent, upscale area, these types of properties are fairly easy to rent.

With keeper properties, you should buy and hold for the long term, with the goal of having the mortgage paid in full from the rental income you collect every month. Even in a worse-case scenario in which the rent barely covers your mortgage without leaving any extra for positive cash flow, keeper properties will continue to appreciate in value.

Property type #2: The temporary hold

A temporary hold property is typically priced in the low to middle range, experiences large increases in a boom or up cycle, and is usually easy to both rent and sell. Generally, temporary hold properties are bought during a down or bottom market and held onto long enough to sell during an up cycle. To cover your mortgage payments, a temporary hold property can generate rental income as well, but the real money comes when you sell the property.

Property type #3: The flip

A flip property is anything you buy just to sell it right away. Usually, you can find flip properties through foreclosures, tax sales, discounted new constructions, or desperate homeowners. The idea is that you buy the property, hold it for a short period of time (usually to fix it up), and then sell, or flip, it.

Although most people associate flip properties with an up cycle, you can buy a flip property at any cycle and make a profit if you buy it right, finance it right, and sell it right. The key is to be selective and to avoid being influenced by the greed of the boom and the fear of the bust. A good deal is a good deal, regardless of the market cycle or anyone's advice.

A flip property is the fastest way to make a profit and put money in the bank. In a hot up cycle, you can make enormous profits in months and sometimes even weeks.

HOLDING PROPERTY LONG TERM

You should look at up and down cycles as seasons. You store what you've harvested in the summer so you can survive during the scarcity of winter.

Similarly, you should sell temporary hold and flip properties (property types #2 and #3) at the peak of an up cycle. This will maximize your profits and give you cash to hold your keeper properties (property type #1) during the down cycle. Plus, you can take advantage of the abundance of opportunities available during a down cycle without putting yourself at too much risk.

If you want to hold property for the long term, focus on keeper (type #1) properties. If you're primarily interested in flipping properties or if you've listened to warnings that all property should be sold at the peak, you may wonder why not just sell keeper properties at the peak and use the profits during the down cycle?

I did this in the beginning of my real estate career. I would sell any property I had when the real estate market was close to its peak, pulling out what I thought was a great profit. But in hindsight, this usually wasn't a smart decision. Why? The reason is that future peaks can be expected to be even higher than the current peak, no matter how ridiculous the current peak may seem now. So if you purchased a keeper property for $100,000 twelve months ago and it rises to $150,000 at the current peak, it may rise to $250,000 in the next peak, and $500,000 in the one after that. If your renters are paying your expenses while you're holding, you've made $400,000 from your initial investment. That's the way to build your future.

Because of this potential, it's critical that you finance keeper (type #1) properties correctly. The first mortgage should be at a fixed rate. Any second mortgages should be used for improvements to make the property more attractive to renters.

HOLDING PROPERTY SHORT TERM

You should purchase temporary hold (type #2) properties toward the end of the down cycle, the bottom, and the beginning of the up cycle, when prices are at their lowest and competition is lean. Because the next peak will likely occur in a few years, you would finance these properties with ARMs or interest-only loans to keep payments low while rents are still likely to be depressed.

Your goal with these properties is to buy low, hold, and then sell high. This type of property can generate profits at different times and helps support any long-term hold properties that you own and rent. Best of all, profits from these gains will also give you the ability to capitalize on fast flip opportunities that abound during the down cycle, without borrowing against your keeper (type #1) properties.

Flip (type #3) properties can be found in all cycles at varying discounts, amounts, and forms. The middle to the end of the up cycle sees a large amount of new construction and a frenzied market of buyers. Some speculators buy new construction properties at the planning stage and sell them after they're built. Because there are no mortgage payments during the building phase, and the first payment isn't usually due until the second month after closing, you can enjoy the gains from the overall increases in property prices during the building phase with your down payment as the only outlay.

Real-Life Story

One of my students used this fix-and-flip strategy in Florida during the 2004 housing boom to do his first deal. He had no money to invest, yet he saw the potential of locking up a new home, not paying any interest or payments on it while it was built, and selling it once it was finished.

So he visited many new developments in his area until he found one that he knew was in a location that was about to expand and that would allow him to sell the property within one year. (During an up cycle, many developers stipulate that you have to hold a new home for one year—this deters some investors.) He found the perfect development and started his negotiations to get a house built for a $5000 deposit. Now he needed the money.

He put together a small breakdown of risks versus rewards, which showed the possibilities of how much money could be made with a $5000 deposit that would be held up for about six months while the house was built. Then he went around to everyone he knew, and even some strangers, to see whether someone would put up the $5000.

He found a friend of a friend who had her money in the bank, getting minimal interest, and she took him up on his offer. They put the $5000 deposit on the house and signed the contract. His timing and thoughts for the expansion of the neighborhood were right on. When the house was completed, they immediately sold it for a $60,000 profit. My student got to make $30,000 without using any of his own money, just by doing his homework, and the woman who invested in the property got to make $25,000 (her $30,000 profit minus the $5,000 of her initial investment). A true win-win for everyone involved.

But remember, homework and cycle analysis are the keys to this type of profit. Without truly analyzing the cycle and the time it has been in an upswing, this could be risky. If you buy too early, buyers can still buy from the developer, and if you buy too late, your house might end up with those on the clearance rack.

Nonetheless, in an environment with double-digit annual price increases, even the six-month or so building period can see a tremendous increase from the original purchase price. A bubble market has a small window of opportunity when it is a great time to make a lot of money fast.

Buying a temporary hold (type #2) property can be great when there's an excess of new construction, usually following a real estate peak. If you buy early enough during an up cycle, you can often buy a home before it's constructed, hold as the price increases, and then sell at a huge profit, as my student did in the preceding example. Then as the market peaks and starts to drop, you can use your profit to buy additional properties. This is being "cycle smart."

When the market falls into a down cycle, many people pull their money out of the market. But if you think a little differently, you can see how a down cycle can be the best time to put your money into the market.

Not only do property values fall during a down cycle, but the number of

available distressed properties (foreclosures, tax sales, and bank-owned properties) increases, which means you can pick up properties at bargain-base-
ment prices. Even better, a down cycle has fewer buyers, so you have less
competition, which means sellers are more likely to make even better deals
with you.

During this time, you can often find homes in better condition needing
fewer repairs due to "friendly foreclosures," where the homeowner just
wants out of the burden of paying for overpriced property rather than being
forced out after a long period of economic distress, which typically causes
neglect. A down cycle is the time to buy a home in top condition at an extremely discounted price, but only if you're prepared and ready for it—
which, after reading this book, you will be.

TRUST YOUR OWN ANALYSIS

Because a bubble is nothing more than the end of an up cycle, and a burst is
really the beginning of a down cycle, let's recap strategies for all the stages
of the real estate cycle. That way, these terms should never discourage or
scare you again.

No matter what type of real estate you invest in, or what cycle you are in,
you can decide the best time to buy and sell to ensure that you maximize
your profits. That's why I've spent so much time talking about understanding real estate cycles before investing. Keep in mind that different markets,
whether they are local or national, can be in different stages of a cycle at the
same time. You can shift your strategies as you feel a shift in the stages of the
real estate cycle.

The main point is that a person needs to use sound judgment when evaluating places to invest. I often play a game with myself where I pretend I
have an investor or partner who cares only about making money. So I need
to support my projections of rental income and expenses, remodeling costs,
and holding costs as well as my assumptions about interest rates, the economic demographic of the type of tenant who would rent the property, the
local economic climate, and trends in the local market. To top it off, I have
to outline the worst-case scenario.

A great place to research job growth in a particular area of the country is
through an area's city and county government offices, including their economic development department. You can review the ups and downs of that
city's job growth over a five-year period by comparing its job growth statistics. Increased job growth, as a whole, increases the demand for real estate,
which in turn tends to increase its value. Decreased job growth has the

opposite effect. Depending on these factors, you can apply the appropriate strategy.

For example, having a company such as Microsoft in a community can have a profound effect on the real estate market. The number of jobs a company creates can increase the demand for housing. Look at the major employers in the area and determine the types of employees they hire: blue collar, white collar, high-income employees, and so on. Low-paid employees will likely rent. High-income employees want to buy. The types of people brought into the community affect they types of properties and strategies you use.

For example, if more employees will be renting, this would be a great area to have a *rental farm,* which is a group of rental properties in the same area that you use primarily for cash flow and secondarily for appreciation. If higher paid employees are moving in, this may be a better fix and flip market. You can look for run-down properties that can be rehabbed to be attractive to a market looking for newer but still affordable homes.

CONCLUSION

Now that you have a clear idea of what a cycle is and what cycle your current area is in, along with brief strategies for how to make money in each cycle, it's time to get started.

I'll show you how to buy property with no money down, how to buy and sell foreclosures and tax sales, what's an REO and how to make money with it, when is the best time to use a lease option strategy, how to manage rental properties, and more.

I'll explain all this, but not just yet. First, I need to give you the foundation to overcome any personal obstacles in your life that may hold you back from achieving your goals.

I don't want this to be another missed opportunity for you. Starting today, I want this to be the start of a prosperous, fulfilled, confident, and exciting life for you and your family. It's time to take control of your life, and to do that you need to set a solid foundation that will help you take action, overcome fears and obstacles, and start profiting from real estate rather than just read about it. I know it may seem like I am getting off-track, but trust me here as I help you set the foundation for life-long success and prosperity. If I can do it, so can you.

PART TWO

Building a Foundation for Success

Even though you may understand the real estate market, that knowledge is useless if mental blocks are delaying action. In this part, I explain how you can overcome problems and mental blocks that stand in the way to success.

CHAPTER 7

PUTTING YOUR FINANCES
IN ORDER

Happiness is not in the mere possession of money;
it lies in the joy of achievement, in the thrill of creative effort.
—Franklin D. Roosevelt

Doing anything for the first time can be scary, so that's why I want to show you how to make real estate investing as safe as possible. The safer you feel and the more control you have, the more likely you'll take action and achieve the success you've always dreamed about.

The first key to successful investing has nothing to do with how much money you can make or how much risk you take. In fact, smart investors know that the best investments don't involve any risks!

Let me explain. Successful investors minimize their risks and maximize their gains. That's what makes real estate so attractive. If you invest $100,000 in the stock market and the market crashes, you might be left with $50,000 in stock. But if you invest $100,000 in real estate, your investment in most cases will always be worth at least $100,000, and that's if you don't do anything at all. Plus in most cases, most of the money is not your own.

Add appreciation and rental income, and your $100,000 investment in real estate will almost always increase over time. You can't say that about most other types of investments.

The key to successful investing is to make educated, calculated risks. That's why I emphasize understanding market cycles in real estate. I don't want you to invest in real estate with hope and luck. I want you to invest with proven, time-tested strategies that greatly improve your chances of making money. Why rely on chance when you can rely on research to make a fortune?

Successful investors don't just know how to make money; they also know how to keep their money. That's why money alone can never make anyone happy or successful.

Did you know that a surprisingly large number of millionaire lottery winners wind

Successful investors don't just know how to make money. They also know how to keep their money.

up bankrupt within less than five years? Money didn't bankrupt these people. Their old habits in handling money bankrupted them. They didn't know how to handle money when they were making only $20,000 a year, so it's natural that they wouldn't know how to handle millions of dollars either.

Money alone can never make anyone happy or successful. A surprisingly large number of millionaire lottery winners wind up bankrupt within less than five years.

These lottery millionaires handled their millions the same way they handled their ordinary salaries. In other words, they spent more than they made and bought things that they didn't need and that would never increase in value. In other words, they spent their money foolishly.

I know you can make a fortune in real estate investment because I have and I've watched countless others do the same. However, I also know that you can lose a fortune if you don't develop a solid financial foundation in your own life. Like those millionaire lottery winners, you can make more money than you've ever dreamed, but if you don't know how to handle money, you could lose all the gains that you make and more.

So in this chapter, I'll show you how to develop a financial foundation that can not only help you develop real wealth but also help you keep it. After you learn how to keep your money, you'll never be broke again no matter how much or how little you have.

DECIDE TO CHANGE

If you don't already have a stable financial foundation, you're going to have to change. You might have to cut back on expenses and pay off debt, or you might have to change how you handle, save, and spend money altogether.

Change can be both physical and mental. On the physical side of change, you may need to create a budget to make sure your expenses never exceed your income. On the mental side of change, you may need to understand that the way you think about money determines how easy (or hard) it is for you to get rich.

For example, I'll bet you probably think about money the same way your parents thought about money. If they thought money was always scarce and hard to get, you probably think the same way. If your parents thought that they never had enough money, you probably think the same way too.

Because your beliefs about money can help (or hinder) your financial foundation, let's take a look at some common money-destroying myths that can keep people from true wealth.

Have you heard people say, "Money is the root of all evil"? I'm sure you have, but guess what? They're wrong! The entire Biblical quote is, "The love of money is the root of all evil." So money itself isn't the cause of evil, but the way people react to money can, for lack of a better word, become evil. See the difference? If you read the quotation correctly, you'll see that evil stems from the love of money. But if you misinterpret the quote, you'll mistakenly think that money is evil.

If you see money as something evil, guess how you'll treat money in your own life? Do you want evil in your life? Probably not, which means you'll do everything you can to keep evil out of your life, which can include keeping money out of your life!

Can you see how negative thoughts and beliefs about money can influence how you'll handle money without even realizing it? You're probably saying, "Dean, I don't think money is evil at all. In fact, I'll take a whole bunch of it please." That's great, but if you don't have enough money now, you have to change your life so you change the way you handle money, both physically and mentally.

If you change only the way you handle money, you might still fall back on your old money habits if you don't change your thinking about money too. Likewise, if you change only your thoughts about money but don't convert those thoughts into action, you still won't have money.

Only when you change both your physical and mental habits about money can you change the amount of money you'll allow into your life. If you really want more money in your life, you just have to change your beliefs about money. It's literally that simple!

I told you we would get off the subject of real estate for a moment, but if I don't share with you all the factors that could allow you to become a real estate millionaire, I am not doing all I can to help affect your life. And I want this to be the day that things start to change for the rest of your life. Together we can do it.

FIND A REASON TO CHANGE

Every New Year, people make resolutions to change. Some people want to lose weight or find another job or quit smoking. Within a few weeks, most of those resolutions are gone and people are back doing exactly what they were doing before they made their New Year's resolutions. So what's the problem?

People want to change and they sincerely mean to change, but until you give yourself a reason to change, your mind is going to keep thinking, "Why bother?" After all, you've lived your life up to this point without having to change, so why do you need to change now?

This is the reason why so many people don't change until something catastrophic forces them to. Sometimes when your life takes a turn for the worse, you have no choice but to change and make something better.

Imagine how bleak life must have looked to a thirty-year-old English woman who had recently become divorced and found herself taking care of a daughter while unemployed and living off welfare. Desperate, she began writing a novel on an old manual typewriter. When she completed her novel, she submitted it to twelve publishers, and all of them rejected it.

Finally, one publisher agreed to publish her novel but warned her that hardly anyone made money writing children's books. This desperate mother, who was forced to change and take a chance out of desperation, would later be known as J. K. Rowling, and her first novel was about a boy named Harry Potter.

When you're desperate, your reason to change is clear: You need to get out of your current situation. But when you think about it, if you aren't truly happy and doing what you want in life, your life is already in a dire situation. You were meant to be happy and enjoy every moment you're alive, and if your life doesn't give you enough free time and opportunities to pursue whatever your dreams might be, you need to change your life. Take action now!

If you don't want to change or, more importantly, don't need to change, you might as well put this book down right now. It's not enough to just *want* to change. You must *need* to change so that changing your life is your only possible option. After you need to change, you'll find that you can reach any goal you set for yourself.

Real-Life Story

Let me tell you the story of one of my students who started out with no money but had a strong desire to change.

"I was making decent money, but I hated my job, which was making me tired of being tired all the time. I was stressed out all the time about money or, to be truthful, not having enough money, and I had bills up to my eyeballs. To further darken my surroundings at that time, I knew that no matter how much money I was squirreling away in my company's 401K plan, it would take me thirty-some years to retire—if I could survive through all the regular layoffs.

"Even then, in thirty years I would get a very, very modest retirement. According to my calculations, even if I saved as much as I was legally allowed and my employer matched a portion of my contributions to the 401K plan, and the 401K plan earned (or lost!) the meager earnings that it had in the past, it would not be enough to retire comfortably. And I would have to wait thirty years to get to that point! For me, I had a strong enough reason to change.

"Once I decided I had had enough, I took action. I knew I couldn't quit my job right away, but I was ready to work harder and smarter during my nights and weekends. I was absolutely ready, so I changed my priorities and made the decision with my wife that we were going to become millionaires and live the life we desired. That's when we got started investing in real estate, and today we are millionaires!"

Of course, that story could be a heck of a lot longer on how they were scared, yet they still went through their first deal, which gave them the confidence to do a second deal, then a third deal, and so on. As a couple, they took the route of buying and renting until the market hit a peak and they ended up owning more than one hundred rental units.

When their real estate income surpassed the income from their jobs, they quit their day jobs with a smile. They ended up waiting until the market started heading up and sold most of their units for an enormous amount of money, and today they invest in real estate full time.

They're both in their mid-forties and semiretired. What made this couple different from most people is that they took action, made the necessary changes, and now they're millionaires who own two $4 million condos in Hawaii. Life is good.

Commit yourself to success right now! Take the next steps to prepare a solid foundation so you can become a millionaire too.

DON'T QUIT YOUR DAY JOB (JUST YET)

Before you do anything, don't quit your day job, even if you hate it. Unless your job is putting your life in physical danger, you need the steady income any job provides while you plan your escape. A job can also help you establish a higher credit rating, which you can use later to get favorable loans. (I show you ways to improve your credit score in a moment.)

One of your greatest assets in real estate investing could be having and maintaining good credit, which is measured as your credit score or FICO score. So if your credit score is good, we need to keep it there. If it is not good, we need to work on improving it. You can, of course, make money with no credit or bad credit, but good credit makes life a lot easier.

A *FICO score* is a credit score developed by Fair Isaac Corporation (FICO) in the late 1950s to determine the likelihood that credit users will pay their bills. The FICO method of scoring has become the most widely accepted and reliable way for lenders to evaluate credit. Basically, a borrower's credit history is boiled down to a single number—a credit score. (Fair Isaac won't reveal exactly how they calculate credit scores.)

Simply put, credit scores are calculated by using sophisticated scoring models and mathematical tables that assign points for different pieces of information based on how thousands, or even millions, of people have used credit.

Credit scores analyze a borrower's credit history and look at factors such as the following:

- Late payments
- Length of time you have had the loan or credit card
- Amount of credit used versus the amount of credit available
- Length of time at present residence
- Employment history
- Negative credit information such as bankruptcies, charge-offs, and collections

Three FICO scores are computed by data provided by each of the three bureaus: Experian, Trans Union, and Equifax. Some lenders use one of these three scores, while other lenders may use just the middle score.

You want your FICO or credit score above 650 and ideally above 700. A credit score above 750 is generally considered excellent.

You can improve your credit score as follows:

- Pay your bills on time.
- Cut down on your consumer debt. Don't purchase furniture or succumb to the many television ads enticing you to buy their products with "no interest for five years." Now is the time to be more disciplined financially.
- Don't buy a new car on credit at this time, if you can repair your old one. Believe me, if you take the time to become a real estate investor, you will have many opportunities to buy a new car and other things you desire.
- Pay off auto loans and other consumer loans early. If that is not possible yet, make sure your payments are sent on time. If you cannot pay off loans early, pay slightly more than the minimum payments. Add an additional $10, $50, or $100 to each minimum monthly payment to show your creditors what a good credit risk you are.
- Don't get caught up with credit card offerings. Having too many credit cards will lower your FICO score because they increase your cumulative available credit. Having two to four cards is good because it shows that you can manage your money and establishes a credit history.
- Don't apply for credit frequently. The more applications you make, the greater number of "dings" on your credit report. Make sure that a mortgage broker shops your loan to many outlets but uses just one copy of your credit score that he or she pulled rather then letting poten-

tially dozens of banks pull your credit report separately. You could end up with many dings on your credit report for one loan.

- Pay off credit card balances early. If you are unable to pay your credit card bill in full when it is due, make sure your payments are on time or, better yet, ahead of time. FICO rewards you for early payments.
- Don't max out your credit cards. Avoid charging more than 50% of your available limit. This shows FICO that you are a good money manager, especially if you pay your credit card in full every month.
- If you don't have any credit or have limited credit, obtain additional credit. Approach your local bank and inquire about applying for a debit or credit card. Not having sufficient credit can actually lower your score.
- Start managing your credit today! You can get one free credit report from each of the three major bureaus in the United States: Equifax (1-800-685-1111), Trans Union (1-800-916-8800), and Experian (1-888-397-3742). You can also get a credit report online by visiting www.Annual CreditReport.com.
- If you see an error on your report, notify the credit bureau. All three bureaus have procedures for correcting information promptly. It's easier and less painful than you might think because you can do it all online. Alternatively, if you plan on working with a mortgage broker or a mortgage company, ask them to help you get your credit repaired. Tell them what you are planning on doing and give them the opportunity to earn your business and trust by helping you improve your credit score. Ask your mortgage person whether you fit the criteria for something called a rapid rescore. A *rapid rescore* gives you a second chance to improve your credit rating by weeding out old data (that could be hurting your credit rating) and giving you time to improve your financial situation (such as by paying down a credit card). And the *rapid* part means that it can be pushed from taking several months to just a few days.

So, if you need a few points higher on a score to qualify for a loan, you may be able to dispute wrong claims on your credit report, pay a credit card or two down a few hundred dollars so the available credit is more than 50%, and do a rapid rescore. Never be afraid to ask for help.

Start today: Credit bureaus look at your past performance to determine your credit score, and your creditors want to see a track record of excellence.

Real-Life Story

Saving money and watching your spending can eventually lead to tremendous wealth, as two of my students found out when they applied these techniques.

"My wife and I both worked, and neither of us was crazy about our jobs. So when we started real estate investing, we kept our jobs to help pay the bills and improve our credit scores. We also drove the same cars for the next six years. She had a reliable compact car, but mine was a twenty-five-year-old pickup truck with no power steering. Fortunately, that truck came in handy for fix-up and remodeling projects.

"We lived our lives with normal expenses and decided not to make any major personal purchases. Instead, we focused on achieving our financial dreams. After four years of investing, we owned fifty-three rental units.

"That was the time my wife quit her job to spend full time with our family and managing rental properties. She did such a great job running everything that she would call me all the time at work and tell me she found another property to buy! We kept increasing our real estate portfolio. After another five years, I quit my job, and since then we have focused all our attention on family, fun, and real estate. Oh, and as for the cars, we have since traded up and paid cash for a Lexus sports car and a Lexus SUV. It was definitely worth the wait!"

SPEND WISELY

One reason why millionaires have as much money as they do is that they've learned to spend less than they make and save or invest the difference. It doesn't matter how much or how little you make. If you always spend less than your income and invest or save the extra, you'll always be rich. There are people making $500,000 a year who are just as broke as someone making $20,000 a year. That's because the person making $500,000 a year has bills that equal $500,000 a year and the person making $20,000 a year has bills that equal $20,000 a year. If your bills always equal (or exceed) your income, you'll always be broke no matter how much you make.

So when I say spend wisely, I'm not saying you can't enjoy the good things in life. I'm saying that you must always spend less than you make. We all want nice things—a new car, a large home, better clothes. But true wealth doesn't come from buying and owning nice things. True wealth comes from being able to purchase what you desire while making more than you spend. Does that make sense?

People who drive around in a new Porsche aren't necessarily rich. They could be in debt and barely scraping by, but they look rich because of the car they drive. Likewise, people who drive an older car aren't necessarily poor. They could be saving and investing their money instead of buying a car that depreciates the second it's driven off the dealer's lot.

I enjoy the finer things in life, and once you start making more, it's hard not to spend more. If you start making a lot of money in real estate but spend more than you make, you could end up right back where you were or even worse.

Grab a hold of a painful memory like the job you dislike, the stress that lack of money causes, or the things you could not provide your family because of lack of money, and let that be your conscience on where to put your newfound wealth. Spend less than you make, invest the difference back into real estate or savings, don't overleverage, and you will be on your way to life-long financial independence.

The next time you want to buy something, just ask yourself this question: "Do I *need* it or do I *want* it?"

If you are saying, "Hey, Dean, I got this book so I could have money to buy the things I want, not to live conservatively," I agree with you. But getting to your desired level of success takes a few changes, and living within your means is an important one. You're not going to live conservatively for the rest of your life—just long enough to pursue your long-term goal of financial independence. As your income slowly grows, so will your available budget of "fun money." And one day you'll look around and realize that you're making more money than you ever thought possible.

TRACK YOUR SPENDING

Most people know how much they make every year, but too many people don't know how much they spend every year. If you don't know how much you spend, it's easy to spend more than you make and dig yourself deeper into debt every month.

So if you really want to get rich, and you currently scratch your head at the end of each month wondering where all your money went, here is a plan that could work for you. Start tracking your spending. Whether you pay by cash, check, credit card, or debit card, keep track of everything you spend. Remember, you can't manage what you don't measure; so track your spending.

You can track your spending on paper, but you can also use a money management program on your computer such as Quicken or an ordinary spreadsheet. I have also created an area on www.deangraziosi.com with free downloads of spreadsheets and other forms and information to help you along your journey to wealth and prosperity.

I know that tracking your spending can seem like a hassle. But ask yourself this question: If the way I am currently running my finances is not making me wealthy and I don't do anything different, what are the chances that next year I will magically get rich? The answer is: If you continue to do the same things you are currently doing, you will end up continuing to get the same results. Here is some incentive. When you start making and "keeping" more money, hire someone to keep track of your spending. So the quicker you start keeping and making more money, the quicker you can hire someone to help.

Following is a computer spreadsheet example from one of my students showing how he tracks his personal spending by category. He fills this out monthly, and then averages his spending by category to determine his average expenses during the year. Finally, he can use those numbers to budget expenses for the future.

| Spending Categories | April | | | | |
	Credit Card #1 3/27-4/26	Credit Card #2 3/10-4/09	Credit Card #3 4/5-5/4	Personal Checkbook April	Total of April Spending
Gifts	$103.19				$0.00
Home Mortgage & related expenses				$2,233.09	$2,233.09
School related expenses					$0.00
Costco				$198.13	$198.13
Home Decorating					$0.00
Auto & Home Insurance		$506.14			$506.14
Medical Costs & Med Insurance				$228.26	$228.26
Auto Repair / Licensing					$0.00
Restaurants		$426.89		$2.58	$429.47
Clothing		$98.30		$111.12	$209.42
Utilities				$37.01	$37.01
Gas—Cars		$9.95		$195.02	$204.97
Walmart & groceries		$57.19			$57.19
Travel—Air					$0.00
Hair/Facials		$11.49			$11.49
Cash Withdrawals				$71.70	$71.70
Entertainment		$24.47			$24.47
Pet related				$21.87	$21.87
Total for the month	$103.19	$1,546.07	$0.00	$3,098.78	$4,644.85

An example of my spreadsheet. Remember blank spreadsheets for this and many other parts of the book are available for free at www.deangraziosi.com.

Even if you keep a log on a piece of paper that you carry in your pocketbook, wallet, or day planner, make this part of you routine. The important point here is to track what you spend by category, and then analyze the results to determine whether you can trim some areas. Just knowing what you spend and where you spend it is valuable information.

If tracking your income and expenses sounds troublesome, remember that you have to track your income and expenses for tax purposes anyway, so you might as well use this information to plan for your financial future at the same time.

Many of my friends and relatives make a lot of money at their current jobs and are successful. But in many cases, they can't understand why they always seem to run out of money every month. When they ask for my advice, the first thing I ask is whether they know where they are spending their money. Most of the time, they don't. So I encourage them to complete this same step to understand where their money is going. When they do this, they're always amazed at how much they spend every month.

I want you to make tracking your expenses part of your routine. Remember, when you start investing in real estate, you will need to track your income and expenses for legal and tax purposes, such as the following:

- Completing your Federal income tax return annually
- State sales and income tax purposes in the states where you own properties
- Managing the performance of your properties, one by one, on an ongoing basis

ELIMINATE THE NEGATIVE

Just because you want to change doesn't mean people around you will accept your changes. When you change, some people might feel threatened to question their own lives; rather than do that, they'll try to stop you from changing.

In my seminars and in my other book, *Totally Fulfilled,* I call these people dream stealers. They want to steal your dream because they don't want to change their own lives.

Real-Life Story

Here is a letter from one of my students, who took some extreme action to protect himself against dream stealers.

"I was full of optimism and naively thought (and I am glad I did) that there was nothing I couldn't do if I set my mind on it. Unfortunately, the negative influence in my

life was my wife. She was a classic dream stealer. Anytime I read the real estate classified ads and wanted to go drive by a property, I would get the, "You and your get-
rich-quick schemes!" lecture. This would last the *entire* car ride and all the way back
home.

"She could steal any enthusiasm from just about anyone with her negativity.
Things hadn't been going great in our marriage to that point, and this constant negative influence was just too much to bear. So I did what was right for me and got a divorce. I have since remarried and my new wife and I share a love for investing in real
estate. Our financial future has never been brighter!"

I'm not recommending that divorce or getting away from people is always the answer. Sometimes making people aware of their negativity is
enough to make them change (or at least stop). Try to get them to read *Totally Fulfilled* or another inspirational book. Seriously evaluate your life and
take a critical look at the negative influences that may be around you. People
could be acting out of love because they feel they are protecting you from
getting hurt or failing, when indeed they are helping to keep you in an un-
happy life. Identify these people and decide that you have to follow your
own desires and that they can't derail your journey.

In some cases it may not be a person. Perhaps a huge debt is constantly
on your mind, or another negative influence is dragging you down. Think
how wonderful life will be when you release yourself from your "ball and
chain."

Real-Life Story

Here is a portion of another great letter I received regarding how someone eliminated a
negative influence.

"My husband and I had spent a lot of time discussing the changes we needed to
make in our lives. We were both equally convinced and committed to making a change,
so our first step was to see a loan officer at the bank. This loan officer (we'll call him
Ron) met with us and listened while we explained our desire to purchase and remodel
a property. We discussed various types of loans that the bank had to offer because we
had little or no cash available for a down payment.

"Ron listened patiently and to our relief agreed to give us the loan. But then he
added, 'But don't expect to become millionaires.'

"We left the meeting both pleased that we had received the loan but also irritated
that our loan officer would throw such a downer on the whole experience. Instead of
supporting and encouraging us, he tried to deflate our dream. We could have given up
on our dream, but we decided on another alternative. We 'fired' Ron and found a more

understanding loan officer to work with us! We have since done countless properties, and yes we are millionaires from real estate. Imagine the business he lost."

The point is that you will encounter many obstacles along your path to becoming a successful real estate investor. Listen to what others have to say but don't let the naysayers discourage you. Pursue your goals relentlessly and I guarantee you will be successful.

CONCLUSION

Just remember that the solution to your problems is not making more money but managing your money wisely. You'll never be broke if you spend less than you earn, but you'll always be broke if you spend more than you earn, even if you earn millions of dollars a year.

When people say they want more money, they're actually saying they want more of what money can give them, which is freedom of choice—the choice to own the best that life has to offer (cars, homes, jewelry, and so on), the freedom to do what they want at any time, and the freedom to reach their true potential.

Money is an important ingredient in happiness, but it's not the only ingredient or the most crucial one. In the next chapter, I'll show you ways to remove mental blocks that might be holding you back from becoming the person you truly want to be and were meant to be. Ready? Let's go!

CHAPTER 8

REMOVING YOUR MENTAL BLOCKS TO SUCCESS

If you think you can, you can.
And if you think you can't, you're right.
—HENRY FORD

I once paid $40,000 to buy land in New York that at a quick glance looked like a swamp. If this sounds as bad as buying the Brooklyn Bridge, that's exactly what everyone else thought when they looked at that same property. Now you may be asking yourself, "Why would Dean buy swampland in New York?" The answer is simple. When other people looked at this property, they saw just a swampy parcel of land. When I looked at that same piece of property, I saw an opportunity.

Most of the wet area filled the edge of the property closest to the road. Anyone driving by could see only stagnant water. At first glance, the land looked useless, but what people didn't see was what lay beyond the swamp.

The swamp actually filled only a tiny portion of the property and it was wet only because a stream that ran through the property was backed up with silt (dirt). The rest of the land past the swamp rose into a small hill that commanded a wonderful view of the surrounding area. All I did was clean out the stream and take the land from the hill and use it to fill in the low-lying areas. By subdividing this supposed swampland, I made hundreds of thousands of dollars and wound up with one of the most valuable properties in the neighborhood!

Hundreds of people had the ability to do what I did, but they didn't for one reason. They looked at the swamp, saw an obstacle, and gave up. I looked at that same swampland, saw its potential, and wound up making a fortune.

Physical obstacles didn't stop other people from doing what I did. Their mental obstacles stopped them.

Most problems or obstacles don't lie outside ourselves, but within. If you want to succeed in real estate, or anything in life, the biggest obstacles to remove from your life are the ones between your ears.

Because you've read this far, you've already seen how real estate investing offers the potential to make a lot of money in a short amount of time with little risk, especially when compared to other forms of investing. But no matter how good any money-making opportunity may be, it's no good until you take action and start using it. Even Aladdin's lamp was useless until Aladdin took the time to pick it up and made the effort to rub it so the genie would come out.

> *Most problems or obstacles don't lie outside ourselves, but within. If you want to succeed, the biggest obstacles you need to remove from your life are the ones between your ears.*

So before examining the details of specific real estate strategies, let's take a moment and examine one of the most important ingredients necessary for your success: You. Specifically, we're going to start by taking away every obstacle that could stop you from succeeding.

Now you may be asking yourself, "How is Dean going to take away all my obstacles? How would he know what they are or how extreme they are? How does he know how many bills I have to pay each month? What does he know about how hard I work every day, how far I travel just to get to my job, or how tired I am when I come home? What does he know about the problems I face every day at home and at work?"

The short answer is that I don't know how many problems or obstacles you have. But here's what I do know: Everyone has obstacles, some much bigger than others. We all have them and they will never go away. Some problems are life-threatening while others are downright annoying. But no matter how big and scary any of your obstacles may be, they all share a common characteristic: You can choose how you respond to them.

> *We can never eliminate obstacles, but we can always overcome them.*

Obstacles will always pop up, so we better learn how to overcome them.

THE POWER OF CHOICE

> *Since we cannot change reality,*
> *let us change the eyes which see reality.*
> —NIKOS KAZANTZAKIS

Helen Keller was born with normal sight and hearing, but she fell ill at nineteen months old and became blind and deaf. She could have chosen to remain an invalid for her entire life, but instead she chose to overcome her disabilities by learning how to read and write.

When you look at the insurmountable obstacles that a little girl named Helen Keller had to face every day, it can help put our own obstacles into perspective. And even though our own obstacles can sometimes feel like an enormous burden, the problem really isn't the obstacle but rather how you handle it.

The main reason people have heard about Helen Keller is not because she was blind and deaf but because of the way she responded to and overcame obstacles. The choices Helen Keller made are the same choices you can make. You can choose to let problems and obstacles overwhelm you and stop you dead in your tracks or you can choose to follow a system to let problems be minor speed bumps on your way to success. It's up to you.

Write down all the obstacles that are holding you back from taking the action you need to change your life. Each of you will have a unique list, but frequent obstacles are lack of time, lack of money, fear of failure, not knowing what to do, being stuck in a job you hate, having an awful childhood, and not having the right education.

Next, look at your list and ask yourself honestly, "Are these things really stopping me and am I going to continue to allow them to control my destiny?"

Okay, now you are saying, "Thanks, Dean. I not only wrote down all my problems and obstacles, now I'm angry about them too." Great! That's the first step. Obstacles can never hold you back. How you deal with obstacles is what holds you back. So here is the lesson that can help you overcome your personal obstacles no matter what they are.

On that sheet of paper where you wrote down your obstacles, I want you to write one of two words: *challenge* or *excuse.* Why? Because if you break down your obstacles to one of these two things, there is no doubt you can overcome them. We have to eliminate the word *obstacle* in our lives. Once you identify what that obstacle truly is, you can work on either eliminating your excuses or conquering your challenges.

Remember, problems get in your way only with permission. Everyone has problems, but people who address their problems properly do not let their problems stop them. Every problem, no matter how big or how persistent, can be overcome if you choose to do so.

The key lies within you. Ultimately, you can handle every obstacle in your life the same way. If the obstacle is an excuse, eliminate it, stop focusing on it, stop saying it, and stop telling people about it.

If the obstacle is a challenge, do what it takes to overcome it. You can overcome a challenge in lots of ways, but the quickest way is to focus all your energy on a positive outcome. So many people spend so much time trying to figure out what went wrong, or why bad things always happen to them, or how hard their life is that they have no energy left to work on a solution.

Take something as simple as spilling a glass of milk. When the glass spills, you can react one of two ways. You can ask yourself why it happened, who's fault is it, why does this always happen to me, will it stain the carpet, and so on, wasting your energy. Or you can simply get a towel to clean it up and get a new glass of milk.

Where we put our focus and energy determines the outcome we will get. If you focus on problems or obstacles, you will continue to have them. If you focus on solutions, you will get solutions.

You can't let problems defeat you and then blame them on your lack of success. If you choose this path, guess what? Not only will you not be able to overcome current obstacles, they will invite even bigger problems into your life (lack of money, lack of free time, lack of ever achieving any of your dreams).

It's time you see problems for what they really are—either an excuse or a challenge. If you're blind and deaf, you definitely have a much bigger obstacle than someone who just hates their job and is stuck in a broken relationship. But as Helen Keller proved, even physical problems can be overcome when you focus on a beneficial solution instead of the problem at hand.

I don't want you to read this book, nod your head in agreement, and put it down. I want you to read this book and use it to spur yourself to take action. Part of taking action is realizing that obstacles will never go away, but if you approach them with the right conviction then achieving your goals is a reality. After you realize that you can succeed in spite of any problem, you're more than halfway to any goal you set for yourself:

- Problems and obstacles are real. Everyone has them.
- Obstacles can slow you down, but they can only stop you with your permission.
- Turn your obstacles into excuses or challenges and then deal with them.
- Give yourself permission to succeed in spite of your problems.

Real-Life Story

I've never seen the power of personal choice demonstrated on such a high level until I met Darrell Scott. He bought my first book, *Totally Fulfilled,* and found it inspirational. One sentence really stuck out for him, "Practice makes what? Perfect!"

Although so many people believe that phrase, it's wrong. Practice doesn't make perfect. Practice makes permanent. So if you practice something the wrong way— from a golf swing to the way you handle obstacles or choices—it will become permanently wrong.

Darrell later told me, "I had to look at this book with some young guy on the cover telling me he had the secrets to be *Totally Fulfilled,* and I am so glad I did, because that quote alone made me have to get in contact with you." Darrell Scott is the father of Rachel Scott, the first child killed in the Columbine shootings. You can only imagine what Darrell and the entire Scott family must have felt like, but they made a choice different than most people. They chose to celebrate Rachel's life, share her incredible story, and start Rachel's challenge (www.rachelschallenge.com).

Darrell went out on the road and trained others to spread the words of his daughter to embrace those who need it, to eliminate prejudice, to spread kind words, and to make it cool to be nice.

Rachel even wrote in her journal that she hoped this kind of compassion would start a chain reaction. That is exactly what the Scott family did. To date, they have spoken in front of millions of children and have undoubtedly helped reduce teenage suicides and school violence, while making a huge positive effect on thousands of people wherever they go.

After the Columbine tragedy, the Scott family could have become very negative. Instead, they *chose* to focus on an incredible outcome from a terrible situation.

The day before writing this, I received an e-mail from Darrell, letting me know that their son Craig Scott—you may have seen him on TV interviews, including one of Katie Couric's most touching interviews when she retired from the *Today Show.* President George W. Bush had appointed Craig to his school safety panel. Isn't it amazing how much a single decision can affect your own life and the lives of others?

Remember, you have the power of choice to respond to any situation positively or negatively. The choice, and the power, is up to you.

BREAK FROM THE PAST

The farther behind I leave the past,
the closer I am to forging my own character.
—ISABELLE EBERHARDT

If I told you that I had a certified check for a million dollars in an envelope and all you had to do to get it was reach in my desk drawer to retrieve it, would you do it? Of course you would. If somebody offered me a million dollars if I just took the effort to reach for it, I'd do it too.

Now suppose that before you reach for the envelope, I remind you about the time in third grade when you were caught reaching into the teacher's desk drawer and got your knuckles rapped with a ruler. Would you let that painful memory stop you from grabbing a million dollars?

Of course you wouldn't, but guess what? People turn away from a million dollars every day because of similar painful memories. Maybe the memories are not as trivial as getting your knuckles rapped with a ruler, but they all share one characteristic: They happened in the past.

Even more important, these memories no longer exist except as thoughts in your mind. Mark Twain once said that if a cat sits on a hot stove, it will never sit on another hot stove again, but it also won't try to sit on a cold stove either. Unfortunately, many people let their past determine their future.

Here's the good news and the bad news about your past. The bad news is that you can't change what's happened to you in the past.. The good news is that everything that has happened to you up to this point is in the past and you can't change it—and it doesn't matter!

Pretend that you woke up today with amnesia and can't remember anything from your past. All memories of your failures are gone, all thoughts about people who did you wrong have vanished into thin air, and all those words that people used to criticize, belittle, and humiliate you have disappeared as if they were never spoken at all. You have the same skills, talent, and dreams as you have right now, but without a memory of anything from your past holding you back. Do you think you could go forward in life with more confidence and achieve your goals without the memories of criticism and past failures holding you back?

Of course you could! Who wouldn't want to be free from all the mistakes and failures of their past? The past has no chains holding you back. No one from your childhood is keeping you from achieving your dreams today. Nothing from yesterday can stop you from doing anything today. Your memories are nothing more than thoughts, and thoughts can't hold you back physically, but mentally they can feel stronger than the thickest steel cables holding up the Golden Gate Bridge.

So guess who's keeping around your thoughts from the past? It's not your parents, your boss, your spouse, your co-workers, the people in your neighborhood, your old elementary school teachers, or your childhood friends.

It's you.

That's both good news and bad news. It means nobody can stop you without your permission. It means also that you no longer have an excuse for why you can't succeed. If you're the only one who can stop you, the simplest way to success is learning to get out of your own way.

I know some people have had horrible childhoods or past experiences with violent, abusive, and controlling people, and I know that past experiences can color the way you see the world today. But if you let your past control your future, you'll be like the person afraid to grab a million dollars right now because of a bad experience with a third-grade teacher many years ago.

In this book, I'm giving you a million dollars worth of real estate advice, and all you have to do is take action and follow my instructions. Don't be afraid to reach for that million dollars. You're worth it.

I know most people don't let a single past experience control their actions today. But the mistake people make about the past is misinterpreting what really happened.

Let's say a third-grade teacher really did hit you on the knuckles with a ruler. So what? Maybe you weren't supposed to reach into the teacher's desk, so she rapped you on the knuckles to teach you never to do that again. At that moment, you learned that if you tried reaching into her desk again, your teacher would probably rap you on the knuckles again. Simple lesson.

Now let's look at how people misinterpret that lesson. Rather than just think of that as a single, isolated incident, people use that incident, along with many others, to "prove" a false conclusion about themselves, such as: they are not worthy; life is hard and they'll never get what they want; only other people can get what they want; or they'll be punished any time they take a risk so why bother trying?

This list of misinterpretations can go on and on, but the pattern is always the same. Take one or more experiences from the past and use them to justify a wrong conclusion about yourself and life in general. After you believe that you're not worthy or that taking risks is too painful, you're letting your past control your future for no reason at all.

No matter who you are, where you live, or what painful experiences you may have had, remember this: You are worthy. You deserve to be happy. You can achieve your goals. You are special. You can do anything you want to do. You deserve to be who you want to be.

The only way the past can hold you back is if you let it. Don't let your misinterpretations of the past create negative beliefs about yourself that dampen your dreams and short-circuit your goals. As long as you believe in yourself, nothing from the past can hold you back again. Forgive the past and move forward with your life.

- The past is over and there's nothing you can do about it.
- The past may shape your life, but you can always determine your future.
- Your misinterpretations about the past, not the past itself, hold you back.

- As long as you believe you are worthy of success you will be, regardless of what happened in the past.

THE FEAR OF CHANGE

When you are through changing, you are through.
—Bruce Barton

Some people say they're afraid of change. That's not true. Nobody is afraid of change. What people are really afraid of is the uncertainty that change can bring.

Remember as a kid when your parents told you they were going to take you to the circus the next morning, and you were so excited that night that you had trouble falling asleep? What was the difference between that night and most other nights? The promise of going to the circus was a change in your life, but you probably embraced it as exciting and fun.

Now think about a time when your parents told you they were going to take you to the dentist the next morning. Did you feel that same sense of excitement, looking forward to the next day when the dentist would stab your cheek with a needle full of Novocain so he could yank your tooth out with a device that looked disturbingly like a pair of pliers? Of course not!

The point is that you probably look forward to some changes in your life but dread other types of changes, so what does that tell you about change? Change by itself isn't anything to fear. What people fear is change that takes part of their life out of their control.

Were you ever the new kid in school? That first day was probably your most frightening because you didn't know what to expect, where to find anything you needed, or even who you might turn to for help. You probably felt isolated and alone. Yet within a few days, you probably started settling into a routine. You made some friends, found your way around the school building, and met different people who could help you. Change is always uncomfortable, but look at the alternative.

If you're like millions of Americans, you may feel stuck in the rut of working in a job you hate, making money that barely covers your expenses, and going home every night feeling exhausted—with no hope for a better future. If this sounds like your life, wouldn't you want to change?

Despite hating their jobs and dreaming of a better life, some people still refuse to change. They prefer putting up with the miseries that they know rather than risk a better life that might force them to face something different.

Because you're reading this book, you're probably not that type of person, but you might know someone who is, so let me tell you a secret about change. You can either choose to change or you can be forced to change.

Let me say that again. You can choose to change or you can be forced to change.

No matter how much you may hate or avoid change, the world is changing around you all the time. You're getting older, some of your co-workers will likely leave for other jobs while new people arrive to replace them, your neighbors will likely move away and new people will take their place, your company may lay off people or shut down factories, your friends may change their routines and see you more or less than before, even the government could pass new laws that can increase the amount of money you make or wipe out your job. Trying to avoid change is like trying to stop the sun from coming up every morning. No matter how hard you try, wish, or complain, you just can't do it.

So if you can't avoid change, what can you do? First, with many types of changes in life, the best you can do is adapt.

Let's say your company suddenly goes out of business and you find yourself unemployed. Rather than wasting time complaining or feeling sorry for yourself, you have to adapt to being unemployed. That could mean looking for another job in the same area or in another part of the country, going back to school to learn a new trade, investing in real estate on a part or full-time basis, or any number of endless possibilities.

Nobody likes any change that disrupts their life, but complaining about it won't make it any better (and will probably make it worse because the longer you complain and resist change, the less likely you'll take action to make your life better). When something in your life that's out of your control changes, you have no choice but to adapt the best you can do. *Adapting* is not the word I want for you. I want you to *embrace* change and even start to look forward to it because it can bring new and exciting things.

There's a saying that when God closes one door, He always opens another. The Chinese word for *trouble* translates to the word *opportunity*. Sometimes what seems like the worst thing that could happen to you winds up being the best thing that could happen to you.

Imagine a young boy growing up in Spain, who dreamed of one thing his whole life: becoming a professional soccer player. One day, he gets into an accident and winds up in the hospital, where the doctors say he will never have the body strength to play soccer professionally again. Can you imagine how terrible this young man must have felt, seeing his lifelong dream crumble before his eyes?

While recuperating in the hospital, this young man spent his time composing music on a guitar that someone gave him to help him pass the time. Soon he found he had a knack for writing and singing songs, and when he got out of the hospital, he decided to pursue a singing career. If you listen to the radio, you've probably heard this young man's music and voice, because he has sold more than 250 million albums and is Spain's best-selling musician of all time. You may not have heard his name when he was striving to become a professional soccer player, but you may recognize his name as the world-famous singer Julio Iglesias.

I'm not saying that if you adapt to change, your life will become as magical as the life of Julio Iglesias, but it could! You'll never know until you take that first step.

Even better, you don't have to wait for change to alter your life because you have the power and choice to change any part of your life right now. Let's say you're afraid that you may lose your job due to outsourcing, corporate bankruptcy, downsizing, or a hundred other reasons out of your control. Rather than hope and wish that nothing will change, take action now and change your life today while you have the choice.

I admit, real estate investing can seem scary at first, but it's no different than being the new kid at school. And the rewards are unlike any other opportunity I have seen in my life.

Real-Life Story

One of my students recently went through a tough divorce, combined with the loss of his company and inevitably bankruptcy. He got remarried and moved to a new state to start fresh. His wife got a decent job, and he started a landscaping business. With their combined income they were getting by. Then they had a few changes.

One change was that his wife became pregnant. The second change was terrible. She lost her job (and benefits) due to corporate restructuring and could not get a new job because she was pregnant.

Obviously, he was scared. But he didn't waste time saying, "Poor me," or "Why does this happen to me," or "Who's fault is it?" He saw my TV show one night and, even though he had bad credit and no money to invest, he took a chance and got my course. Through my teachings and, even more importantly, his desire, his ability to take action, and probably his desperation, he made things start to happen.

On his first deal, he made $30,000 without using any of his own money. Fast-forward two years and he's now a full-time real estate investor who works from home, his wife is a stay-at-home mom, they live in beautiful home, and he gets to spend time with his family. The last we spoke, he had raised his net worth an additional $400,000 and had a tremendous amount of positive cash flow from apartments he owned.

Do you see how his reaction to change was so important? He used obstacles as fuel to move forward. He was cutting grass, his wife out of work, she was pregnant, he had no money to invest, and he had bad credit. But by focusing on a better future, he overcame his fears and gave real estate investing a try. I'm sure it wasn't always easy, and I'm sure he was scared a lot—but the result is amazing because he made it amazing. My techniques were the tools, but he was the craftsman who put them to use.

Remember, if you do exactly what you're doing right now and never change, all you'll ever get in your life will be more of what you already have. If you want more out of life—a new home, more money, extra time to spend with your family—you have to change something in your life. It might mean waking up earlier, going to bed later, reading more, learning how to talk to people, making phone calls to people you don't know, or a thousand other things.

Many people associate change with fear, helplessness, being uncomfortable, and other negative feelings. They avoid any type of change just to avoid those feelings. Who would blame them?

The key to adapting to and inviting change into your life is to no longer accept those negative associations. Rather than see change as something that disrupts your life, look at change as a way to get you one step closer to your goals. When you see change from that point of view, doesn't change suddenly seem so much more appealing?

Change isn't something to fear. Change is the path that can take you one step closer to your dreams:

- The fear of change is nothing more than the fear of uncertainty.
- Change is inevitable. Either you choose to change or you will be forced to change.
- Some changes are out of your control. You can only adapt to those changes.
- Some changes are completely in your control.
- Alter the emotions you associate with change and you can alter the way you respond to change.
- You cannot reach your dreams until you change.

THE FEAR OF CRITICISM

Any fool can criticize, condemn, and complain and most fools do.
—BENJAMIN FRANKLIN

You may be reading this book so you can take action and change your life. Many people decide to forgive their past and accept that change can lead them to a better life, but they still don't change and improve their lives. What happened?

Getting out of a rut isn't easy. In the early days when roads were made of dirt, rain used to make the roads muddy. When wagons would roll over the muddy roads, they would leave behind tracks, or ruts. As the sun hardened the mud, the ruts would remain in the now-dry road. Other wagons riding on that same road would often fall into one of many ruts hardened in the road. If your wagon wheels fell in the wrong rut, the tracks might take you in a different direction, which meant you had to make an extra effort to get your wagon out of its current rut and back in the direction you wanted to go.

So when people get stuck in the same routine, we call it a rut. Like a rut in a road, getting out of your own rut can take just as much extra effort. If you have a lot of people around to help you, getting out of a rut can be much easier. On the other hand, if a lot of people are telling you to stay in your rut and are criticizing or mocking you when you try to get out, can you see how you might want to just give up?

That's the problem with criticism. Constructive criticism can point out your mistakes and guide you in the right direction. Destructive criticism can destroy your initiative and short-circuit your desire. So the next time someone criticizes what you are doing or want to do, ask yourself whether that person is trying to help you or hurt you.

If someone's trying to help you, ask whether that person is qualified to help you in the first place. When I started investing in real estate, I got all kinds of advice from well-meaning people who knew nothing about real estate. People warned me that I would lose all my money, that real estate was only for rich people, that I could invest in real estate only if I had a license, or that the real estate market was going down and I would lose my investment if I tried to buy now.

If I had listened to those people, I might still be fixing and selling cars for a living. It wasn't a bad way to make a living, but it's not as much fun or nearly as profitable as investing in real estate.

The next time someone offers you advice, find out that person's qualifications. Don't throw away your own dreams based on well-meaning but incorrect advice from people who really don't know what they're talking about. If you're going to listen to anybody, listen to successful people who have done or are currently doing what you want to do.

A newspaper reporter once asked several expert stock analysts to choose the stocks they thought would increase in value the fastest in the next year. Then they gave a monkey a pencil and let him scribble on the newspaper's stock listings. Whatever stock name the monkey's random scribbling touched, that was the stock the newspaper tracked for the following year.

By the end of the next year, most of the stock analyst's picks had increased in value, although a handful had decreased. But the monkey's stock picks wound up increasing the greatest amount within that same year.

So the next time someone gives you advice, listen politely and see whether it helps you. If so, great. Thank the person and ask additional questions if you think that person can help you even more. But if that advice is nothing but criticism, thank that person and forget what he or she said. You might as well have had a monkey giving you advice.

Often it's not the criticism that stops people. It's the desire to be liked by the person doing the criticizing. If your husband or wife criticizes you for wanting to start your own business, for example, you have a choice. Start your own business and risk further criticism from your spouse, or don't and avoid further criticism. Unfortunately, life doesn't work so neatly. People who criticize mercilessly will continue to do so no matter what your dreams may be. If you want to start your own business and your spouse criticizes you, you may decide not to start your own business. But then if you dream about investing in real estate or going back to school, that same spouse is going to criticize that dream too.

Negative people aren't just criticizing your goals; they're criticizing every goal that anyone might have. My advice is to get that negative person to change his or her mind (if it's your spouse), learn to ignore that person's criticism, or get away from that person and find a more supportive group. They say birds of a feather flock together. When was the last time you met a successful businessperson hanging around people who grumbled and complained about their problems all day in a bar?

I recommend finding a mentor, someone who can teach you what he or she knows. The right mentor can give you advice that will help you avoid problems and find answers that took the mentor years or even decades to learn. If you can't find a mentor, feel free to visit my web site at www.dean graziosi.com or give my office a call at 1-800-315-7782.

Although some people can succeed by themselves, most people rely on others to help them to change and succeed. Surround yourself with positive people who will encourage you to pursue your dreams. These people may not be able to provide advice that directly helps you reach your goals, but they can provide encouragement when you feel frustrated and offer advice when you feel you can't go on anymore. Just as friends and relatives can destroy your dreams through criticism, so can positive, motivated people push you closer towards your goals through their encouragement and advice.

Real-Life Story

Here's a story about my friend Doug, who met me while I worked in an auto body shop. Doug was initially afraid to pursue his dream until he literally just changed his mind.

"I worked in a lawn business and would see Dean whenever I'd stop by his auto body shop to pick up money for work I had done. During those visits, I always saw Dean multitasking and running four or five businesses from his desk. I didn't want to appear nosy, but one day I just had to ask how he did it.

"Dean told me, 'Don't ever say no to any work. Tell people you'll take care of it and if it is out of your league, hire someone to do the job for you.'

"That was when I started to realize that I was being held back by the people in my life who were afraid and uncertain of themselves. My parents would constantly tell me, 'You don't know anything about that. How are you going to do that job?' Or 'You're getting in over your head. You don't want to make a mistake or you'll go broke.'

"I struggled with this type of mentality in the small town where I lived. Many of the men I looked up to owned small businesses and made a decent living, but they only drove average cars and paid their bills and never really got ahead. Sure they had some money, but not enough to have a fruitful retirement other than rocking on the back porch, because there was no money to travel and enjoy the golden years.

"By working with Dean, I purchased my first piece of property and started to build the house I live in today. This same house, which I built for $200,000, is worth more than $500,000 just six years later. After more advice from Dean, I secured a deal where I subdivided a piece of property, making three lots out of one.

"The property owner kept the lot with the house on it and sold me the other two lots for $75,000. I sold one lot for $125,000, walking away with $50,000, and later sold the second lot for $135,000.

"I used this money to buy my first rental house and another piece of property, which I again subdivided into four lots. I'm in the process of buying more rentals and property to develop, but if I had listened to the small-minded individuals in my town as well as my family members, who were just trying to protect me, I would not have any of this property and the money I've made just by taking action and pursuing my dream."

The simplest act of reaching for your goals will change your life for the better. If you don't believe me, try it and see. You may be surprised at the results:

- Consider the source and motive of any criticism.
- People who criticize others are often using their criticism to justify their own failures in life.
- People can help or hinder you. Choose to be around people who can help you.
- A mentor can give you invaluable advice that can save you years of trial and error.
- Birds of a feather flock together. Fly with the eagles and leave the turkeys behind on the ground.

THE IMPORTANCE OF PERSONAL INTEGRITY

The most important thing for a young man is to establish credit—
a reputation and character.
—JOHN D. ROCKEFELLER

Are you like many people whose mental blocks act like brakes on their dreams? Fear of change and letting the past control you can be tough mental blocks to overcome, but the most devastating mental block is the lack of personal integrity.

Personal integrity refers to setting standards for yourself and then following them, regardless of the consequences. Two of the most important standards of personal integrity are responsibility and honesty.

Taking responsibility for your life means eliminating excuses. If an important phone call needs to be made, for example, you do it yourself or you make sure someone else does it. If the other person fails to make the phone call, you don't blame that person but instead take responsibility for doing what you can to make sure the phone call gets made.

Responsibility doesn't mean accepting the blame. It means making sure that certain tasks get accomplished so you never have to blame anyone in the first place. Tasks get done now or later, but they get done. If they don't get done at all, the responsibility lies with you and you alone.

Most people don't want to take responsibility for their life because if they don't like their life, it's up to them to change it. Most people would rather shift the responsibility for why they aren't living a fulfilled life to their parents, their spouse, the economy, or their company. When you give up responsibility, you give up control of your life.

Responsibility is a promise to yourself. Honesty, another standard of personal integrity, is a promise to others. When you're honest, you gain the respect of everyone, including yourself. When you are honest and say you're going to do something, you do exactly what you say. No excuses.

If you take responsibility for your life, people respect you. If you're honest with yourself, your self-esteem strengthens and you feel good about yourself.

Self-esteem is what you think about yourself. Reputation is what other people think of you. If you take responsibility and remain honest, your reputation and self-esteem will take care of themselves.

Imagine the tremendous feeling of self-worth and power you will feel if you can face yourself in the mirror and smile at the person looking back at you. When you can do that, you'll know that anything is possible:

- Personal integrity means setting standards for yourself and never lowering them. Ever.
- Taking responsibility for your life means taking control of your life.
- A responsible person may have problems, but he or she never uses them as excuses.
- Always be honest with yourself. After all, you're the one person you can never fool.
- If you're honest and responsible, you're more than halfway to your goals.

CONCLUSION

The most powerful fighter is an ordinary man
with laser precision focus.
—Bruce Lee

I know you have everything in your power right now to succeed. Throughout this book, I want you to see me as your friend and mentor, encouraging you to pursue real estate and showing you what to do and how to do it. Anything is possible as long as you take action and never give up.

To help you reach your goals, I spend the rest of Part II helping remove the most common excuses people use to short-circuit their dreams. By the time you are finished reading those chapters, I want you so fired up about the potential in your own life that you'll be ready to tackle any challenge.

CHAPTER 9

ELIMINATING THE FEAR
OF FAILURE

I'm not afraid of failing.
I'm afraid of living a boring life.
—Roy Edwards

Everyone has great ideas. You've probably had a dozen great ideas in the past year alone. Getting a great idea is the easy part. The hard part is turning your great idea into something that can make you money.

Perhaps one of the biggest mental blocks that stops people from acting on their great idea is the fear of failure. We've had the fear of failure drilled into our heads since childhood. If you took a test in school and got 75% of the questions right, you were still penalized for getting 25% of the questions wrong. The teacher didn't pat you on the back and say, "Great going! You got 75% of the questions right, which proves you're a smart kid. Now let's see how we can improve your score so that next time you get 80% of the questions right, then 85%, and maybe even 90% or 100%!"

That probably never happened to you. I know it never happened to me. Instead, the teacher probably handed your test back with 75% marked at the top in red ink along with the letter *C* printed like a scarlet letter of shame. If you're like me, seeing 75% at the top of a test didn't make you feel like a winner. It made you feel like a loser. Given a choice between taking another test or avoiding it altogether, guess which choice offers the quickest way to avoiding failing?

If you answered, "avoiding a test altogether," you're right! Unfortunately, that's the same attitude people take with life. Rather than take a chance and succeed, they choose the safer route of not trying, just to avoid any possibility of failing. Here's the quick cure for overcoming your fear of failure: If you don't try, you've already failed!

The quick cure for overcoming your fear of failure is this: If you don't try, you've already failed!

Your options are simple. You can take action and have a chance at success, or you can avoid taking action and guarantee failure. Given a choice between the possibility of success or the guarantee of failure, why would anyone choose the guarantee of failure? But that's exactly what people choose when they don't take action on their great ideas.

Everyone who enters the Boston Marathon, for example, has a chance of winning. Some people have a better chance than others because of training and experience, but nobody has ever won the Boston Marathon by standing on the sidelines.

If you want to achieve a dream of gaining life-long financial independence through real estate—or achieve any goal for that matter—the only way to avoid failing is to take action and give it your best shot. So take action on your dreams right now!

FAILURE IS THE STEPPING-STONE TO SUCCESS

It is better to have enough ideas for some of them to be wrong,
than to be always right by having no ideas at all.
—EDWARD DE BONO

The fear of failure can actually motivate you to take action. Of course, whenever you take action to achieve any goal, you'll almost always run into problems. If your goal is to lose weight, your problem might be finding the time (and energy) to wake up one hour early to jog or visit a health club. If your goal is to find a better job, your problem may be finding the time to create a resume.

To achieve any goal, you have to take action, but you can rarely reach most goals in a single step. People who fear failure see every step as one more chance where they can fail. People who crave success see every possible problem as just one more stepping-stone that takes them closer to success.

People who fear failure see every step as one more chance where they can fail. People who crave success see every possible problem as one more stepping-stone that takes them closer to success.

Think about your favorite sports team or athlete. Everyone cheers when Tiger Woods wins another golf tournament, but how many people would cheer if Tiger Woods had a bad putt at the ninth hole, threw down his clubs, walked away, and gave up? Or how many people would cheer Tiger Woods if he never tried to play in the first place?

Tiger Woods succeeds because he feels there is no such thing as failure; there are only temporary setbacks. Tiger Woods doesn't win every golf tournament, but he doesn't give up and call himself a failure. He learns from his mistakes, gets back on the golf course, and enters another tournament to try again.

That's exactly what you need to do if you want to reach any of your goals. Success is less a destination than a process. As long as you're trying, you're succeeding. If you never try or if you give up, you've failed. It's as simple as that.

Do you want to succeed or do you want to fail? If you want to succeed, simply try and keep trying until you reach your goal. Don't look at obstacles as problems. Look at obstacles as lessons for you to learn. Each time you learn another lesson, you move closer to your goal. Unlike school lessons, life's lessons let you keep trying until you succeed. If you keep trying and learning from your mistakes, eventually you will succeed. That's guaranteed.

When you think about it, fear of failure is nothing more than a learned behavior. As a baby, did you try to stand and walk on your own two legs over and over again until you succeeded? Or did you wobble on your two legs, fall down, and then decide right then and there that you would never try to walk again so you would never have to feel like a failure at walking? Of course not! Children know that problems are only minor setbacks, but many adults associate every setback as a failure and use that as an excuse to stop trying. If babies can reach their goals, think how many goals you can reach too.

FAILURE IS FEEDBACK

A failure is a man who has blundered but is
not capable of cashing in on the experience.
—ELBERT HUBBARD

Fear of failure is natural. Nobody wants to fail. However, the only way to succeed is to fail.

Failure is nothing more than feedback that tells you what not to do. Look at the team that wins the World Series or the Super Bowl. Do you see them playing perfectly every play? Does the winning team never make a mistake? Of course not! Every winning team makes mistakes, but what defines the winners is that they learn from their mistakes and try not to make the same mistakes again.

Don't think of failure as something that stops you from reaching your goals. Think of failure as something that redirects you towards your goal from another direction. If you've ever become lost while trying to find a house or a restaurant in a strange neighborhood, did you stop and ask for directions? You could look at stopping and asking for directions as a sign of failure or as feedback that points you towards the fastest and shortest path to your goal.

What matters is not how few mistakes you make but whether you get to your goal. Each mistake inches you closer towards your goal. If you never make a mistake, chances are you'll never reach your goal either. People have a special name for those who reach their goal no matter what mistakes they've made. They call them winners.

> *Nobody cares how many mistakes you make. People have a name for those who reach their goal no matter what mistakes they've made. They call them winners.*

FAILURE IS NEVER PERMANENT

There are no failures—
just experiences and your reactions to them.
—TOM KRAUSE

Watch any major sport championship and see what happens at the end. All the cameras are focused in the winner's locker room, where they're spraying champagne over each other and laughing. Notice that nobody ever sends TV cameras into the locker room of the losing team? What message does that send? Right! If you lose, nobody wants to talk to you, let alone be anywhere near you.

No wonder so many people fear failure! But if you look carefully, people aren't really afraid of failure. They're afraid of the outcome of failure. If teams could keep playing the Super Bowl or World Series over and over until they won, do you think they would do it? You bet!

Now guess how many chances you have to keep reaching for your goal? Do you have only one chance like a Super Bowl or World Series team? Or can you keep trying, over and over, until you succeed? You can keep trying until you finally succeed.

Doesn't that make a huge difference in the way you look at failure? The only way you can fail is if you quit trying. That means failure and success are both in your hands. If you're afraid of failure, great! Use that to motivate you to keep trying until you succeed.

Nobody likes to fail, but even failure has a way of turning into success. When Thomas Edison tried inventing the lightbulb, he failed thousands of times, but he looked at each failure as another way not to invent the lightbulb. Thomas Edison didn't fear failure because he knew that each failure was taking him one step closer to his goal.

As Thomas Edison learned, failure is nothing more than a temporary setback. Even the teams that lose the Super Bowl or World Series come back the next season ready to try again. Failure is only permanent if you stop trying. So the only way to overcome your fear of failure is to keep trying until you finally succeed.

I'm not saying that you have to like failing or that failing feels good. I am saying that once you succeed, everyone forgets how many times you might have failed. Think about that. One success can wipe out thousands of failures.

When a team wins the Super Bowl or World Series, nobody asks the players how they felt when they lost last year. Everyone wants to know how they feel right now as winners. That shows you how quickly the world forgets your failures when you finally succeed.

Failure is never permanent, but success is. Every team remembers the year when they succeeded and won the championship. Nobody dwells on the years when they lost. Failure is fleeting. Success is here to stay.

And what is amazing about having a book like this or a mentor to help you succeed is that in many cases you can learn from other people's failures and mistakes. Believe me, I didn't become successful in real estate overnight; I made countless mistakes. But I was lucky enough to learn from them. Looking back, the mistakes I made in life and in real estate were the foundation for my success.

FACE YOUR FEARS

Courage is going from failure to failure without losing enthusiasm.
—WINSTON CHURCHILL

When you try to avoid failure, you're running away from your fears and letting them overpower you. Each time you run away from your fears, your fears seem to get bigger and stronger. Even worse, your fears aren't a physical place or object that you can run away from. Your fears are in your head, so no matter where you go, you always take your fears with you.

If you don't overcome your fears, they will overcome you. The only way to overcome your fears is to face them head on. Sound scary? Trust me, it's not.

Now I don't know what your fears may be, but I do know this: Most of what people fear isn't even real. Most people fear their own thoughts of what might happen. I'm willing to bet that almost all the time, your greatest fears never even come true. So when you fear failure, you're really scaring yourself with imaginary fears.

But imaginary fears are just as scary as real fears, so you wind up scaring yourself either way. That's why the only way to overcome your fear is to face it. The first step to facing your fear is identifying exactly what you're afraid of.

Let's say you're afraid of investing in real estate. Why? Maybe your biggest fear is that you could wind up losing all your money. Now that you've identified your greatest fear, you're halfway to overcoming it. Could you really lose all your money by investing in real estate? Possibly, but not likely when you have a guide like this book or a model from other successful investors. So what's the answer? It's right there in your fear. Do your research to avoid the risks and make sure you don't overextend yourself.

Now the fear of losing everything you own in real estate has suddenly shrunk, and you've done nothing more than think about your fears differently. By setting a limit on exactly how much you're willing to invest, you can lose what you've invested and still be within your acceptable limit of loss. You can not only identify your greatest fear, but also take active steps to make sure your greatest fear never happens.

If you're afraid of losing money in real estate, make sure you learn everything you can before buying a piece of property. This can mean reading books or getting advice from qualified experts. (Anyone can give advice, but not everyone is qualified to do so.)

The more you learn, the more confident you'll become and the less likely your fears will come true. By facing your fears, you can learn exactly what you need to do to overcome them.

TAKE ACTION

Action may not always bring happiness,
but there is no happiness without action.
—BENJAMIN DISRAELI

Here's a little secret. Everyone's always a little afraid. Fear of anything new and different is natural. Most people want to wait until their fears go away before taking action. But because everyone's always afraid, this means too many people never take action at all. The solution is to take action regardless of your fears. The more action you take, the more your fears will go away. Action is the only cure for overcoming fear.

Let me tell you about a property I bought in my hometown. As a kid, I lived on the Hudson River in New York, and every year, the locals would go out with their boats and their nets to catch a fish called shad, for its eggs. Shad roe is like a cheap version of caviar. As a kid, I remember my grandmother taking me to this little shack where they'd collect the shad and sell fresh shad roe.

Even though I now live in Phoenix, I still like to go back to my old hometown and scout for properties since I'm still familiar with that area. Every now and then, I'd drive by the old shad roe shack, which looked like it had been abandoned for years and ready to collapse at any moment.

I knew the history behind this shack, but more importantly, I like to zero in on distressed properties where the weeds have grown over the grass, rusted cars litter the lot, or a faded For Sale sign droops in the front yard like it's been there for years without anyone bothering to call. When you see a distressed property like that, you know you could get a potential bargain.

Is buying distressed property scary? Of course! Buying a freshly painted home with a landscaped lawn is easy because you know you could always turn around and sell it if you need to. Buying a distressed property is scary because you know it will take work just to improve it enough so you could even sell it again, but that's what makes distressed properties so attractive. By thinking differently, you can buy a distressed property way below market value and sell it later at a much higher price than the amount of money you would ever have to put into it.

While visiting my hometown, a friend of mine casually mentioned, "Did you hear about that old shad roe house? I think it's going to foreclosure." I felt like kicking myself because I had driven by this condemned building and never once thought about buying it myself. I was thinking more about the memories of going there with my grandmother. I immediately went to the town clerk's office to find the address, section, block, and lot number, which uniquely identifies a piece of property. (Depending on where you live, you may be able to search for this information online through your town or city's web site.) More importantly, I also found out the name and address of the person who owned the property. Within a half hour, I called the owner and asked whether the property was for sale. He said he was having trouble with the bank and was in danger of losing the entire property unless he could pay off $30,000 worth of debt on the property.

I told him, "I'll give you $35,000.00 for the parcel." Obviously that caught his attention. Not only was he going to be able to pay off his debt, but he would also walk away with $5000 profit.

Then I called my attorney and told him to do a title search, which basically makes sure that no other outstanding debts are on the property. My attorney ran the title search and I found out the only debt owed on the property was the $30,000 to the bank.

It took some time and negotiating on the seller's end with the lender, but after a few months, I became the proud owner of a condemned shad roe house for $35,000. The shad row shack would have to be torn down, but the land was the important part of the deal because empty lots in that area were selling for $125,000 to $150,000.

For an extra $10,000, I will tear down the building and clean up the entire parcel of land. My total cost will be $45,000, but the land itself is worth nearly three times that amount. Now I can either sell the land as is, build a house on it and rent or sell it, or just let the property sit there until that area booms again. Buying distressed property, or any property, can be scary because you can let your mind worry you to death about what could go wrong. But if you just take action and study the problem and focus on the beneficial solution, you'll soon see that your fears melt away.

I was worried that I could be the owner of a weed-infested lot with tons of additional debt attached to it. So that's why I had my attorney do a title search. When I found that no additional debts were attached to the property, that fear disappeared.

I didn't do anything that you couldn't do either. Hundreds of people probably drove by that same condemned shack, but I was the only one who took action and overcame my fears.

After completing this real estate transaction, will I feel any fear with the next one? Probably! But now I know that experience and action will help me overcome any fears I might feel, and now you know that too. And the best part is that the more deals you do, action you take, and obstacles you overcome, the more confident you will get and the more you can handle. I promise you that. I bet there is a "shad roe shack" type of property that you have driven by many times that may be a money-maker waiting for you to take action.

FEAR OF SUCCESS

Procrastination is the fear of success . . . Because success is heavy,
carries a responsibility with it, it is much easier to procrastinate
and live on the "someday I'll" philosophy.
—DENIS WAITLEY

Ironically, one of the greatest fears of failure is the fear of success. It's not that people fear success itself. They fear that if they succeed, their life will be worse off than before.

Let's look at this rationally. Could you reach your wildest dreams and wind up worse than before? Sure. You see it happen all the time with athletes or lottery winners who suddenly go from owning practically nothing to having millions of dollars overnight. But did success really ruin these people?

I don't think so. What ruins people isn't success but how they handle success. The way you handle problems right now determines how you'll handle your life after you achieve success. In other words, success won't spoil you without your permission.

If you succeed once, people will not only expect you to succeed again, they'll also expect you to reach even loftier goals next time. When people succeed once, they often worry whether they can do it again. My answer to that is, "Does it matter?"

I'm not being flippant. I'm saying that the only person you should be worried about is you. Other people may want you to succeed, but don't lose sight of your own goals. Don't be driven to succeed based on what other people think about you. Be driven to succeed based on what you think about you.

Think of the team that wins the World Series. The next season, everyone calls them the champs, but what usually happens? Everyone expects the champs to win every game, and everyone criticizes their performance when they don't. Yet trying to succeed the second time is no different than trying to succeed the first time. You try, you make mistakes, you try again, and you keep making mistakes. Success isn't a destination; it's a process. As long as you're trying, you can never fail no matter what anybody else may say or think.

Remember, true success is not a trophy or a championship but knowing that you're reaching for your goals no matter how many setbacks you face. People who fear success don't trust their own abilities and dreams. But if you strive for a goal and overcome obstacles in your way, you gain trust and respect in yourself and your abilities. Then when success finally does come, you know you've not only earned it, you've worked for it, and you'll welcome as much success as possible.

If you really want to overcome your fear of success, take action. You can never fail until you stop trying.

CONCLUSION

My favorite quote is from Winston Churchill, "The definition of success is going from failure to failure without losing your enthusiasm." Life isn't easy. We all have unique circumstances and issues we need to deal with that help promote fear of failing. But as I look back on my life and the failures and successes I have had, I realize that getting though my failures and learning from them is one of the biggest reasons I can write this book with the confidence of knowing that you can do anything you want with the right action plan.

Fear is paralyzing. To be paralyzed keeps you exactly where you are, which is probably not the place you want to be. I still fear failure on a certain level with each new venture. But fear has only hindered my growth, while going for it and embracing failure has allowed me to grow financially and personally beyond where I ever thought I would be as a kid.

Growing up with a single mom who made $90 a week, wearing hand-me-downs, and moving from a trailer park to rented homes and in and out of my grandparent's house, I used to dream of someday making enough money to help support her and to go to a fancy restaurant once a year. Fortunately, I could focus on solutions and overcome my fears. It is amazing to know that if you try and fail, it's okay. It just means you'll be better at it next time.

I share this with you to stress the importance of knowing that if I can do it, so can you. Don't fear failure. Fear of failure is basically a desire to protect yourself and a desire for perfection. Nobody's perfect, and once you realize that failure is nothing but a stepping-stone to success, you'll know that failure simply shows you the path to success.

So what do you want, failure or success? I think you know the answer, so let's tackle another common obstacle that stops most people from achieving success: the perceived lack of time, which I'll talk about in the next chapter.

CHAPTER 10

FINDING THE TIME TO IMPROVE YOUR LIFE

How we spend our days is, of course, how we spend our lives.
—ANNE DILLARD

I have no doubt you have said to yourself that you just don't have the time to make things better in your life. We've all felt that feeling of overload, when we believe that we have much more than we can handle at the moment. Even if you don't feel you have time, I want you to finish reading this chapter because I'm going to show you how to make more time for yourself so you don't miss out on the real estate opportunities I describe in Part III.

The last thing I want is for you to get all excited about investing in real estate, only to do nothing because you don't have time or don't believe you have time. We all have twenty-four hours in a day, yet some people seem to squeeze more productivity and happiness in a day than others. How do they do it? This chapter shows you how.

I want you to realize that with a few tweaks, you can find the time to build wealth and financial security. After that happens, time will never be an issue in your life again. So use that as your motive to find enough time now so you can have a lifetime of it in the future.

THE TWENTY-FOUR-HOUR TIME TRAP

If you're happy with the way your life is right now, you can keep your life exactly the same by not changing a thing. However, if you're not happy with the way your life is going, you need to take time to change and do something different.

Many people want to change and even make plans to do so but they never follow their plans because they never find the time. If you want to change your life, you're going to have to set aside time to change, and that means eliminating something in your life. You don't have to eliminate anything that you enjoy. Simply eliminate the things in your life that you don't enjoy and that don't help move you towards your dream.

We all have twenty-four hours each
day no matter who we are, how much
money we have, or where we live. How
you manage your time determines the
quality of your life. If you're like most
people, you may feel you have a ton of
things to do and not enough time to do
them. That's a normal feeling, but it's
also wrong. Let me show you three
ways you can squeeze more time out of
each day.

If you want to change your life,
you have to eliminate the things
in your life that you don't enjoy
and that don't help move you
towards your dream.

First, let's look at three ways most people spend their time:

- Unavoidable tasks, such as sleeping, eating, commuting, and working.
- Nuisance tasks, such as mowing the lawn, cleaning the house, and visiting with unpleasant relatives.
- Leisure tasks, such as reading, watching TV, and spending time with
friends and family.

Unavoidable tasks are those that you absolutely must do, such as working
eight hours a day in a job or sleeping a certain number of hours each night.
You can't eliminate unavoidable tasks, but you can minimize their effect on
your life.

For example, most people have to work eight hours a day and also commute to work, which can often add another hour or two, for a total of up to
ten hours a day. Given this time restriction, what can you do?

You may have a fixed, eight-hour time period that you absolutely must be
at work, but can you shorten your commute? Arrive at work earlier and
avoid the morning rush-hour? Or leave work later and avoid the afternoon
rush-hour? Either way can shorten your commute and thus save you time.
Now here's the trick. If you arrive early or stay later, use that spare time to
read about or study real estate. You can't eliminate unavoidable tasks, but
you can rearrange them so you don't waste any more time doing them than
necessary.

How about your lunch hour? Could you find a way to make real estate
calls, research properties, read and learn more, or call realtors? I had a student who once told me how much he loved everything about real estate investing, but he had no time to get started. Something as simple as adjusting
his lunch break changed his life forever.

By not taking a coffee break in the morning, he got an hour and a half for
lunch. Each day he had been going to lunch with a group of guys who did

nothing but complain how the company was unorganized or how their boss didn't know what he was doing. I suggested that he break away from this group, bring his own lunch, and find a comfortable place such as a coffee shop or park. If he ate his lunch in fifteen minutes, he could spend an hour and fifteen minutes each day working on his goals and dreams. He could read about new strategies, contact agents, make appointments, create new relationships with mortgage brokers, call on homes for sale, or just browse through the classified ads looking for properties to buy. With a cell phone or a laptop computer, he could work anywhere.

Typically, the lack of time isn't a problem. Rather it's organizing your time. This gentleman found the time he needed and is on his way to financial freedom. And it all started with a lunch break. He had time; he just wasn't using it properly. To take it one step further, he realized that he had a lot more time in his life once he adjusted his way of thinking towards doing something productive that would better his life.

After you get creative in managing your time with unavoidable tasks, it's time to look at nuisance tasks, which you can often eliminate. Hate mowing the lawn? Hire the neighborhood kid to do it. You get the job done and you get extra time to work on something more productive.

Ask yourself what your time is worth. If it costs you $35 to get your lawn mowed and it saves you two hours a week, what could that time be worth if you could buy and sell your first home for thousands of dollars in profit? Whenever I see someone spending countless hours on tasks that could be done by someone else for very little money, I think of the phrase, "Don't step over quarters to get to the nickels."

You are valuable and you were valuable before reading this book. Now add the knowledge to make money with real estate and know that you are worth a fortune each and every hour. So try to spend some time seeing whether certain tasks are eating up time that you could be spending on changing your future.

You may not be able to pay someone else to do a nuisance task, but you may be able to do creative bartering. Maybe your kids, your spouse, a relative, or a friend can help eliminate some of your nuisance tasks, and in return you could make them a small partner on future deals. Find something of value you can offer. I once had a neighbor who mowed my lawn each week, and in return I let him put his garbage in my container each week. I was already paying for the dumpster and his garbage was minimal, so it didn't cost me a penny more. He gained by not paying for garbage removal and I didn't have to mow my lawn. Think outside the box, be creative, and find that time. You need it to reach your goals.

Finally, there are leisure tasks. You may enjoy fishing, watching TV, or lying on the beach, but you have a choice. Can you reduce the amount of time you spend on leisure activities so you can spend more time on tasks that could change your life, such as studying real estate investing? I bet you could. I'm not asking you to eliminate everything you enjoy doing. Just reduce some of the time you spend on leisure activities now and devote that spare time towards pursuing your dreams. This will lead to the opportunity to have a lot more leisure time in the future.

So you see, you can carve more time for yourself in two basic ways:

- Sacrifice time from something else.
- Rearrange activities to free up larger blocks of time.

Sacrificing time means you stop doing one activity to make room for something new. This is easier than it sounds, although you may feel you have no activities you can replace with something new.

For that reason, more people are likely to find rearranging their activities more appealing. When you rearrange your activities, you free up time by either grouping similar activities together or by doing the same activities but at a different time to avoid the crowd.

Grouping activities can save you time by eliminating wasted trips. For example, rather than drive to the supermarket and come home, then drive to the video store later that same day and then drive home, you do both tasks at the same time. This is only one example of many things that can chip away at your schedule, freeing up time for you and your dreams.

The difference between people with plenty of time and those with no time isn't the amount of activities they do during the day. The difference is how they plan their day. If you plan your day and follow your plan, you'll be much more organized than someone who simply reacts to every distraction and winds up feeling exhausted without getting anything done.

WHERE DOES YOUR TIME GO?

Before you can plan your day, you need to know how you're currently spending your time. I know planning and tracking your time might seem to take even more time away from your day, but you can't use your time more efficiently if you don't know where it's going in the first place.

Time is money, so you need to watch your time as carefully as you watch your money. People who don't watch their money tend to spend too much and wind up poor. Likewise, people who don't watch their time tend to waste their time and get nothing done.

For one week, carry a notepad with you and keep track of when you start and stop something. For example, if you start driving to work at 8:00 and arrive at work at 8:30, write that down. Don't worry about being too exact, such as arriving at 8:32. You want an approximate idea of how you are spending your time.

People who don't watch their money tend to spend too much and wind up poor. Likewise, people who don't watch their time tend to waste their time and get nothing done.

Some tasks, such as driving to work, are straightforward. Other tasks may not have a definite beginning and end. For example, you may spend the first hour at work making phone calls. But halfway through returning phone calls, you stop and chat with co-workers about the morning news or last night's TV shows. Stop! You've just started another task, so write down the time you started (and stopped) returning phone calls and now write down the time you started chatting with your co-workers.

Is this a nuisance? You bet, but that's the point. By forcing yourself to track the time you start and stop another task, you're forcing yourself to be aware of how you really spend your time.

You may have thought you always spent two hours making phone calls, but you are actually spending thirty minutes making phone calls, twenty minutes socializing with your co-workers, another ten minutes making phone calls, and then another sixty minutes browsing the Internet for the latest news or sports scores.

Once you know how you're actually spending your time, you'll have a much better idea why you feel like you never have enough time. You will get different results if you make twenty minutes of phone calls compared to sixty minutes of phone calls.

Now you have a choice. You can either accept getting twenty minutes' worth of results or you can spend less time socializing and browsing the Internet and more time making phone calls. And you'll no longer fool yourself into thinking you're putting in sixty minutes of work but only getting twenty minutes of results.

Now take the time to track your non-work activities. Do you stop by the local bar for happy hour? What do you do with your weekends? Do you sleep in even though you really feel best with seven or eight hours of sleep rather than ten? Do you have friends you spend time with who are enjoyable but often unproductive? Why not have fun with them while you bounce reinforcing positive ideas off each other? Or maybe get them interested in real estate.

By tracking your time, you can see how much time you're putting towards your important tasks and how much time you're wasting throughout the day.

PLAN YOUR TIME

When you need to do something important such as see the doctor or get your car fixed, you probably make an appointment. Appointments are nothing more than fixed times during the day when you plan to do something for that entire length of time. Although people make appointments to see a doctor or a car mechanic, they rarely make appointments with themselves to perform important tasks.

Not only are most people unaware of how they really spend their time, but they also fail to plan their time. They may set aside time to work or study, but if someone calls or drops by to chat, most people stop whatever they're doing and allow themselves to be distracted. Yet when people make a doctor's appointment, they don't allow a phone call or a friend to keep them from going to their appointment. They make sure they get to their appointment and they push all distractions aside. That's how you need to treat your planned activities.

Planning your schedule means more than just blocking out time for certain activities. To plan your day successfully, you need to plan your day around activities that are most important to your life right now.

Because you're reading this book, let's assume your goal is to learn more about real estate investing. I know understanding different real estate strategies can seem complicated at first, so set aside a small chunk of time, say around ten to twenty minutes a day, to identifying the different factors that can affect the real estate cycle in your area.

After you've identified your goal, you need to identify an activity you can do every day (or at least on a regular basis) that can bring you one step closer to achieving your goal. Maybe this means talking to at least one real estate agent or property seller a day. Maybe it's talking to a loan officer to see what type of loan you can get. Each day you might have a different activity, but if all your activities support a single goal, every day you'll inch your way closer and closer until one day you'll achieve your goal.

Reaching your goal may take you weeks, months, or even years, but I'd rather you reach your goal however long it takes rather than have you go through another year or two with nothing changing in your life, leaving you wondering where all the time went and why nothing ever seems to get done.

While running my businesses and writing this book, I have ten property deals in the works in New York and Phoenix, so I fly back and forth at least once a month. I am finishing a TV infomercial for my new real estate course at www.thinkalittledifferent.com, I am working on a few new web sites and a new real estate mentoring course for people who want a personal real estate mentor.

I also have everyday life issues, and I will be a first-time dad by the time you read this. I don't say that to brag, "Look how great I am." Instead, I share that with you because without time management, I could not do all those things. You know the old saying, "If you want something done, ask the busiest person you know." I think that is really saying, "If you want something done, ask the person with the best time-management skills and it will get scheduled and done."

MANAGE YOUR TIME

After you've identified where your time goes and scheduled activities each day that will help you reach your goals, the final step is to manage your time. Taking the time to plan your daily schedule is useless if you don't follow it.

Too often, it's easy to get distracted by interruptions such as phone calls, unexpected visitors, or sudden crises at work. If you allow anything to interrupt you from your schedule, chances are good you'll never get anything done. Generally, people waste time for three reasons:

- They don't know what to do.
- They're avoiding doing something else.
- They schedule their time poorly by emphasizing the trivial over the productive.

If you don't know what to do, what are the odds you're going to do the right thing? Probably zero, which is why it's so important to identify your goals and then plan each day to move one step closer to them.

If you're wasting time to avoid doing something important, guess what? Avoiding any problem simply prolongs the agony of worrying about it. If you had a sore tooth, would you rather have it yanked out right away or suffer in pain for weeks and then have it yanked out? Surprisingly, many people will procrastinate, choosing the latter option and suffering for weeks before having their tooth yanked out anyway. Procrastination seems to work because it provides immediate gratification, but it delays your goals even more in the long run. Procrastination pushes your future further and further away.

Finally, you may understand the importance of scheduling your time and you may actually do it, but if you don't plan your schedule properly and then stick to your schedule, you might as well not have done it at all. If you don't make time for your dreams, you'll never have time to reach them. It's as simple as that. So when you schedule your day, first schedule time for your most important goals (however much you can squeeze in each day), and then schedule the tasks you absolutely must do, such as sleeping and driving to work. By creatively rearranging your must-do tasks, you can often open up extra time so you can pursue your real dream.

Don't forget to schedule in some leisure time. You don't want to work twenty-four hours a day and deprive yourself from enjoying life. Just make sure that your leisure time doesn't crowd out your important goals for each day and you'll be fine.

TIPS FOR GUARDING YOUR TIME

If time is money, would you leave your wallet open so anyone can drop by and yank out a few twenty dollar bills? I doubt it, but that's exactly how people treat their time. They may have the best intentions of scheduling their time and following their schedule, but the phone suddenly rings and they wind up talking to a friend only to let another twenty minutes slip away.

From now on, I want you to guard your time the same way you would guard your wallet. Every time a co-worker drops by just to chat or you see an interesting story on the Internet that you want to read, think of a taxicab meter slowly ticking away the dollars you're losing each second. Ask yourself, "Is what I'm doing bringing me closer to my goals or taking me further away from my goals?"

Tame the telephone

You may have heard of Dr. Ivan Pavlov. He was a Russian scientist who discovered that if he rang a bell while feeding his dogs, the dogs would associate the ringing bell with food and start salivating. Then Dr. Pavlov took away the food, rang the bell, and the dogs salivated even though there wasn't any food. Dr. Pavlov conditioned his dogs to salivate whenever they heard the ringing of a bell.

As silly as this sounds, human beings train themselves to react the same way whenever they hear the ringing of a telephone. Just because someone calls doesn't mean you have to drop what you're doing and answer the phone; that's why we have answering machines and voice mail. Too many people start working on an important project and stop every time they hear their telephone ring. When you act like that, you're no better than Pavlov's dog, salivating at the sound of a bell.

Here's what you can do to tame the telephone. Don't answer it. Then set aside a block of time to receive and return phone calls at your convenience. By doing this, you're putting the telephone back in your control and not at the convenience of another person.

A cell phone can be an even greater tool or a major annoyance, depending on how you use it. First, nobody should have your cell phone number unless it's somebody you want to talk to. Second, treat calls on your cell phone the same way. Don't answer them except at your convenience. A cell phone can be your biggest asset because you can make real estate calls from anywhere at anytime, but use this tool as a time-saver, not a time-killer.

If you need to talk to someone, treat your time on the phone like any other part of your schedule. Make an appointment to talk to someone when it's convenient for both of you. After you schedule a time to talk, schedule a time limit so both you and the other person know how much time they have to talk. Without a time limit on phone calls, a five-minute phone call can stretch into twenty minutes or more.

One of the biggest time-wasters is playing telephone tag, where you keep calling someone else and never reach them, and they keep trying to call you and never reach you either. You can solve this problem in two ways. When you make a call, leave your name, phone number, a time you can be reached (such as during the time you schedule to return phone calls), and why you're calling. If you're returning a phone call, ask the other person to tell you why they're calling. Once you know why someone else is calling, you can often stop playing telephone tag and just do whatever needs to be done.

Another way to eliminate telephone tag is to eliminate the telephone altogether. Rather than make a phone call, use e-mail or the fax machine. By writing down your communication, the other person can read what you want at their convenience. Then they can respond using e-mail or the fax machine too.

Delegate and replace yourself

I once read a story about a Fortune 500 CEO who cleaned the rest rooms every night because he felt it was important to show he wasn't any better than the average worker. Although this might sound noble, it's an incredible waste of time. If you were paying a CEO millions of dollars to run your company, would you want him or her wasting time cleaning the rest rooms when you could hire a janitor to do that same job for $10 an hour? If your time is valuable, it's worth paying someone to do the trivial tasks so you can do the important ones.

Too many people fill their days performing trivial tasks and then don't have any time left to pursue their dreams. Patching your own roof or building a backyard patio yourself might save you money on construction and labor costs, but you could actually be losing money if those tasks take away time you could be using to make more money.

Deal with information overload

Everyone's drowning in information. You can spend every day reading journals and magazines just in your field and still never keep up. So what's the answer?

Don't even try. I'm not saying don't keep up in your field. I'm saying don't let it overwhelm you. You can't read and know everything, so it's important to choose what's important and what isn't.

The next time you pick up a magazine, newspaper, or book, read the parts that interest you and throw the rest away. You'll get through more books and magazines this way and you won't waste time on parts that you don't care about.

Often times, you may read something that you'll want to save. Don't throw it in a pile that you'll never be able to find again. Organize your information. Get some plastic containers, label each one, and dump your newspaper, magazine, or book pages in those plastic containers.

If the information is really important, you'll be able to find it again by browsing through the right plastic container. If the information isn't that important, you'll forget about it; at the end of the month or the year, dump that plastic container in the trash and start all over again.

The idea is to be ruthless with information. If the information can't help you right away, ignore it. If it might help you sometime in the future, save it and then decide whether you can throw it away. The key is not to let information overwhelm you but to control the flood of information down to a trickle.

Rather than waste time and money buying newspapers or magazines, you can often find the same information on the Internet. Then you can save the information as a file on your hard disk and it won't take up any physical space at all.

Remember, if you feel overwhelmed by information overload, take control of your life and filter out the information that reaches you. Many people like the idea of touching a piece of paper only once; then they decide to keep it or throw it away.

Don't be afraid to throw things away. The less clutter in your life, the more freedom you'll have, so be ruthless and throw away everything you can.

Use the Internet sparingly

Like cell phones, the Internet can be a great convenience or an incredible nuisance. It's tempting to browse the Internet and look at the latest news and sports scores, then the entertainment gossip columns, and suddenly an hour's gone by and you've accomplished nothing except learning what the New York Yankees and Britney Spears did this past weekend.

Use the Internet as a tool to help you find information and ignore all the irrelevant news that won't help you in your goals. I know browsing the Internet can be fun, but make sure it doesn't distract you from what you need to do right now.

Perhaps one of the greatest advantages of the Internet is e-mail. But like telephone calls, e-mail can be a time-saver or a time-waster.

First, schedule time to read and respond to e-mail. You don't need to check your e-mail every five minutes. Second, when writing e-mail, be clear about what you want. If you need to ask questions, make sure the person knows exactly what your questions are. If you bury your questions within paragraphs, chances are good that the other person will answer only one or two of them. But if you make it clear which questions you want answered, you'll often get a reply within one e-mail. Here's a sample format you can use when asking questions by e-mail.

Start with a polite and quick introduction such as the following:

> Hello. In regards to the XXX project, can you answer these questions so we can keep things moving forward?
>
> • Question #1:
> • Question #2:
> • Question #3:
>
> I look forward to your response. Thanks in advance for getting back to me in a timely manner.

When you lay out your questions in a list that's easy to see, you increase the chance that the other person will answer all your questions.

When you write e-mail messages, make sure you use proper grammar. I know people like using acronyms and symbols when writing e-mail, but keep those to a minimum.

Finally, get separate work and personal e-mail accounts. That way, when you browse through your e-mail, you're not distracted by answering work-related e-mail and personal e-mail at the same time.

Remember, any form of communication can be a time-saver if it stays under your control. The minute you let it control you, you've lost control of your time.

INCREASE YOUR DISCIPLINE

Go to any store that caters to business executives and you'll find dozens of time planners, contact organizers, and efficiency tools in both paper and computer format. In case you're wondering which of these systems is best, I'll answer that question for you. All of them, but they'll only work as well as you do.

Nobody's going to manage your time for you. Actually, everyone is more than happy to manage your time for you, but it's rarely going to be what you want. If you want to manage your time, you have to start by learning to say no to unexpected phone calls, unwanted visitors, and unnecessary distractions such as newspapers and the Internet. After you develop the self-discipline to plan, schedule, and manage your time, any system will work for you, whether it's a $100 program on your computer or a $1 pack of index cards you carry in your pocket.

A well-known consultant once approached the millionaire Charles Schwab and offered him the most valuable productivity tip he knew. If Charles Schwab didn't think the tip was useful, he could keep the tip and pay the consultant nothing. If he thought the tip was useful, he would pay the consultant $25,000.

The consultant gave Charles Schwab the tip, and a week later, Charles Schwab wrote the man a check for $25,000. Here was the tip that Charles Schwab thought was worth $25,000:

Make a list of the ten most important tasks you need to accomplish every day. Then do them.

Every day, schedule time to reach for your goals. Every amount of progress, no matter how small, will bring you one step closer to your goal. Simply set aside the time and then do it.

CONCLUSION

You can turn time into money by using your time wisely on productive tasks that will take you one step closer to your goals. No matter how busy you may be, I urge you to set aside some time every day to work towards achieving your dreams. All it takes is consistent and persistent effort. The closer you get to your goals, the more time you'll want to devote towards reaching them.

It's time to turn your dreams into reality, so take the time now to put your dreams into action.

CHAPTER 11

MAKING YOUR GOALS
A REALITY

*The trouble with not having a goal is that you can spend your life
running up and down the field and never score.*
—BILL COPELAND

Would anyone watch the Super Bowl if both teams just went out on the playing field and threw the ball around? How many people would have watched the movie *Rocky* if Rocky just shadow boxed a few times and decided it was too hard and went home?

Sporting events and movies are only exciting if there's a goal. In the same way, you can make your own life exciting just by choosing the biggest dream you can imagine and then going for it.

How do you feel every morning when you wake up and the only thing you have to look forward to is another day at work? Not very exciting, is it?

Now think about how different you feel on the first day of your vacation. Just knowing that you're about to travel someplace fun and enjoy yourself for the next week or two makes that day seem so much better than any other day of the year. What's the difference?

When you wake up to go to work, you feel as if you have nothing to look forward to. But when you wake up on your first day of vacation, you have plenty of things to look forward to. That's how goals can energize your life.

Sadly, most people plan their vacations better than they plan their lives. You probably know someone who can tell you exactly how many vacation days they have and where and when they're going to use them. They may even have checked flight schedules and airfares and found the most convenient or cheapest ones. But ask that same person what goals they have for their own life and what their plan may be for achieving them, and don't be surprised if they stare back with a blank look.

> *If you want to make your life exciting, you need a goal to look forward to.*

If you want to make your life exciting, you need a goal to look forward to. Then every day can feel as exciting as the first day of a vacation.

GOALS GIVE YOU A DIRECTION

Right after you finish reading this paragraph, I want you to jump in your car and start driving. I don't care where you go. I just want you to drive within the speed limit and keep driving.

I seriously hope you didn't do the preceding exercise. But did it make you wonder, "What's the point?"

Just hopping in your car and driving is pointless because you don't know where you're going. If you don't know where you're going, you'll probably wind up someplace where you don't want to be. You might wind up in a pleasant spot, or a tolerable spot, or a really awful spot.

Not knowing where to drive is how life can be without goals. If you don't know where you want to go, your life can feel aimless, directionless, and meaningless. There's a huge difference between people who know where they want to go in life and those who wake up every day with no direction. People who know what they want out of life may not get everything they want, but those who have no idea what they want out of life usually have to take whatever chance gives to them.

To choose what you want out of life, you need a goal. The best part about choosing a goal is that there's no limit. As a kid, you may have wanted to grow up and become a fireman, an astronaut, a jungle explorer, or a movie star. You could choose anything and start playing make-believe.

You've grown up, but that doesn't mean you have to stop playing make-believe. Now you can play make-believe for real.

Choose any goal. It doesn't matter what you choose as long as you truly want it. Don't worry about how outrageous your goal may be, what someone else might want you to do, or whether or not you feel you deserve your goal.

If you're having trouble deciding on some goals, ask yourself what you would like to do before you die. Would you like to travel around the world? Learn to fly? Move to another country? Live in the house of your dreams? Win the World Series?

Even though some goals, such as winning the World Series, may seem impossible, don't censor yourself. You can dream anything you want. What you should do right now is choose a goal to give you a direction. Later, I'll show you how to refine your direction to help you get there as fast as possible.

Choose a big goal. The bigger your goal, the more exciting your life can be. There's a big difference between wanting to play the lead role in a high school play and the lead role in a major motion picture.

When you choose a goal, you're giving your life direction and purpose.

Just as driving your car is pointless if you don't have a direction and a purpose, so can life feel pointless if you don't set any goals.

Right now, before you go any further, write down at least three goals that you want to achieve sometime during your life.

In my life, I want to achieve these goals:

1. _____

2. _____

3. _____

4. _____

5. _____

CHOOSE REALISTIC GOALS

Congratulations! Just the act of writing down your goals sets you apart from 97% of the rest of the world. In 1953, Yale University asked their graduating class what their goals were and discovered that only 3% had any written goals. Twenty years later, Yale surveyed that same class and found that the 3% who had written their goals had earned more money than the other 97% combined.

The moral is simple. If you know what you want, chances are good you're going to get it.

Earlier, I told you not to worry about whether you thought you could achieve a goal. Now it's time to examine each goal to clarify what you really want out of life. If you wrote down a goal of winning the World Series but you're eighty-nine years old, there's a good chance you'll never win the World Series. Does that mean you can't have your goals? Absolutely not!

Remember, goals can give you a direction. Your goal of winning the World Series might show you that your real goal is to be involved in baseball, so how can you achieve that dream? Perhaps you could work with World Series players at a baseball fantasy camp for children. Or work at the stadium where the World Series champs play. Maybe you could open a sports store that sells autographed sports memorabilia that includes autographs from World Series players.

The point is that goals don't have to be a destination; they can point you in the right direction. Nobody can achieve every goal they dream about, but everyone can achieve some of their goals. We all have limitations, so our goals have to fit within our limitations.

Realistic goals are any goals that you can achieve within your physical limitations. A seven-foot-tall man will probably never become a racing jockey, and a midget will probably never become an NBA basketball star. If physical limitations stop you from achieving one goal, find a more realistic goal that you can achieve.

Nothing is wrong with modifying a goal. Any goal is better than no goal at all. Just make sure you're modifying a goal because you can't achieve it rather than because you're afraid to achieve it.

Let's take real estate investing as an example. Suppose your goal is to make a million dollars in real estate. First, check to see whether your goal requires any physical limitations. Nope, so making a million dollars in real estate sounds like a realistic goal.

Besides physical limitations, time limits can turn a realistic goal into an unrealistic one. Making a million dollars in real estate is certainly possible, but if your goal is to do this by next Friday when you've never invested in real estate before, it's not realistic. (If you're an experienced real estate investor, however, making a million dollars by the end of the week actually could be a realistic goal.)

Ideally, a realistic goal is one that you can physically achieve within a reasonable time period. Choose goals that force you to stretch but aren't so far out of reach that they discourage you. Making a million dollars in real estate is challenging but possible. Making a million dollars in real estate by the end of the week is setting yourself up for disappointment.

Make yourself proud. Choose a big goal that you want to reach and know you can reach. I guarantee you that you'll surprise yourself one day.

> *Make yourself proud. Choose a big goal that you want to reach and that you know you can reach if you only try. I guarantee you that you'll surprise yourself one day.*

FIND A REASON BEHIND YOUR GOALS

Okay, so you've chosen some goals, weeded out or altered the unrealistic ones, and turned the others into achievable ones. Just remember that writing down goals is the first step. The second step is to take action to pursue them.

But wait! Have you ever seen people make New Year's resolutions but they never reach their goal? They haven't given themselves a reason to do so.

Goals give you a direction, but if you can't think of a good reason to pursue a goal, chances are good that you won't, no matter how important that goal may be.

Hundreds of thousands of people have bought my real estate course over the years, but the only ones who benefit from my program are the ones who take action.

The people who wish to get rich often buy my real estate course, browse through the material, and then put it on the shelf. They may want to get rich. They may dream about getting rich. But until they give themselves a reason to get rich, they won't move one step closer to their goal.

With other people, it's different. They buy the same real estate course and have a strong reason to change and a goal to reach. Maybe they are sick of the rut they're in and have decided they're going to get out of this rut as soon as possible. Maybe they've lost a job or are about to lose one. Maybe they're just tired of barely scraping by and want a better life for themselves. Maybe they want to finally live life on their terms and have no limits. Whatever the case, people who take action have a reason. Once you have a reason to change, you'll take action. If you don't have a reason, you probably won't change. It's as simple as that.

The only reasons that matter are the ones you choose for yourself. If you find a personal reason for achieving a goal, you greatly increase the odds that you'll reach it.

Write down two personal reasons for each goal. First, write down a positive benefit that you'll get if you achieve your goal. If your goal is to invest in real estate, one positive benefit might be the fact that you could make enough money in real estate to buy a nicer car and live in a better house, or your spouse could quit a job to stay home with the children.

Next, write something negative that could happen if you don't achieve your goal. If you don't invest in real estate now, maybe you will become bankrupt if you don't find a way to start paying your bills fast. Or worst yet, you will live a stagnant life filled with disappointment.

By writing down both a positive benefit (that can pull you towards a goal) and a negative consequence (that can push you towards your goal), you'll have two personal reasons for achieving your goal.

If the idea of buying a fancy sports car doesn't motivate you to pursue your goal of real estate investing, the threat of losing your job or being stuck in a dead-end job certainly might. The more reasons you can create for why you should achieve your goals, the more likely you'll take action.

In my life, I want to achieve these goals:

1. _____

     a. Positive reason _____

     b. Negative reason _____

2. _____

     a. Positive reason _____

     b. Negative reason _____

3. _____

     a. Positive reason _____

     b. Negative reason _____

4. _____

     a. Positive reason _____

     b. Negative reason _____

5. _____

     a. Positive reason _____

     b. Negative reason _____

MAKE COMPATIBLE GOALS

Now that you have at least two reasons for achieving each goal, take another look at your goals. Ideally, you want all your goals to support each other. If you have conflicting goals, you'll need to either modify one or both goals or drop the least important one.

For example, you might have a goal of losing weight and a second goal of becoming a gourmet chef. Now it's possible to become a gourmet chef without becoming overweight, but can you see how both goals might interfere with each other? As a gourmet chef, you'll have to surround yourself with food all the time, which isn't the wisest strategy when you're trying to lose weight.

The more compatible your goals, the faster you can achieve them. Suppose one of your goals is to invest in real estate and a second goal is to get a college degree. You can make the two goals mutually compatible and supportive if you get a college degree in a field you can apply to real estate, such as accounting, law, or business. Then the skills you learn in college can support your other goal of investing in real estate.

The more you can make your goals support each other, the more you can achieve in the same amount of time. Even if some goals don't appear to support each other, find a way to link them.

For example, if one of your goals is to make a million dollars in real estate and a second goal is to sail around the world, look at the achievement of one goal as a way to help you reach the other one. As you invest in real estate and make a profit, use those profits to take sailing lessons and rent or buy your own boat. Then when you finally reach your goal of a million dollars in real estate, use that money to take a year off to achieve your second goal of sailing around the world.

The more goals you can link together or achieve at the same time, the faster and more likely you'll take the necessary action to reach them all.

TAKE ACTION WITH MINI-GOALS

Without action, even the simplest goal will remain forever out of reach. With action, even the toughest goals can be reached.

I urge you to choose the biggest, greatest, wildest goal you want to achieve. Don't hold yourself back. Just remember that no matter how big or outrageous your goal may seem, you don't have to reach it in one step.

So if your goal is to invest in real estate, I don't expect you to make a million dollars on your first deal, even though it is possible and I would love a call from you telling me you did.

At the time of this writing, I'm working on a deal that could make me $1.2 million without using any of my own money. I'm doing nothing more than using the strategies that you'll be learning in the following chapters.

I'm locking up property on contract, and then if all goes as planned I will be assigning the contract to another company for a huge profit. I have been trying to lock up this property on contract for five or six years. Not a lot of work—maybe a few hours a year—but consistent work. I was not sure how or if it would happen, but it was a goal of mine to get it, and now my goal is to make more than a million dollars on this one deal without using any of my own money. Although the deal is not finalized, I believe it has a 97% chance of going through.

Obviously, deals like this don't come around everyday, but they do happen. Just remember this: The more real estate deals you put together successfully, the more money you'll make. Eventually, you could become a millionaire in real estate too. Some people might make a million dollars after ten real estate deals. Other might make a million dollars after twenty or thirty deals. It doesn't matter how long or how many steps it takes for you to reach your goal. The important thing is to reach it.

In the beginning, any goal can seem intimidating and out of reach. That's only because it is something you have not experienced yet. The trick isn't to tackle your goal all at once, but to divide your main goal into smaller goals that each take you one step closer to where you want to go.

Let's say you want to lose twenty pounds by next year. Nobody's going to lose twenty pounds overnight, and most people aren't going to lose twenty pounds in three months. Try losing one pound every three weeks. By the end of sixty weeks, or a little over a year, you'll have lost twenty pounds.

The key to reaching any goal is to create a series of mini-goals that you know you can achieve. As long as you keep working on your mini-goals, you'll eventually get to your main goal, one little step at a time.

VISUALIZE YOUR GOALS

It's easy to write down a goal, but it's much harder to stay motivated to keep working towards a goal. So besides breaking a large goal into several mini-goals, make your goal more enticing by using visualization.

Visualization is like a creative form of daydreaming. As a kid, do you remember pretending to be a fireman or a policeman? You didn't just see yourself as the word *fireman* or *policeman*. You probably saw yourself in a uniform and a shiny badge, throwing ladders against the side of a burning building so you could carry a hose closer to spray on a roaring fire. Notice how much more descriptive your imagination can be compared to the plain words *fireman* or *policeman*?

That's the same way visualization works. You don't just write down and read your goals. You imagine yourself achieving your goals and visualize yourself living them. If your goal is to make a million dollars in real estate, how would you feel? What would you do with a million dollars? Where would you go? What would you buy? Who would you help? The more vividly you can see your goals in your imagination, the more exciting your goal will appear, spurring you towards achieving it.

To remind yourself of your goals, cut out pictures from magazines and newspapers that represent your goals and paste them where you can see them every day. If you had a million dollars right now, maybe you would take a trip to Hawaii. Find a picture of Hawaii with the sun shining over palm trees along a beach where people are sunbathing.

Visualization helps you see what you want before you even get it. Think back to Christmas as a kid. You might have seen a doll or an action figure on TV that you absolutely had to have. The more you saw that toy in your mind, the more you wanted to get it.

The same principle works with your goals. The more you visualize your goals, the more you'll find yourself wanting them, and the more likely you'll take action every day to move one step closer to reaching them.

CREATE MEASURABLE GOALS

While browsing through an old high school yearbook, I wondered what each person thought about after they graduated from school. Some people even had their goals printed under their name. One boy wanted to be a doctor. One girl was planning to study the environment. What struck me the most was the girl who simply wrote that her goal was to live a long and happy life.

That sounds like a noble goal. After all, who wouldn't want to live a long and happy life? Unfortunately, this vague type of goal is useless because how long is long, and what exactly would make this girl happy?

If you don't make your goals concrete and measurable, you'll never know how close (or how far) you are from achieving them. That's why I suggest you make goals that anyone can look at and know, without a doubt, whether you have achieved them or are moving closer to them (or further away).

If one of your goals is to "be happy," how would you measure happiness? Would you be doing a certain type of work and making a certain amount of money? Would you be traveling around the world, visiting exotic locations?

You can't measure a goal of "being happy," but you can measure a goal of having a million dollars in your bank account or owning a million-dollar home on the beach.

Go back over your goals and make sure that each goal is something you can accomplish without a doubt in anyone's mind. Can anyone verify if you've reached a goal of losing twenty pounds? Yes. Can anyone verify if you've reached a goal of buying and selling at least one house within a year? Yes. Can anyone verify whether you're rich or happy? No, because it all depends on your definition of rich and happy.

Measurable goals give you concrete targets to aim for. When you know what you're trying to achieve, you'll know when you've achieved it.

DEVELOP A PLAN—FIRST!

For every goal you want to achieve, develop a plan. Everyone has different goals, so it's important that you know what you want to achieve. Maybe you want to create additional monthly cash flow from rental properties. Or you might want to invest your way out of debt. Whatever your goals, write them down now, and then create a written plan that will help you reach your goals.

Make your goals as specific as you can. For example, one goal might be, "I will create $500 per month in net positive cash flow over the next twelve months." Another example might be, "I will purchase and sell four houses in the next five years." The more specific and concrete your goals, the easier it will be to know when you're heading in the right direction to reach them and when you're heading in the wrong direction and getting distracted.

Determine what you need to do to achieve each goal and list that below the goal along with the specific time frame. For example, "I will correct all errors on my credit score and try to raise it to 700 by next year." Or if your goal is to create $500 per month in net cash flow in the next twelve months, you should decide how many properties that represents. The clearer your goals, the easier they will be to achieve.

Create your plan so that you can achieve your goals. Don't be afraid to dream big. I did, and I'm still dreaming!

By completing these steps, you'll know what you want to achieve, how you plan to achieve it, and how long it should take to achieve each step. Now put your goals into action.

YOUR GOAL OF REAL ESTATE INVESTING

Because you're reading this book, I'm sure that one of your goals is learning how to make money investing in real estate. Now that you've chosen a great real estate goal, give yourself some reasons for why you want to succeed in real estate. For some people, real estate is like a giant game of Monopoly. For others, real estate offers them a way out of their job and provides them a brighter future.

Now that you have a reason (or two) for why you want to succeed in real estate, break your goal into mini-goals. If you know nothing about real estate, what should your first mini-goal be? (Maybe finish reading this book!) What's your second mini-goal? What's your third mini-goal? Make sure every mini-goal moves you closer to your ultimate real estate goal, whatever that may be.

Now ask yourself if your goal and your mini-goals can be measured. Define exactly how you'll know when you reach each mini-goal and your real estate goal. Will it be through the number of homes you buy and sell? The amount of money you make? Whatever your criteria, make sure you know exactly what you want to achieve.

Finally, visualize your ultimate real estate goal. Picture yourself stepping inside the house of your dreams, cashing a check for a certain amount of money, or quitting your job once and for all.

CONCLUSION

Whatever goals you set for yourself, I'm certain you can reach them. What's even more exciting is that once you reach one of your goals, you'll gain the confidence and experience to reach for bigger and better goals. The more goals you reach, the more goals you'll want to reach, and each goal can change your life for the better.

I guarantee it.

Date _____

Goals for the next year:

_____
_____
_____
_____
_____
_____
_____
_____
_____
_____
_____

Goals for years two to five:

_____
_____
_____
_____
_____
_____
_____
_____
_____
_____
_____
_____
_____

Signature _____

Date _____

PART THREE

Creating Real Estate Wealth

In this part, I explain how to apply the knowledge of Part I with the mental tools of Part II to create wealth in real estate by understanding cycles, strategies, and when to apply the right strategy for maximum profit.

UNDERSTANDING THE DIFFERENT TYPES OF REAL ESTATE INVESTMENTS

*Property is the fruit of labor; property is desirable;
it is a positive good in the world.*
—ABRAHAM LINCOLN

If you're going to buy new shoes or a new car, you need to know your choices. You may want to spend a lot of money buying the best pair of shoes or car you can find, or you may need something less expensive. Real estate is no different. You need to know what you can buy based on what you want to own.

At the simplest level, there are two types of real estate: residential properties and commercial properties. Residential properties are anything that people can live in, such as single-family homes, duplexes, condominiums, and apartment buildings. Commercial properties are places where people do business, such as office buildings, retail storefronts, and warehouses.

This book focuses exclusively on residential real estate investing because everyone needs to live somewhere, which makes residential properties much easier to buy and sell. In addition, residential properties are usually priced lower than commercial properties, making them easier for the average investor to buy with little or no money down. Best of all, residential properties can be not only an investment, but also a place for you to live. If you buy a duplex or an apartment building, you could live for free on your own property while your tenants' rent pays the mortgage.

You can buy four types of residential real estate:

• Houses
• Condominiums
• Rental units (duplexes, apartment buildings, etc.)
• Empty land

Houses are basically single-family homes on a plot of land. Condominiums are basically apartments that you own instead of rent. A condominium is typically in a building with several other condominium units.

Any home can also be a rental unit, but rental units are typically duplexes or apartment buildings where multiple people live under the same roof. A duplex, triplex, or quadplex consists of two, three, or four living units, respectively. You can think of duplexes, triplexes, and quadplexes as miniature apartment buildings. Apartment buildings typically contain multiple rental units.

Finally, there's empty land. Although empty land may seem to offer no immediate source of income besides holding and selling later for a profit, you can make money with empty land, or any type of property, by being creative and thinking a little differently.

MAKING MONEY WITH REAL ESTATE

There are a lot of incredible strategies on how to make money from real estate. But with all the strategies you are about to learn, real estate investing really boils down to a few simple tasks. You can buy property and sell it later at a profit, you can buy property and rent it, or you can do both. For example, you can buy a home and rent it. While you're making money collecting rent, the property value is likely to increase every year. When the property value is high enough, you can think about selling and making a profit. I've simplified these two strategies, but I want you to see that you can get creative by attaching a unique strategy to each purchase and sale.

You see, most people make money in real estate by accident. They buy a house in a great location that they can move into right away with minimal changes or improvements. They live in that house for several years and then sell it for a profit.

Although there's nothing wrong with making money by turning your home into a profitable investment, this method alone takes too long for you to become a successful real estate investor. You want your home to appreciate in value while you are buying and selling or buying and renting other properties. I don't know about you, but I don't want to wait ten or twenty years before making money in real estate. I want to make money now, and I'll show you how you can make money in just a few years, months, or even weeks. The amount of money you can make in real estate depends entirely on you.

In Chapter 15, you will learn that you can also make money with lease options and by assigning a contract to another buyer. But right now I stick with the most common approaches to profiting from real estate.

Making money buying and selling

You can make money buying and selling your own home, but for most people, that takes too long. So why not speed the process by improving the house to increase its value right away? If your area is in an up cycle, you can buy a house and make improvements while your home's value increases. When the improvements are finished, put the house on the market and sell it. You can do the same in any cycle as long as you are paying significantly less than what other homes in the area are selling for.

Both your improvements and the up cycle will have raised the house's value so you can make a quick profit in a short amount of time.

This is a strategy I used recently with a home I found on a cul de sac in a decent neighborhood. Although the neighborhood was prosperous, this particular house seemed like it didn't belong because it was not being cared for as well as the neighboring houses. The landscaping contained weeds and dead plants and the exterior paint was faded and cracked.

When looking for a house to buy, it's best to buy the worst house in a great neighborhood than the best house in a bad neighborhood. A bad neighborhood can drag the value of the best house down while a great neighborhood can raise the value of even the worst house on the block.

Through the realtor who represented the house, I found out that the owner didn't live in the area and had rented the house to tenants. Renters usually take minimal care of a property because they don't want to sink their own money into improving a home for their landlord. The carpets were ruined with pet stains and odors, the countertops were ugly, cracked, and faded, the garage doors were crooked, and the inside walls of the house had ugly stains.

> *Buy the worst house in a great neighborhood rather than the best house in a bad neighborhood. A bad neighborhood can drag the value of the best house down while a great neighborhood can raise the value of even the worst house on the block.*

Most buyers are scared off from such a property because they are unsure how much money they will have to spend and how much time it will take to fix the property and make it ready for resale. Not me. Where others saw problems, I saw an opportunity.

Despite the house's condition, it was still in a nice neighborhood. It was also on a cul de sac, which appeals to many people because it means less traffic. Families particularly like cul de sacs because the reduced traffic means it's a safer area for children to play. The potential of the house looked much brighter than its current condition, so I made an offer.

To pay for the house, I used 100% financing, which meant that I didn't spend any of my own money. Obviously, 100% financing means you're going to pay more on interest, but because I was planning to have the house back on the market in about a month, the little bit in extra interest did not bother me. Before making an offer, however, I got a home inspection. I knew that besides the apparent problems, other things were probably neglected as well. I could use these problems as leverage when I submitted an offer. After making a list of the negatives of the home over and above its obvious appearance, I made an offer.

Because the seller was motivated to get rid of the property, part of the offer was for him to give me 2% of the sale value back at closing. This 2%, commonly called a *seller's concession,* can be used to pay closing costs (such as title insurance, future taxes, insurance, title agency fee, and attorneys' fees) and even go towards a down payment if needed. This ensured that I would not have to use any money out of my pocket. In fact, I got cash back at closing for this property. I got cash back at closing because the seller's concession was more than my expenses. So when you hear people say that they got cash back at closing, this is one way to do it.

Now remember, the seller gave me a concession only because I asked and justified my claim with evidence. If you just ask for a concession because you want to pay less, the seller would likely get insulted and not sell you the property.

I got a good but neglected home for less than the asking price and I used 100% financing, so I didn't spend a dime of my own money.

I then hired a handyman to make minor improvements, such as changing the countertops to a more modern color, putting in new carpeting, painting the inside, and even plugging in room fresheners around the house to make it smell fresher.

In the back yard, the handyman trimmed the bushes, weeded, and threw out the dead plants. After a couple of weeks' work (the handyman's work, not mine!), I put the house back for sale and sold it for about a $25,000 profit. I basically made $25,000 for less than ten hours of physical work on my end. If I had held out, I could have made more because this area was starting to boom. But I had a lot of properties at the time and I was in this for a fast buy and flip.

During an up cycle, everyone's buying houses, but they want a nice house. I found a house that was run-down and on the market for quite some time. The longer a house remains on the market, the more the seller will be motivated to make concessions to sell. Having an up cycle made the seller even more frustrated because people were buying every house but his.

When you buy a house and fix it, make sure that the cost of the improvements don't outweigh the potential profit. That's why I kept my improvements to a minimum.

The key is to find homes with just enough things wrong that they will turn most people away, but not enough things wrong that you can't fix them at a minimal cost. The ideal fix and flip occurs when most of the things wrong are small cosmetic flaws such as painting or cleaning.

If the thought of taking out a mortgage on a second house seems too risky, find a house that you want to live in. After all, you need to live somewhere, so why not make your home your investment at the same time?

After buying a house, you can slowly fix it up and improve it. The improvements don't need to be major, such as installing a swimming pool or building a second story. Sometimes improvements can be as simple as putting in new windows, painting the house a brighter color, or installing new kitchen countertops.

After making improvements and living in the house for a few years, put it on the market and sell it for a higher price than what you paid for it. If nobody is willing to pay that amount because the real estate cycle is down or near the bottom, it doesn't matter because you'll still have a place to live. If someone buys the house, you can look for a new house and start the process again. I did this many times and made hundreds of thousands of dollars in the process.

Making money with rental income

Although making $25,000 buying and selling a house for a few hours of work is great, those opportunities may not be readily available in a down market. The homes may be available but not selling as fast. You can make a steady, predictable source of income in real estate through rental income. You own the property and someone else pays you rent to live there.

You can rent any type of living area. At the simplest level, you can rent a spare bedroom in your own house, but most real estate investors rent separate units, such as homes, condominiums, duplexes, or apartments.

When you buy any property, you'll have to pay a monthly mortgage. So the goal with rental property is to charge rent that exceeds—or, worst-case scenario, equals—your monthly mortgage and all your expenditures, such as taxes, insurance, and maintenance. That way, your renters pay your bills and provide you a little extra every month as positive cash flow while the value of the property increases.

Let your renters pay your bills and provide you with a little positive cash flow every month while the value of the property increases.

Rental properties gave me my jump start into the real estate investing world. Can owning rental property be challenging? Of course, but anything that can reward you with such big dividends is always challenging. To assist you in your current or future rentals, I dedicate an entire chapter to managing properties. In my early twenties, I had close to thirty rental units and managed them all myself, so you will learn firsthand what to do as well as what to avoid.

UNDERSTANDING PROPERTY INVESTMENTS

Now that you have a brief insight on how to make money selling property or renting it, it's time to look at the different types of property investments. Each type of investment property offers advantages and disadvantages. Some people specialize in just buying and selling homes. Others prefer buying and selling rental properties, and still others do both, depending on the opportunities.

After you review the different types of properties you can buy, you can decide for yourself which types of properties you find most attractive. In real estate, there is no single "right" way to make money. The only "right" way to make money is to always make a profit.

Single-family homes

Everyone needs a place to live, and when most people dream about owning their own home, they usually think of a single-family home with a front and back yard. When you buy a single-family home, you can rent it (at much higher prices than an apartment or a condominium) or you can hold it long enough to sell it at a tremendous profit.

Home renters tend to be more responsible and affluent than typical apartment renters, which means you should normally have fewer problems with tenants if you choose to rent your property. When the real estate market is in an up cycle, selling a house is easy. When the real estate market is in a down cycle, renting a house is easy because fewer people have the money to buy one.

If you can buy a home whose mortgage and other expenses are less than what you can charge for rent, you most likely have a winner. Or if you can buy a home at a discount (because it needs work or the previous owner went through financial hardship), you can fix and flip it.

Buying distressed properties is one of the easiest strategies for new investors to make quick cash and start to learn the business. If you just keep your eyes and ears open, you can find properties that look terrible but need only a quick facelift. And the money you can make buying and then reselling this type of home can be incredible.

Real-Life Story

My friend Steve and his wife have purchased and sold sixteen handyman's specials. He used the no-money-down principles that you'll soon learn. His strategy was to buy a run-down house in a neighborhood that was expanding and fix it up himself. Then he'd turn around and sell it. On his first house, he made almost $40,000. (He still has a copy of the check framed on his wall.) Now he's averaging an extra $10,000 a month in pure profit by flipping homes.

As Steve became more experienced, his skills became more refined. Now he's finding homes that haven't been remodeled since the 1950s. He purchases them and hires a team of people to rip up the carpet and put down tile, paint the walls, put in new countertops, paint the outside of the house, and mow and manicure the lawn. This makes the house look a hundred times better. He puts an average of $10,000 into each house and sells them for a profit of between $10,000 and $40,000 each—with no physical labor on his part.

Initially, Steve's credit was terrible, his wife's credit was terrible, and he had no money to get started. But they learned how to invest in real estate by taking action. Surprisingly, they do this part time. Steve loves his full-time job as a pilot. Steve's wife quit her job and stays home with their young son while helping out with Steve's real estate investing in her spare time.

If you wanted to be a runner, you wouldn't run one day and expect to be fast, would you? No, you'd understand that you have to practice. Well, the more you do the things I'm teaching you, the more you'll sharpen your skills. You'll also expand on my ideas, making them your own.

Condominiums

Like single-family homes, condominiums are easy to sell in an up market and easy to rent in a down market. Unlike houses, condominiums are much less expensive to buy. For the price of a single house in a typical city, you may be able to buy three or more condominiums.

Condominiums are most popular in crowded areas, such as the downtown area of a popular city. If you live in a rural area, condominiums may be hard to find or nonexistent.

Many condominiums are former apartments turned into separate units. Because of their lower price, condominiums offer first-time buyers a chance to buy property of their own. Because condominiums don't have a front or back yard, maintenance is generally easier.

Families tend to rent single-family houses, and couples and single people tend to buy or rent condominiums. Condominiums may be less expensive than single-family homes, but they also lack the privacy of a house on its own lot.

Real-Life Story

Scott is a twenty-one-year-old college student. He knew that real estate made people a ton of money, but he thought he would need to be older or have a lot of money to get started. Scott also had a few obstacles, such as having no credit, no experience, and no income.

He had been reading about real estate and purchased my course. That's when he realized my most important lesson: You have to take action.

At the time, Scott was renting an apartment near Arizona State University's campus. His landlord owned close to twenty-five condos in the same complex, which Scott knew was a great investment because it was so close to the campus and the restaurants and bars. One day, when he was paying his rent to his landlord, Scott mentioned that if the landlord was ever interested in selling any of his units, Scott would be interested in purchasing one.

The landlord called him about a week later and said that he would sell Scott one of his two-bedroom units for $270,000. Scott told him that he was very interested and would get back to him within the week. Scott said, "When I hung up the phone, I was so excited I could have jumped through the roof, but then I was quickly grounded when I realized that I didn't have $270,000—or so I thought."

The property was worth around $300,000 to $320,000, so a lot of profit was in the deal if he could find an investor. Scott called everyone he knew and finally found two real estate investors who were looking to purchase property near the college campus.

Scott worked out a deal that if the investors would put up the money, he would do the painting and cleaning to have the place ready within thirty days. Scott was also willing to pay for all the cleanup and half the mortgage payment if it did not sell before the first payment was due.

The investors agreed to give him 40% of the profit, so together they bought the property. Within eight days, Scott cleaned the property and had it looking like new. Because the area was experiencing a major upswing market, they had two offers the first day they put the property on the market. One offer was for the full price of $325,000. The investors and Scott sold the property, without ever making a single payment, and wound up profiting $27,000 after the closing costs and the cost of the materials they put into the property. Scott's share was a little over $10,000. After this success, Scott is currently working on his second deal.

Rental units

Rental units are properties specifically designed for renting, such as duplexes, triplexes, and apartment buildings (although you can always rent a house or a condominium).

Unlike houses and condominiums, rental units also offer you the chance of living on your own property while letting your renters pay part or all of your monthly mortgage, essentially allowing you to live cheaply or even for free. In high-priced areas such as New York or San Francisco, this advantage alone can make rental units a great source of income and a cheap place to live at the same time.

Although tenant turnover is greater in multiple-unit dwellings, you have the convenience of many units in one place. I have owned quite a few multiple-unit dwellings throughout the years, most of which I sold during peak cycles, and I have always made money on them.

Like single-family homes and condominiums, a rental unit property's location can be crucial. If your rental unit is near a university, you can expect a steady stream of student renters in the fall, winter, and spring, and a sudden absence of renters in the summer.

Buying and selling rental units may not be as easy as buying and selling single-family houses or condominiums. Generally, only other investors want to buy rental units. When most families or couples want to buy property, they usually think of a house or a condominium. As a result, selling a rental unit, especially a large one, can be difficult in any market because there will be fewer buyers. But with proper planning and long-term goals, rental units can be an incredible boost to your real estate investing career.

As mentioned, one unique advantage of rental units is that they give you a chance to live for free. I probably overstate this fact because I have lived in my own rental units for free on several occasions and have helped others do the same. For example, I once bought a parcel of property that had five rental buildings, but one was in bad shape and needed to be torn down. I fixed four buildings and put up a duplex (a two-family house) on the space left vacant from tearing down the fifth building.

My sister-in-law had lived at home her entire life because she couldn't afford a mortgage. So I said, "Listen, if you don't mind the inconvenience of getting some calls and renting and managing all five rental units, I can show you how to live in a new house for free." She was happy to have the opportunity. So I told her exactly how much I was making from all the rental income. I showed her that if she bought all five units, the rent coming in could cover her mortgage, taxes, and insurance, with a little bit left over for maintenance.

Basically, she could live for free and build equity, but she had to be the property manager of the remaining four rental units. She'd keep a pager at her side and a list of people she could call to come and fix things when needed.

Well, that's exactly what she did. And while she was living there for free, her tenants were building her net worth and she built her credit. She lived there for two years and then sold it. This was perfect because she sold it at a profit and put the money down on another house where I acted as general contractor.

She learned a valuable lesson, and when we were designing her new house, I said, "How about making it a two-family house?" And that's what we did. We designed the house strategically, and you couldn't even tell there was an apartment in the house. She now gets $1200 a month from rent, and it pays a good chunk of her monthly expenses.

Compromising a little can make the difference between having to struggle and being able to spend money as you like. My sister-in-law likes to travel, and she can use the money she saves to go on vacation. She also has a timeshare on a Caribbean island. She would never have enjoyed herself as much or had as much flexibility if she hadn't learned how to compromise. It taught her lessons that will last a lifetime.

You can make money with real estate in a million ways. My best definition of a real estate investor is someone who is open minded, not afraid to go for it, knows personalities and people, isn't afraid to ask, and makes things happen.

Making money with rental units can come in many forms. Just be aware of the cycle you are in and the available buying strategies, and your mind will open up to a new way of thinking and making money.

Vacant land

Vacant land poses a particular challenge. On the one hand, most people shy away from empty land because they can't rent it to generate income, they can't live on it, and it's more difficult to get a loan. On the other hand, empty land offers unique opportunities that single-family houses, condominiums, and rental units can't offer.

I have made a great deal of money in my real estate investing career by buying vacant land, holding it for a short time, and flipping it for a profit or subdividing a bigger parcel into smaller sections. If you know your local market and the cycle you are in, you can buy vacant land for a great discount and sell it for a profit.

I always keep my eyes open for vacant land with a unique circumstance attached to it that I can resolve inexpensively. For example, remember the story I told in a previous chapter of buying a piece of property that looked like swampland from the road? Once you got through the wet area, the property was gorgeous. I simply used the dirt from the higher areas to fill in the lower regions, and the property was immediately worth three times more. I subdivided the property into five buildable lots and sold each lot at a tremendous profit. But even if I had just fixed the property and flipped it, I would have made money.

In general, I suggest that you buy and sell vacant land after you get experience investing in real estate. First, build up some equity and cash from other ventures. Then consider investing in vacant land when you have more experience and extra money to invest. However, don't rule out strategies such as lease options and locking up property on contract, which can allow you to make huge profits from raw land.

CONCLUSION

As you can see, every type of investment property offers unique opportunities and challenges for making money. Now that you know the different types of residential properties you can buy and the unique profit potential of each, it's time to look at different strategies for buying them in different real estate markets.

CHAPTER 13

IDENTIFYING LOANS AND FINDING SOURCES OF MONEY

Money for me has only one sound: liberty.
—GABRIELLE CHANEL

If you don't have any money, that doesn't mean you can't get started investing in real estate. In this chapter, I show you how to find cash from a variety of sources so you can choose the one that's best for you.

When you think about it, buying real estate is no different than buying anything else. If you're going to buy a new TV, for example, you need money. You can pay for it in cash or you can buy it on credit, essentially borrowing the credit card company's money to pay for your purchases.

That's the same process you can use to buy real estate. Because real estate prices can be several hundred thousand dollars or more, almost no one buys real estate with their own money. Instead, they use loans, which they can get from a variety of sources, such as banks, private lenders, and even government agencies.

With a little creativity, it's possible to buy real estate with no money down, just like you do when you buy something using a credit card. Of course, eventually you have to pay back the lender, such as the credit card company. Real estate is the same except with bigger numbers and the chance to resell your purchase for an enormous profit. You can buy property with little or no money of your own; begin paying back that money you borrowed, plus interest, over a fixed period of time; sell the property for a profit; use the profit to pay back the lender; and still have money left for yourself.

To make sure you pay back the money you borrowed, lenders use a legal document called a mortgage in some states or a deed of trust in other states. Mortgages and deeds of trust serve the same purpose—making sure the lender either gets paid or has the right to seize your property if you fail to pay them back—but have a few important differences.

WHAT IS A MORTGAGE?

Although we commonly refer to loans as mortgages (and I do as well in this book because it is common jargon), technically a mortgage is not a loan. A *mortgage* is a security document that protects the lender's interests in your property because he has lent you money.

A mortgage is an agreement between you as the borrower (the mortgagor) and a lender (the mortgagee). The mortgage creates a lien on the property, which acts as collateral for the money you borrowed. The lien is recorded in public records, probably at your county courthouse.

Until you pay back all the money borrowed, you cannot transfer ownership of your property to anyone else, unless your mortgage specifically gives you that right, which is rare. (If you sell the property, you use the money first to pay back the remaining amount you borrowed. The rest of the money is yours to keep as profit. Then the new owner must take out a new mortgage on the property.) If you fail to pay back the lender, a mortgage gives the lender the right to sell the property to pay your debt. This sales process is called a *foreclosure*. Foreclosures must usually go through the court system; this type of foreclosure is called a *judicial foreclosure*.

WHAT IS A DEED OF TRUST?

A *deed of trust* is a special kind of deed recorded in public records such as in your county courthouse, where it tells everyone that a lien is on your property. Unlike a mortgage, a deed of trust involves three parties: you as the borrower (the trustor), the lender (the beneficiary), and a neutral third party (the trustee), who holds temporary (but not full) title on your property until the lien is paid. When you pay your loan in full, the deed of trust is cancelled.

If you do not fulfill your payment or contractual obligations, the trustee has the power to foreclose your property without going through the court system, making it easier and quicker than foreclosing on a mortgage.

WHERE TO BORROW MONEY

Most people borrow money from a bank, but you can borrow money in many ways, such as from

- Institutional lenders
- Mortgage brokers

- Government agencies
- Private lenders

If some of these terms sound unfamiliar, don't worry. I'll explain them all soon. I just want you to realize that you have a variety of sources where you can get money to buy real estate. After you know how to borrow money from one or more lenders, you can mix and match your options to fit each deal.

Institutional lenders

Institutional lenders are banks, credit unions, savings and loans, mortgage brokers, mortgage bankers, and REITs (Real Estate Investment Trusts). When most people buy real estate, they typically turn to an institutional lender first.

For years, institutional lenders offered relatively few choices in borrowing money. But during the housing boom that flooded the market with buyers, lenders had to compete by offering more flexible loans. Rather than require a down payment, institutional lenders started offering up to 107% financing loans, interest-only loans, and even fifty-year amortization (which means you can take fifty years to pay back your loan, which reduces your monthly payments).

Institutional lenders usually base their decisions on the four Cs of lending:

- Credit. Does your credit history show that you pay your financial obligations in a timely manner? What is your credit score? (I've had things pop up on my credit report that were wrong and lowered my credit rating. To correct this problem, I either supplied proof of payment or proved that the report was wrong. So get a copy of your credit report and make sure it's correct.) We talked about this in an earlier chapter and I repeat it here because no matter what your credit score, you can always improve it.
- Collateral. Does the property you are offering for security have enough value to offset their risk? This is usually determined by an appraisal.
- Capacity. Is your income, or the income from the investment, adequate to offset their debt-to-income (DTI) ratio? Different types of loans have different ratios. For instance, for conventional home loans with traditional lenders, your monthly PITI—principal, interest, taxes, and insurance—usually cannot exceed 26–28% of your gross monthly income.
- Compensating factors. What other things can offset the lender's risk? Will the property generate income from rents? Do you have a strong

employment history, residual income, assets, high net worth, or a previous history of success in investing?

Loans from institutional lenders can vary dramatically. Basically, the more risk a lender takes, the more they expect in return. Unlike some old school thinking, if a property has the potential to produce significant income, I lean towards getting a loan with a high interest rate rather than shy away from a loan altogether. It's my practice to do whatever it takes to buy property that I think is a good deal rather than let an opportunity slip away by not getting a loan. Even better, it's possible to take out a loan at a high interest rate and then refinance later at a lower interest rate.

Because institutional lenders can often take time to evaluate a loan, many people prequalify for loans. This means that they show the lender proof and history of employment, income records, assets, debts, and so on. Based on this information along with your credit rating, an institutional lender can prequalify you for loans up to a certain amount. After you prequalify for a loan, you'll be able to borrow the money you need in a hurry if a real estate opportunity suddenly pops up.

Just remember that there is a big difference between preapproved and prequalified. In a *prequalification,* the lender looks at your income and credit history but does not verify it. A prequalification gives you an idea of how much you can borrow, but no funds will be disbursed until the complete loan file has been submitted to the underwriting department of the lender and signed off by an underwriter.

To get preapproved, you may need to wait an additional three to six weeks, depending on how busy the lenders are. Becoming *preapproved* gives you the ability to shop like a cash buyer. The only documentation required by the lender after preapproval is the purchase contract, appraisal, and title report. Those three items can be generated within a couple of days, especially if you've established a relationship with your appraiser, title agent, and real estate broker. After you have decided on a property, you can close within a week if you are preapproved for a loan.

To become prequalified or preapproved for a traditional loan, you need to provide the following:

- Two most recent years of W–2s, showing continuous employment in the same or a related line of work.
- Last thirty days of pay stubs. They won't accept handwritten pay stubs.
- Last three months of bank statements for checking and savings (all pages, front and back).

- Most recent statements from all other asset accounts (CDs, 401Ks, retirement, Social Security).
- Recent credit report. Generally, the lending institution will run your credit report.
- Purchase contract on the property you are attempting to buy.
- Recent appraisal on the property you are purchasing. Usually the lender will arrange for this to be supplied.
- Divorce decrees, including division of assets if applicable.
- Bankruptcy papers if applicable.

If you are self-employed, you need to provide additional information to the lender, as follows:

- Last two years' tax returns. Business owners who write off everything and show little or no taxable income can't use institutional lenders.
- Profit and loss statement and balance sheet for two full years.
- Business license or letter from a CPA indicating two years' business history.
- Most recent business checking and savings statements (all pages).

Mortgage brokers

You can borrow money directly from an institutional lender, such as your own bank, or you can find a lender through a mortgage broker. A *mortgage broker* works with several lenders to find the best loan for you. If one lender turns you down, the mortgage broker can submit your loan application to another lender, who may approve you.

One reason a bank may turn you down for a loan is because of something known as seasoning. *Seasoning* means the bank requires that you hold a piece of property for a certain period of time, such as six months or a year, before they'll let you refinance it.

In Chapter 4, I told you about a foreclosure I purchased for less than $60,000, immediately turned around and refinanced. After closing costs I wound up with $188,000. I also mentioned that I had to find a bank that did not worry about seasoning. Fortunately, using a good mortgage broker allowed me to get over that hurdle. To get this property, I needed to close fast and there was no time for a loan. So I paid cash and immediately put in an application to my mortgage broker to get a loan on the house.

I paid less than $60,000 for the property, but it was appraised for $220,000. I wanted to borrow 90% of the appraised value, so I could pay myself back and have money to rehab the property and additional money to invest in other properties. However, most banks turned me down because they considered my loan a refinancing (because I already owned the property after paying cash for it), and they wouldn't approve a loan because the property wasn't seasoned.

Seasoning is just one criterion a bank may have. Banks generally want proof that you could pay the costs of the house for six months or a year before giving you more money. Most banks have this as part of their criteria, but not all.

I could have applied for a loan from multiple banks myself, but I let the mortgage broker find me a bank that would loan me money instead. Another advantage is that with a mortgage broker, he or she will run your credit once and use that to submit to many banks. If you went to different banks yourself, each bank would run your credit and that can lower your score. (Each time someone requests your credit report, it is a negative ding on your overall credit score. The number of times someone requests your credit report is one of the determining factors credit bureaus use to calculate your current credit score.)

Even though getting approved for the loan required paying a higher interest rate (because the property wasn't seasoned), I found that the rents from the property would still cover the mortgage. Even with my credit score heading towards 800 and a great income, if a bank has a policy that they can't do a certain loan, they can't do it. So having the ability to access a multitude of banks and lending institutions through a mortgage broker may be a smart move when doing a nontraditional real estate transaction.

When considering a mortgage broker, ask how long the mortgage broker has been in business and how many banks he or she works with. Most importantly, find out how much the mortgage broker charges for application and origination fees. Application and origination fees (also called *points*) are a percentage of the entire loan amount that is paid to the bank or the mortgage broker at closing. One point equals 1% of the total loan.

Most mortgage brokers charge from .5% to 3%, so it is important to ask what they charge. Some mortgage brokers also receive additional money from the bank that is lending the money, which is called the *back end*. Don't be afraid to ask mortgage brokers how they make money because they are required by law to disclose that to you. You want to pay a mortgage broker for his or her services, but you want to keep your expenses to a minimum.

Government agencies

The government wants people to become homeowners, so they have many city, state, and federal agencies designed to help people buy their own home. Two government agencies that help home buyers are the Veteran's Administration and the Federal Housing Administration.

The Veterans Administration (VA) helps eligible veterans get loans through a bank by guaranteeing a portion of the loan. The VA guarantee effectively replaces the down payment (typically 20% of the property price) that the lender normally requires before approving a conventional loan. This means eligible veterans can obtain up to 100% financing to purchase a home at a competitive interest rate normally reserved for conventional loans that require a down payment.

The Federal Housing Administration (FHA) allows you to buy a house with as little as 3% down, instead of the typical 10% or 20% required to secure a conventional loan. The FHA doesn't make home loans—it insures them. If a home buyer defaults, the lender still gets paid from the FHA insurance fund. To qualify for the FHA program, you need a good credit history and sufficient income. Your monthly housing costs should not exceed 29% of your gross monthly income. Total housing costs include the mortgage as well as principal, interest, taxes, and insurance (known as PITI).

Example (Maximum PITI)

Monthly income x .29 = Maximum PITI
   For a monthly income of $3000, that means
   $3000 x .29 = $870 maximum PITI
Your total monthly costs, adding PITI and long-term debt, should be no more than 41% of your gross monthly income. Long-term debt includes such things as car loans and credit card balances.

Example (Maximum monthly costs)

Monthly income x .41 = Maximum monthly costs
   For a monthly income of $3000, that means
   $3000 x .41 = $1230
   $1230 total − $870 PITI = $360 allowed for monthly long-term debt

The ratios for an FHA loan are more lenient than for a typical conventional loan. For conventional home loans, PITI expense cannot usually exceed 26–28% of your gross monthly income, and total expense should be no more than 33–36%.

To learn more about FHA loans, go to my web site at www.dean graziosi.com and click the link for FHA loans.

Private lenders

Many people think that a bank is the only place where they can get a loan, but you can borrow money from anyone. Private lenders can be individuals or groups that loan money to fund what they think will be profitable investments, such as real estate.

Private lenders typically advertise in daily newspapers, and most have relationships with realtors, mortgage brokers, and bankers to handle their paperwork requirements and to bring them prospective clients. In exchange for risking their money, private investors typically charge a higher interest rate than banks and may also request a portion of the profits. Keep in mind that many private lenders are also real estate investors, which means they could make a good partner for the right project. Some of my most successful students started out lending money to other real estate investors.

When you borrow money from a private lender, you typically use a legal document called a promissory note (often called just a *note*). Basically, a *promissory note* is a contract outlining the promise by one party (the maker) to pay a sum of money to the other (the payee). The terms of a note typically include the principal (the amount owed), the interest rate, the maturity date (when the note will be paid off), and any collateral used to secure the loan.

Collateral can be anything of value, such as a car, jewelry, or a rare coin collection. If the maker defaults on payments, the payee can take possession of the collateral and sell it to recover the money owed. Typically, the value of the collateral is greater than the money owed on the promissory note.

Remember that private lenders will analyze (actually overanalyze) your deal because they are the ones at risk. Because you are using them rather than the bank, they worry that there could be a problem somewhere. Maybe you have bad credit or the property has problems. They will typically do their own analysis, crunch their own numbers, check the title, order an appraisal, and so on. If they don't find any problems and they lend you the money, that could be a good indication that you have found a great deal.

CONVENTIONAL FINANCING TECHNIQUES

The number of conventional and nonconventional financing techniques is virtually unlimited. But I want to begin this section by explaining some of the better-known conventional lending programs available through Fannie Mae (Federal National Mortgage Association, or FNMA) and Freddie Mac (Federal Home Loan Mortgage Corporation, or FHLMC).

The federal government set up Fannie Mae and Freddie Mac to purchase mortgages made by banks, mortgage banking companies, and mortgage brokers. They are not insurance companies, like FHA or VA. They are the source of additional money for lenders to loan to their customers. In the conventional lending business, they are considered the voice of authority and have set down a list of rules, or *lender guidelines.* If lenders want to sell their mortgages to these two institutions, they must follow these guidelines.

Fannie Mae and Freddie Mac are commonly known as the *secondary market.* When a lender bundles up their loans and sells them into the secondary market, they sell the loans at a discount. When loan portfolios (literally thousands of mortgages) are accepted by either institution, they send money back to the originating source, less the discount they charge, so those lenders can keep loaning money to the public in the form of new mortgages.

Now, let's talk a little about some of the most commonly used terms you'll see when considering different types of loans. First, there's the principal, which is the total amount of money you're borrowing. So if you want to buy property that costs $275,000, you would take out a loan where the principal of the loan would be $275,000. (If you put a down payment such as $27,500 on the property, the principal of the loan would be $247,500.)

Second, when lenders loan money, they expect to be paid back within a certain time, such as fifteen or thirty years, although the specific time frame can be negotiated. Third, to make it profitable to loan money, banks and other lenders charge interest.

So, when taking out a loan to buy property, you need to consider the following:

- Principal
- Time frame to pay back the loan
- Interest rate of the loan

The more you borrow, the higher your monthly payments will be. The longer the time frame, the lower your monthly payments. The higher the interest rate, the higher your monthly payments. By adjusting these three factors (principal, time frame, and interest rate), you can adjust your monthly payments to make them affordable.

One way to lower your interest rate is to live in your investment property. Generally, lenders offer a lower interest rate if you're buying a property as your residence than if you're buying property as an investment. The theory is that you're more likely to pay a loan for your own house, so you'll be a lower risk of defaulting on your loan.

You can legally get around this rule by being innovative and creative, but it does require some potential inconvenience on your part because you will have to live in the property you are buying for at least a short period of time. If you already own a home, you'll have to turn it into an investment property by renting it out. In this way, you can legally get a lower interest rate while investing at the same time. For this to work, you should be increasing the purchase price of each new property because lenders probably will not believe that you are moving from a higher-priced property into a lower-priced property.

Adjustable-rate versus fixed-rate mortgages

In a traditional loan, you borrow a specific amount of money that you can pay back within fifteen or thirty years at a fixed interest rate that never changes throughout the life of the loan. Adjustable-rate mortgages (also known as "ARMs") were created to reduce the monthly payment obligation of the borrower so that your monthly payment is lower than a fully amortized tradition loan. ARMs have lower interest rates than traditional fixed rate loans. ARMs usually have interest rates that are fixed for a shorter term, such as three years or five years. During this three-year period for example, the loan payment is interest only for a predetermined period of the loan, and no principal is amortized in the payment. Then the principal portion of the monthly payment will kick in (or start amortizing) later as defined in the loan documents. ARMs have predetermined minimum and maximum interest rates (known as a "cap" and a "floor,") that state the highest and lowest rates that the rates might adjust to over the life of that loan. These ARMs usually have built-in periodic adjustment "collars" where the interest rate will not adjust more than a certain amount, such as 2% annually or as defined in the loan.

In the most recent three-year period where property values increased rapidly, home buyers turned to ARMs as a preferred method of financing their investments to keep their monthly payments lower, especially if they didn't plan on holding onto their property for very long.

The most common adjustable-rate mortgages adjust the interest rate periodically in one of three ways:

- Monthly adjustments. The interest rate is recalculated monthly.
- Six-month adjustments. The interest rate adjusts every six months.
- 1/1, 3/1, 5/1, 7/1 and 10/1 adjustments. The interest rate remains fixed for a certain number of years and then adjusts annually thereafter. For example, a 5/1 adjustment means the interest rate remains fixed for five years, and then adjusts annually after the fifth year.

Although adjustable-rate mortgages can cost you more money than a fixed-rate loan when interest rates change, ARMs can make sense if you're going to own property for less than five years. So it's possible to get an ARM at a lower interest rate than a fixed-rate loan, buy property, improve it, and then sell it less than five years later at a profit. Then you pay back the money you borrowed though the ARM and keep the extra money as profit. In this way, you sell the property before the next interest rate increase or decrease could affect you.

Private mortgage insurance

Private mortgage insurance, or PMI, is basically an insurance policy that you pay as part of your monthly mortgage payment. PMI insures the lender that, if they have to foreclose on the property due to nonpayment of the loan, they will receive the remainder of their loan from the insurance company. Basically, PMI protects the lender but costs you extra money. That's why most investors try to avoid PMI.

Generally, the higher your initial down payment, the less likely the lender will require you to pay for PMI because you'll have a financial stake in making payments (otherwise you'll lose your initial down payment as well).

Prepayment penalty

When a lender makes a loan to someone, they expect to receive payments for a specified period of time. This amount is known as the *yield*. To ensure that they receive the yield they expect, many lenders state that if the borrower pays off the loan earlier than expected, they have to pay a prepayment penalty, which can be as much as six months to one year's worth of interest. If you are planning on keeping your property for an extended period of time, you probably don't need to worry about the prepayment penalty because you won't want to pay off your loan anyway. One advantage of a prepayment penalty is that if you accept it as a condition for the loan, you can often negotiate a lower interest rate with the lender.

However, if you're planning to buy property, fix it up, and resell it later, you could be hit with a prepayment penalty when you sell the property and pay back the original loan.

NEW CONVENTIONAL MORTGAGES

Many people just getting started in real estate have no idea what's available through institutional lenders or how flexible some of those lenders have become with their lending programs. My goal in this section is to give you an idea of some of those creative financing programs.

With a competitive marketplace, most of these new conventional mortgages allow minimal or no-money-down purchases, enabling beginning investors a chance to get into the market. As long as you have a decent credit history, you should qualify for most of these loan programs. Remember, always raise your credit score by paying off your debt.

103%–107% new first mortgage

Rather than finance 100% of the purchase price, lenders may offer you 100%

financing plus an additional 3% to 7%, which you can use to pay off debts, make improvements to the property, or spend any way you like.

The loan period is typically for thirty years, with no private mortgage insurance and an adjustable-rate mortgage where the interest rate remains fixed for two or three years before adjusting annually afterwards.

Here are the exact numbers for a home I recently purchased, knowing I would need to do some minor repairs before I could sell it again. Instead of using any of my own money, I went with a 106% loan. The sale price of the house was $455,000 but because I got a 106% loan, I borrowed $482,850. The remaining balance was $27,850:

1.5% points to the mortgage company	−$7,230
School taxes until the end of the year	−$8,005
Mortgage tax of .5%	−$2,414
Title insurance	−$3,039
Attorney fees	−$1,000
Administration and miscellaneous fees	−$1,850
Insurance	−$1,250
Money left over	+$3,062

Now as crazy as those expenses seem, they're typical of the closing costs necessary for any real estate purchase, although costs can vary from state to state. Although I paid an extra 0.5% origination fee to get a 106% loan from the lender, the rest of those fees would be due even with a traditional loan. But in this case, by doing my homework and knowing what the home was worth, I was confident doing the deal this way and walking away with money in my pocket.

For my loan, I paid an interest rate that was probably 1.5% higher than a traditional loan, but a few months of payments with higher interest was not significant enough to tie up my own money. After fixing up this house, I have it under contract.

I put about $10,000 into the house, and after paying all the fees, such as taxes and insurance, expenses, and realtors' commissions, I should make around $60,000 profit. With this type of 106% loan, I was able to make that kind of money without using a penny of my own money to purchase the place.

80/20 new first and second mortgages

LTV, or loan to value, is the bank's term for letting you know how much of the value of the home they will lend you. Many lenders allow for 100% financing for a new first mortgage that does not exceed 80% LTV and a new second mortgage that does not exceed 20% of the total LTV. You can use these programs to avoid paying private mortgage insurance (PMI). In this case, they would be lending you 100% of the value of the home.

The 80/20 mortgage is basically two different loans, one for 80% of the appraised value of the home and a second mortgage for 20% of the value of the home (or asking price, whichever is lower). Together, this makes up 100% of the sale price.

If you don't have any money for closing costs, you can ask the seller to give you a seller's concession for the amount of the closing costs. If your costs for title insurance, loan discount fees, taxes, and so on are $2000, for example, ask the seller to pay that out of the money he or she will receive from the sale.

80/15/5 new first and second mortgage with 5% borrower contribution

The 80/15/5 loan is a variation of the 80/20 mortgage. The borrower comes up with 5% towards the purchase price and the lender gives a first mortgage that does not exceed 80% LTV and a second mortgage for the remaining 15% of the LTV. This program is also used to avoid PMI. You can still ask the seller to help with closing costs.

So on a $100,000 purchase, you would need $5000 as a down payment. In the next option, the 80/10/10 mortgage, you would have to come up with $10,000 for a down payment.

80/10/10 new first mortgage

The 80/10/10 loan is another variation of the previous two programs. In this one, the borrower comes up with a 10% down payment of the purchase price and the lender gives a new first mortgage that does not exceed 80% LTV and a new second mortgage for 10% LTV. The less risk the lender is asked to take, the better the interest rate on both the first and second mortgages.

Mortgage renovation loan

A few lenders offer *mortgage renovation loans,* which not only loan you money to buy property but also provide you with the funds to renovate the property. These programs have specific guidelines as to LTV (up to 95% with great credit), the renovation period (usually up to six months after closing to complete the work), and the use of licensed contractors to perform the work.

IT PAYS TO HAVE GOOD CREDIT

If you have excellent credit, "the world is your oyster." Lenders perceive a person with an excellent credit history as their lowest risk because of the borrower's ability to pay everything on or before its due date. Borrowers with credit scores exceeding 700 sometimes have to provide little or no income documentation to secure a loan. A couple of examples follow.

Stated income mortgage

All credit-worthy borrowers have to do with a *stated income loan* is state their income without proving where it comes from. This is probably the most popular loan for self-employed people. Most lender guidelines limit borrowers to 90% LTV for purchases with no income documentation. A mortgage broker can help you through the process of getting the documents you need for this type of loan.

I use a stated income loan whenever I know that I am going to fix and flip a property quickly. With a stated income loan, you may pay a little higher interest rate each month, but there is significantly less paperwork and time involved in getting the loan.

Stated income/stated assets mortgage

With the *stated income/stated assets loan*, the credit-worthy borrower has the freedom to simply state their income and indicate how much they have in the bank. According to the guidelines, you do not have to prove your assets. The interest rates on these programs are a little higher, but if it makes the transaction work, go for it.

No income, no assets mortgage

A *no income/no assets* (NINA) loan is the granddaddy of them all because if your credit score is high enough, and the LTV is low enough, you don't have to tell the lender how much you make or how much you have in the bank. These rates are even higher than the stated income and stated income/stated asset loans, but again, if it works for you and allows you to qualify and close the loan, that's the main thing.

CONCLUSION

Can you see how many lending options are available? With so many different types of loans available, lenders can tailor the best loan for your needs. If one lender turns you down, you can choose from plenty more. In fact, the job performance of loan officers is based on the number and quality of loans they make, so they have an incentive to loan people money.

More money is available now than ever before. As long as you have a good, or even average, credit rating, you should be able to use one or more of the loans described in this chapter to finance your next deal.

Because your credit rating determines the number and type of loans you can get, I strongly recommend that you watch your credit score. Regularly review your credit report and clear up any errors. Think of all the interest you will save if you receive better (or even preferential) interest rates that banks make available to clients with excellent credit. Manage your credit score aggressively, develop relationships with lenders, explore the options with those lenders, and establish your credit options before you purchase a property.

If you develop relationships with different lenders and understand the variety of loans you can use, you'll be able to pounce on the next real estate opportunity you see and walk away with a hefty profit.

CHAPTER 14

BUYING REAL ESTATE WITH NO MONEY DOWN

A creative economy is the fuel of magnificence.
—Ralph Waldo Emerson

Believe it or not, you can buy real estate without spending any of your own money, and I'm going to show you how. In this chapter, I'll show you some of the techniques that I and others have used to build tremendous wealth in any real estate cycle. This chapter complements the traditional and creative financing techniques you learned in the preceding chapter. So as you read this chapter, keep in mind that many financing techniques you just learned can be mixed and matched with some of the techniques you are about to learn.

Sometimes borrowing money from a single lender makes sense; sometimes borrowing money from several lenders may make sense. Every real estate transaction will be different, so by understanding your financing options, you can choose the options that work best for you.

LEVERAGE IS AN ASSET

Leverage means the ability to spend a small amount of money for a large asset. The more you can use leverage to buy a property, the more money you can keep for improving the property to increase its value as well as for other investments.

The main advantage of leverage is that it reduces, or even eliminates, the amount of down payment required to buy property. However, it also increases your monthly (and total) debt. If you plan on using high leverage, make sure the income from your real estate investment can cover your expenses—and also make sure you have the ability and resources to make up any shortages if it doesn't.

The basic idea behind buying real estate with no money down is to get creative. One, you can find an alternate source of money to buy real estate, or two, you can offer something just as valuable and useful to the seller, such as:

- Submit your offer to purchase, specifying that the real estate agents carry all or a portion of their commissions on a note, with an interest rate that is attractive to them.
- Tap the equity in a property you already own, either by refinancing or by asking the seller to accept that equity as part (or all) of the down payment.
- Have the seller carry a portion or all of the down payment.
- Use traditional and nontraditional loans and funding in whole or in part, as described in the preceding chapter.

More creative financing techniques are available than conventional techniques. You just have to know what to look for—and what to do with the information after you've found it. I'll show you my techniques, but I want you to develop techniques of your own because every real estate deal is unique.

The greatest thing I can teach you about buying property with no money down is that there is no one-and-only technique. If you can buy property without using your own money and you do not overleverage, you are a winner.

HOW I MADE $100,000 IN FORTY-FIVE DAYS

Let me walk you through a deal in which I used none of my own money. I was driving home one afternoon when I saw a realtor putting up a sign across the street from a house I already owned. I quickly pulled over, spoke with the realtor, and found out that the sale price was $525,000.

Now I asked whether I could take a quick walk through the home. I already knew that it was built in 2001 (the same time as the one I already owned) and that it probably had similar features, so I was in and out in minutes. I asked when the house was going to be put on the market and where the owners were moving. From these simple questions, the realtor told me that the man who lived there had passed away and his two children now owned the house and one of his children lived out of state. The realtor was going to put the house on the MLS (Multiple Listing Service) the next day.

This immediately sparked my interest. I knew the sellers were probably extremely motivated, but I also understood that they were going through a difficult time. I needed to let the sellers know that I wanted to help . . . and fast.

Knowing this information, I drove across the street to my house, wrote an offer, and faxed it to the realtor. The exact letter I wrote was as follows:

Dear XXXX,

Here are my thoughts. I paid $525,000 for the house I own across the street, which equals $214 a sq. ft. This is a great comparison because it is directly across the street and the houses were built the same year by the same builder. My house has a lot more options and benefits than the one you have listed.

At $214 a sq. ft, the house you are representing would be listed for $471,428. However, I know you need to go by what you can get and what supply and demand will allow, not by my house as a comparison. But this is what I am using as my basis.

With that in mind, here is what I would like to offer:

Sale price $513,000.

Seller concession of 3% (sellers to pay 3% of the sale price either to me or toward my expenses at closing)

Because I won't bring in a realtor on my end, you could represent both sellers and buyer. With that, though, I would like 1% back from you at closing.

I can have a credit line of approval faxed over this weekend.

I can close in less than thirty days.

I would take as is. No cleaning, no repairs, and so on.

This offer might be a little different than most, but it is my nature to be creative.

Thanks for your consideration,

Dean Graziosi

Within an hour after talking with the realtor, I faxed over my offer. By that same afternoon, the realtor got back with me and said the sellers had accepted the offer. That was great news because I knew that this particular area in Phoenix was still in an upswing cycle—heading towards the peak but not quite there yet. I knew that the house needed a little care and could be flipped for a great profit.

I called my mortgage broker, told him that I thought the house would be appraised above the asking price, and said I wanted to do 100% financing. I see no reason to use my own money when you have the opportunity to use other people's money.

You may be wondering why the realtor would sell the house at a reduced rate and give me 1% back. In most cases, residential homes are listed at 6%—typically 3% goes to the buyer's agent and 3% goes to the seller's agent. My offer was a good deal for him because he could represent me as the buyer's agent, so he made a total commission of 5% (after giving me 1%) instead of 3%. In addition, he had spent almost no time on the deal and already had a solid buyer lined up.

After the great news of the sellers accepting my offer, I hit my first obstacle. My mortgage broker found a creative financing deal and I got my approval for a 100% financed loan. But when the bank saw that the owners and the realtor were giving me a total of 4% of the sale price at closing, they didn't want me to get that much back and would not do the loan that way. In my experience, banks don't want you to leave a closing with too much money because they fear you already have a profit and may walk away from a property if trouble arises.

To me, this was just a little bump that needed some creative thinking. Because the sellers had already agreed to the 3% concessions at closing for expenses or cash back, I went back to them and offered a new deal. I explained that the bank was not willing to do the deal with these concessions, so I asked them to deduct it from the sale price and showed them how they would receive the same amount of money. The sellers agreed and I asked the same of the realtor, who agreed as well. Now we had a deal.

Now the actual sale price was reduced by 4% (3% that the sellers were giving back towards closing fees and 1% from the broker), so I was buying the house for $492,480. Instead of getting the money at closing, it would simply be deducted from the sale price. So here is how the deal was structured after the obstacles were addressed. Because the house was appraised for much more than I was paying, I went to the bank and got 100% financing for the purchase. This was an 80% first mortgage and a 20% second mortgage.

I put $7500 into the house before I put it up for sale. I installed new stainless steel appliances, slapped on a coat of fresh paint on the inside, and used my credit card to pay for all the upgrades. Then I asked a realtor friend if she would be willing to sell the house for 1% commission rather than the standard 3%. She agreed because she knew the house would sell quickly, reducing the time she would be investing. Often realtors will reduce their commission if you will accept only limited services (meaning they may just list it on MLS and put up a sign but not spend any money on advertising or promotion). This realtor knew that when I get a house ready to sell, it has major curb appeal.

I listed the house with her two weeks after closing on it. The loan did not have to be paid for forty-five days after I closed, so when I sold the house within a few weeks, I never made a single payment. This is a perfect example of how you can make a fortune without having to come up with a huge down payment as long as you know the cycle of the area you are investing in and use the proper strategy.

When investing in real estate, it's important to have a backup strategy in case your first plan doesn't work out. Let's assume a worst-case scenario where I couldn't sell the house. The logical backup strategy would be to rent the property to cover the interest payment (because it was an interest-only loan)

> *When investing in real estate, always have a backup strategy in case your first plan doesn't work out.*

plus property taxes, insurance, and homeowner's association fees. This backup plan falls short because the rent probably won't cover the monthly costs. But based on the up market cycle, the odds were in my favor that I could flip the house quickly.

What makes a deal like this possible? You have to be ready for an opportunity. When I saw the realtor putting the For Sale sign up, I took action by approaching him and understanding the situation. When you find a great deal, you have to move fast. I knew the area and knew that the house was undervalued. I also solved a looming problem for the sellers. These factors allowed me to have an agreement with them just hours after seeing the property.

The result was that I walked away from the closing with a check for $109,000. After deducting my costs and expenses, I still profited more than $100,000 in less than six weeks without using any money out of pocket. How's that for incentive?

THE ABCS OF CREATIVE FINANCING

It really is as simple as ABC (and D) to determine whether a property will fit into your portfolio of investments. To develop your own creative financing techniques, you need to do four things:

- Analyze the situation (price, property, seller, buyer, profit potential, and leverage factor).
- Be sure to identify benefits.
- Choose the right strategy.
- Develop a relationship with the seller or broker so you know the magic buttons.

And I will add a fifth: Understand the market cycle.

Every time you analyze a property and use your financing resources to set up a deal, the benefits of creative financing become more obvious.

That's why I give you so many of my personal experiences, and describe all the different ways and places where you can get money. Remember, I had never used most of my creative financing methods before. I didn't have a guide like you have to point me in the right direction. I learned these techniques through trial and error, by not being afraid to ask, and by thinking a little differently. So you get a huge head start!

As you become more familiar with the strategies and techniques of creative financing, you will soon become skilled at choosing the right combination of resources to make the deal work for all parties. You'll have all the ingredients; you just need to know how much or which ones to use in a particular recipe. My intention is to give you so many ingredients that you can make any recipe (and any purchase) a reality with creative thinking and action.

BE CREATIVE AND THE MONEY WILL FIND YOU

In Chapter 13, you learned about traditional financing and some newer loan types that enable you to get 100% to 107% financing. Now let's look at some less conventional methods of accomplishing your goals. Not everyone reading this book will have the credit to obtain conventional mortgages, so they will need to find alternate ways to secure financing.

If you want to become a successful real estate investor, you should learn how to use every possible financing resource available. If the deal makes sense, I do everything in my power to make it happen. Again, make a list of all your ingredients and mix and match them to come up with creative financing that works. By thinking a little differently and being creative, you can combine the right money sources that will benefit everyone.

> *To be a successful real estate investor, use every possible financing resource available.*

The most important thing to remember about being creative with financing is that you must never be afraid to ask! It always amazes me what some sellers are willing to accept just to get the property off their hands and to get a sense of security that they will be paid as agreed.

Following is a list of additional or alternate financing resources:

- Seller carryback financing
- Seller-carried second mortgage
- Property potential
- Assumption of mortgages

- Assumption of mortgage with seller-carried second and bonus
- Wraparound mortgage
- Equity partners
- Real estate agent and broker
- Home equity line of credit
- Whole life insurance policy
- Personal property equity
- Credit cards
- Assuming the seller's debt
- Promissory note
- Distressed properties can equal flexible sellers

Seller carryback financing

Without question, using the seller as your financing source can be the easiest way to finance a property, and that's true even if you have the credit to go to an institutional lender. But seller financing is rarely the least expensive form of financing because you tend to pay a little more interest to entice the seller to hold the note. But when calculating a deal, if seller financing is available it is usually the best way to go.

If the seller is going to accept monthly payments instead of cash upfront, he or she will want to receive an interest rate higher than what they might get through a traditional savings account. Seller-carried notes can be accomplished simply: just two people agreeing to the interest rate, terms, and conditions they want; drawing up the paperwork; and closing on the property.

Although seller financing can allow you to purchase property with no money down, the interest rate will often be higher. But if you have no money or you do not have the best credit, you may still end up on the positive side when you calculate your traditional closing costs compared to using the seller as the financier. These calculations definitely come into play when you factor in how long you plan on holding the property.

Seller financing can come in many forms, but it is usually a first or second mortgage on the property. For a seller to carry a first mortgage on their property, they must either own it free and clear (have no mortgage on it) or have a first mortgage that doesn't prevent the seller from creating a wraparound mortgage (which I discuss later in this chapter). Let's assume the property owner is having trouble selling a piece of property due to a down market and poor property location or condition. If the property owner owns the property free and clear, you can ask the seller to sell you the property and take back a mortgage on it.

From the seller's point of view, the only drawback is that he or she won't get all their money at once. The advantages include making more than the asking price of the property due to the added income from interest, earning a higher interest rate than banks might pay if the seller put that money into a savings account, and having the guarantee of using the property itself as collateral. If the seller doesn't need the money right away, this method, known as *carrying a note on the property* (also referred to as *the seller carries the paper, the seller holds the paper,* or *carryback financing*), is a can't-lose proposition for the seller!

If you default on your payments on the promissory note, the original property owner can take back the property and resell it. So the original property owner is protected while you get a chance to buy property for no money down.

Now, I can hear you asking me, "Dean, does seller financing really happen?" All I can say is, "Absolutely!"

Suppose you've driven by a property for quite a while and have noticed it's been sitting vacant. You do what you can to contact the owner or you ask your realtor to pull the ownership records on the property and complete a comparable market analysis of similar properties that have sold in the area within the past six months. Upon getting the report on comparable sales, you discover that the property is owned by someone outside your state, and homes that are fixed up in the area are selling for between $100,000 and $105,000 depending on the amenities. You also find out that the ownership records do not indicate any mortgages on the property, and the records show the mailing address for the tax bill with an out-of-state phone number.

Then, when you speak with the out-of-state owner by phone, you discover the property belonged to his brother who died six months ago. The out-of-state owner inherited it, and he just hasn't had the time or resources to follow up on the matter. He tried to rent the property once but never received the rent on time, and his situation requires that he be able to count on regular monthly payments. You also find out that he will be going into a rest home next month and is in need of an extra $600 in monthly income to cover his monthly bill there.

During the conversation, you convince the seller that you are a reliable source of the income he needs if he would be willing to accept $90,000 for the property and carry a first mortgage at 8% interest. That would give him what he needs—and you've just bought a property for no money down!

This example may sound too simple, but similar things happen every day and for any number of reasons. Typically, seller-financing works whenever the seller is motivated to sell the property, so they offer financing as an additional incentive. Just remember, don't assume that someone will not accept what you offer and don't be afraid to ask.

Real-Life Story

Here's a real-life example of mine. A wonderful older woman had recently become a widow. Her home consisted of her living area plus an additional two apartments. She lived in upstate New York and was ready to move south to a warmer climate, so she needed to sell her home. This property was perfect for me to buy because I already owned the piece of land adjacent to it.

Well, she put the house on the market for about $10,000 more than it was worth. And by asking that extra $10,000, she had no takers. I figured I would wait it out and when she dropped the price I would move in. But after some time, she still had not dropped the price, so I knew it was time for me to find out why.

Because we were neighbors, I didn't have to introduce myself when I went to her house to get more information. I simply sat down and told her I had some interest in the property and would love to come to an agreement that worked for both of us. But I also told her that I thought the house was overpriced and the fact that it was not selling proved I was correct.

We had a great conversation and she invited me back for dinner later that week. While at dinner, I did more listening than anything else. I found out that she knew the house was overpriced, but before her husband passed away he told her that was the price she had to get for the property, and she wanted to follow his wishes. I also found out that she wanted to move down south with her daughter and son-in-law, she owed nothing on the house, she wanted security to pay her new mortgage, and having a lot of cash upfront was not necessary. In other words, I learned her magic buttons.

After putting all the pieces together and considering all my options (the same options I am teaching you here), I came up with an offer that pushed a few of her magic buttons while I asked for a few of my own. I said, "I think we both know that your house is overpriced, but I understand your circumstances and why you need to get that amount, so I will pay you full price." She was ecstatic.

I added, "But I also want to make you aware that your property is not worth what you are asking. So for giving you full price and satisfying the other things you need, I would like you to be flexible as well. Because you don't owe any money on the house and you're moving down south, I would like to buy the house with no money down. You can keep the property in your name, or you can be the mortgage holder. I am going to start putting money into the property immediately to fix it up. So the worst that can happen is that you'll get monthly payments, and if I can't keep up the payments, you'll get the house back in much better shape than it is now. Another plus is that you'll be getting the full amount of money you wanted." I asked her what amount of money she would need every month to feel comfortable, and it was very reasonable. I knew that the rents from the three apartments would cover that, plus some.

To make a long story short, we agreed on the deal, and she sold me the property for no money down. In fact, it was her suggestion that I not even pay interest. And the best part is that I spent a few dollars renovating the place, the tenants' rent covered what I owed her every month, and I ended up owning the property free and clear.

Seller-carried second mortgage

If you want to buy property but can't come up with enough cash, ask the seller to carry a second mortgage. For example, if the asking price for a piece of property is $200,000, but you can come up with only $160,000 in financing with a first mortgage, ask the seller to accept a promissory note for the remaining $40,000. This gives the seller his or her asking price, and if you spread out the promissory note payments over at least a five-year period, the bank will treat the promissory as a second mortgage.

Keep in mind that the less money you can pay upfront, the larger the amount of interest you'll need to pay on the promissory note. Basically, the seller wants confidence that you will follow through and pay according to the terms of the note. If you are successful, you can purchase the property with a first mortgage plus a seller-carried second mortgage without using any of your own money.

Property potential

Sometimes the property itself can be used for a portion or all of the down payment. If you can spot the profit potential in a property and can come up with a solid plan to make money, you can attract investors to contribute to the down payment.

For example, I was shopping for property on which to build my own home. The property I found was raw land with fantastic views. But I had one obstacle: Because of other investments, I had little available cash to use as a down payment. However, by keeping my eyes and ears open, I had learned of two people who were looking for lots on which to build their own homes. So I made an offer on the land that the owner accepted, and with a small down payment and a contract I was able to lock up the property for a month so no one else could buy it.

I met separately with the two people who were looking for lots. I told them I was in the process of purchasing beautiful property with great views, that I was going to subdivide the property, and that I needed to raise capital.

Then I offered them the following deal. If they would give me a refundable deposit on an approved buildable lot, I would sell it to them for 20% to 30% less than it was worth. We were pushing each other's magic buttons: I needed money and they needed land with a view, and I could offer it to them for a huge discount if they would pay upfront and have the patience to wait several months while I subdivided the land.

One individual loved the property so much that he paid me in full for the choice of any lot. The other individual paid me 50% of the money upfront. That was enough money for me to purchase the property. No banks, no loans, no hassles.

Attorneys drew up contracts to protect their investment. It may have been risky for them, but there's no payoff without risk. Just preselling those two lots gave me all the money I needed to purchase the property, with some left over to start the subdivision process. I ended up getting five buildable lots out of the property—and made a fortune.

So you see, there is no one set way to find financing and buy with no money down. It's all about thinking a little differently, being open to what is around you, and taking advantage of the knowledge you are about to gain.

If there is a parcel of land you could possibly subdivide and sell, see whether you can you find a buyer who would be willing to pay upfront—or a portion upfront—for a nice discount. Then use that money for the down payment on the property. Or maybe you can find a partner who would be willing to provide the upfront money because you found the desirable parcel.

Maybe there's something valuable on the property that you can presell. A friend of mine once bought land, and then presold the trees on the property for lumber. From the money he made preselling the trees, he got paid more than the cost for the entire property. How's that for thinking differently?

Assumption of mortgage

I've explained how you can use seller financing, with a promissory note, to buy property with little or no money down. Now what happens if someone uses a no-money-down technique to buy property, and then turns around and wants to sell it to you? You have two options. First, you can pay the property owner cash (through a traditional loan or other source of funding). Second, you can assume the mortgage, which basically means you take over payments on the existing mortgage or promissory note.

To reduce delinquent payments and foreclosures, most bank mortgages have due on sale and no assumption clauses. These two clauses mean that if you sell your property, you must pay off your entire mortgage. In other words, the buyer must create a new mortgage from scratch and cannot assume your current mortgage. So most assumptions of mortgages occur when the current property owner used a promissory note to purchase property—you assume payments on that original promissory note.

Some promissory notes may include a qualification provision. That means if someone is making payments on a promissory note, they can't let someone else assume payments without the promissory note holder's permission.

So if someone bought property with a promissory note and suddenly wants to sell the property, you can assume their promissory note payments (with the note holder's permission) and purchase property with no money down.

Assumption of mortgage with seller-carried second and bonus

Next to using seller financing, assuming a mortgage is probably the most cost-effective way to own property because you pay no loan costs as part of the transaction. Let's say you found a property with an assumable first mortgage, but you have little or no cash available for the down payment or closing costs. You can assume the first mortgage (meaning you take over payments on the existing mortgage or promissory note) and negotiate with the seller to take out a second mortgage for their equity in the property, as explained in the previous section, "Seller-carried second mortgage."

As an enticement to the seller to accept your offer, you can agree to pay an additional amount of interest over and above what the seller is currently paying on the first mortgage, as well as negotiating the second mortgage interest rate to accommodate the seller's needs.

For example, suppose a seller has a property with a value of $140,000. The property has an existing first mortgage in the amount of $102,000 at 6% interest with a monthly payment of $612 that you can assume.

When you negotiate the purchase, you would ask the seller to carry a second mortgage in the amount of 8% (interest only) and agree to pay the seller an additional amount of 1% of his or her first mortgage (for the same time period of the second mortgage) as a bonus for carrying the second mortgage, allowing you to purchase the property for no money down. The bonus would not be part of the second mortgage, because it is an incentive to the seller to get creative with the financing. The benefits to the seller are as follows:

$38,000 second mortgage at 8%	$253 monthly
$102,000 at 1% (bonus)	$85 monthly
$102,000 assumption	$612 monthly
Total payment	$950 monthly

The effective rate on this type of financing technique for the second mortgage becomes 10.68%. An easier way to accomplish this loan would be to just write the second mortgage for the higher interest rate. Incidentally, all the mortgages and the bonus you are paying go away when you refinance the property.

Wraparound mortgage

Normally when you buy property, at least one mortgage is already in place. Instead of qualifying for a new first or second mortgage or both—which can take a lot of time and include a lot of extra money in closing costs—some creative buyers use a financing instrument called a wraparound mortgage.

Instead of paying off the original mortgage and getting a new one, a *wraparound mortgage* keeps the original mortgage, which the seller must continue paying. Then you as the buyer make payments to the seller.

As an alternative to paying the seller and trusting that the seller will use the money to pay the existing mortgage, you can use a third-party escrow company. You pay the escrow company and the escrow company pays the seller's mortgage and sends a check to the seller for the difference.

This type of creative financing does not require you to qualify with the current lender, but there is a drawback. If the existing lender finds out about it, they have the option to call the loan due and payable immediately. Sometimes they will just renegotiate with the new interest holder and keep the loan (or modified version) in place, but they do have the right to call it in. That lender's position and rights in the property override any agreement you may have made with the seller.

A wraparound mortgage works particularly well with property owners who want to sell right away. In a wraparound mortgage, you can get title to the property in your name (depending on the state you reside in), but it is not a clean title. The original mortgage stays in the seller's name because you are not paying off the original mortgage holder. Until that original mortgage is paid, the terms and conditions of the original first mortgage cloud the title.

It is important to mention again that if you ever consider using a wraparound mortgage to buy a piece of property, make sure arrangements are made to get the original mortgage paid on time. You never want to send the payment directly to the seller; instead, use a title officer, a bank, or preferably a third-party escrow company. If you pay the seller directly and he or she doesn't use it to pay the mortgage, you could lose everything when the original mortgage holder forecloses on the property for nonpayment. Any money, including monthly payments, down payment, repairs, or other work that you have put into the property would disappear. And you couldn't do a thing about it because you would have been a party to the fraud carried out against the original lender.

Additionally, many title companies will no longer allow the use of wraparound mortgages because of their increased liability with this type of transaction. As you can probably tell, this is not one of my favorite ways of financing property.

I know you're probably thinking, "Dean, why would anyone use a wraparound mortgage?" Well, as the saying goes, "desperate times give birth to desperate people." This type of mortgage can solve the immediate needs of both parties to the transaction, and if the monthly payments are made on time and everyone does what they say they are going to do, there probably will never be a problem. People with terrible credit or no money might see this as their only option, and if they are willing to take a calculated risk, it can get them into property ownership. Just make sure you are aware of every aspect in a deal like this.

Equity partners

Let's say you find a piece of property that you know will make money, but the price is far out of your price range, such as an apartment building selling for $1,000,000. Although you may not be able to afford to purchase this property by yourself, you can team up with other investors and create a legal organization called a *partnership* or a *limited liability company*.

Get nine investors willing to invest $111,111 each so each investor gets to own 10% of the apartment building. Nine investors times 10% apiece ownership equals 90%, yet 100% of the asking price has been paid. So where does the other 10% go? In your name because you found and organized the deal!

If you don't have the money, offer to manage the property. You get your 10% ownership with no money down in exchange for finding, negotiating, and managing the property. In return, your partners get a property manager they can trust because you also have a financial stake in the property.

Real estate agent and/or broker

Real estate agents and brokers typically earn commissions ranging between 5% and 10% of the selling price, depending on the type of property listed. Residential property commissions average 6%, and commercial and investment property commissions average 8.5%.

However, all fees are negotiable and sometimes so are the terms with which a real estate agent will participate. If the agent doesn't need the commission immediately, you can get creative.

For example, if the agent should receive a $10,000 commission upon closing, he or she might consider accepting a promissory note for $13,000 (instead of $10,000 cash today) due and payable twenty-four to forty-eight months after the sale. The property will appreciate enough (5–15% annually, depending on your area and the improvements made) to cover these additional costs upon refinancing or selling the property. You can even negotiate a discount on the note if you pay it off early. Basically, a promissory note to a real estate agent or broker lowers your initial up-front costs in buying real estate.

Home equity line of credit

Your existing home can be a great source of investment capital because many lenders will lend in excess of 100% of the value of your home at attractive rates. When you borrow against your existing home, that's called a *home equity line of credit, or HELOC*. You should apply for the maximum HE-LOC possible because you pay interest only on the portion you use and not on the maximum limit.

Let's assume your home is worth $250,000, and your mortgage with the bank has a balance of $180,000. That means you could get a HELOC totaling $70,000 from your local bank. Your HELOC would let you write a check for up to $70,000. If a deal comes up where a fast closing could save you a ton of money, this would give you readily available down payment money. New and seasoned investors alike can use this strategy for fast convenient money. Many of my students who thought they had no money to invest used a HELOC to kick off their real estate investing career.

Whole life insurance policy

In many cases, you can borrow a down payment against a whole life insurance policy at an attractive interest rate. If you don't own a whole life insurance policy, find someone who has one and offer an interest rate 2–4% higher than he or she would have to pay when borrowing against the policy. As an additional incentive, you could offer part ownership in the property (such as 5% or 10% ownership), payable at the time of sale or within a time frame you both agree on.

Personal property equity

Instead of offering cash, you may be able to offer a seller personal property for part or all of a down payment. Personal property can include stocks, bonds, jewelry, automobiles, boats, recreational vehicles, or timeshares—anything the seller perceives as valuable. Don't assume a seller won't want what you are offering, and don't be afraid to ask!

When you offer personal property, you have to negotiate with the seller on the value of the property you're offering. Offering personal property lets you use what you already own in place of cash while lowering your down payment. As an alternative to giving your personal property to a seller to lower your down payment, you can also use your personal property as additional collateral, which is called a *pledged-asset mortgage.*

Let's say you want a piece of property, but you don't have the cash to make the down payment. So you need to convince the seller to accept payments (seller-carryback financing). Such an arrangement protects the seller because you're using the property as collateral. If you fail to make payments, the seller can take back the property.

As an additional incentive for the seller, you can include your pledged-asset mortgage as well. This tells the seller that if you default on payments, the seller can take back the property plus any personal property (car, boat, and so on) that you included as collateral.

Credit cards

You can also use available balances on credit cards to generate the cash you need for purchasing properties. The use of available credit can increase your debt-to-income (DTI) ratio, so be careful not to overextend yourself and thereby disqualify yourself in the lender's view because your existing debt is too high for their guidelines. Also be aware of the high interest rates most credit cards charge for interest.

Still, you can use credit cards to provide additional cash in a hurry, which can be handy when other sources of funding can't completely cover the amount of money you need to close a deal right away.

I know most people may cringe when I suggest using credit cards to purchase a piece of property or to come up with a down payment. I've used this strategy for years, such as for buying vacant land that I couldn't get a bank loan on. Typically, you pay a higher interest rate and closing costs on vacant land, so it was actually cheaper and easier to get cash advances of my credit cards for a short-term loan.

Not everyone has $10,000 or $20,000 in cash-ready credit card limits. From having worked on improving my credit and from applying for a few high-limit cards, in my early twenties I had about $40,000 available at any time. I had those high credit card limits, but I was disciplined enough to use them only as an opportunity to make money. I kept one card for personal use and the rest sat there for real estate purchases, almost like a home equity loan even before I bought a home.

I bought several pieces of property in my early investing days by taking cash advances from my credit cards, seemingly paying cash to the seller and then either selling the property for a profit or refinancing the property later to lower my monthly payments.

I once had the opportunity to buy a tax parcel of land for $12,000. This was a transaction that had to happen fast. So I grabbed three of my cards, called the number on the back, and pulled out $12,000 in cash in a few hours and was able to buy the land. I think the highest interest rate of all three cards was 10%, which wasn't that bad if you consider the closing costs I would have had to pay with a bank loan.

I held onto this property, tightened my budget, and aggressively paid the debt down each month until I paid it off. Then I sold half the property for about four times what I paid for the whole thing, and I still own the other half. The value keeps rising each year, so I am in no hurry to sell.

Assuming the seller's debt

If the seller owes money unrelated to the property, such as a high credit card balance or a car loan, you can offer to assume this debt by making monthly payments. By taking over the seller's debt, you can further entice the seller to sell you the property and accept monthly payments instead of a lump sum, thereby allowing you to buy the property with no money down. If you pursue this approach, you will need to enlist the services of an attorney to protect your interests.

Promissory note

A *promissory note* is a legal document between an individual borrower (the maker) and the lender (the payee). Usually, there is also a provision for collateral that the payee can collect if the maker defaults on payments. When you use seller-carryback financing, you're using a promissory note and using the property itself as collateral, although you could use anything of value, such as a car, boat, or coin collection.

Now if someone owes you money, you will be the payee on a promissory note, which means someone else is paying you a steady monthly income. Because a promissory note represents guaranteed income, you can use your promissory note to purchase property in three ways:

- Sell the promissory note to someone else at a discounted price. So if you hold a promissory note that says someone owes you $10,000, you could sell it for $7000 and the new owner of the promissory note would receive payments worth $10,000. You would essentially lose $3000 on the promissory note, but it might be worth it if selling the note allows you to buy property that could make you a lot more money.
- Use the promissory note as additional collateral for seller-carryback financing. This gives the seller added security of using both the original property and your promissory note to ensure that the seller receives payment in one form or another.
- Use the promissory note payments to make payments to the seller. This helps convince the seller that you can and will make monthly payments.

Promissory notes give you one more way to use your financial assets creatively to help buy property to make a down payment or to convince a seller to accept payments in lieu of a lump sum.

Distressed properties

Often, as a result of financial stress, owners of distressed properties will be open to considerable discounts in their prices and terms. As I have mentioned, not all distressed properties are run-down. A property can be distressed for a variety of reasons, such as illness, death, relocation, or poor property management. However, when any one of these is a factor, the property usually will be run-down to some extent, because of the owner's mental state or lack of funds to maintain the property.

Now I don't want you to take advantage of people who are facing a tough time. Instead, you may have the opportunity to do the opposite: take a burden off someone's back and help them solve their problem. Many distressed properties are vacant, with someone still responsible for making mortgage payments, and they are probably not easy to rent due to their condition. So the owner may have a big mortgage to pay on the property every month and may not be receiving any financial benefit from owning that property. If you show up and offer them a way to make money, they'll often jump at your deal.

When you research a property, it's important to determine how long it has been vacant and the existing monthly payments. If a property has sat vacant for six months with $1000 monthly payments, those owners have already lost a ton of money, with no prospect of the money drain ending anytime soon. If you come up with an offer that solves their problem, using the creative financing techniques you are learning, you may be able to not only purchase the property with no money down but also get the property at a greatly reduced price. And in most cases, getting the property burden off the seller will be a win-win solution for everyone.

Getting inside the owner's head is important because you can find out all sorts of things that will work to your advantage in the negotiations for this type of property. This is also where being a problem solver for the seller and thinking a little differently can pay big dividends.

DISCOUNTING THE PAPER

The phrase *discounting the paper* means asking a promissory note holder to take less than the face value of the note they are carrying on a piece of property. The advantage to the promissory note holder is that they get quick cash now. The advantage to the new owner of the promissory note is that they'll eventually earn more money than they paid for the promissory note.

A lot of people make a business out of discounting paper; you can see ads in the classified section of your newspaper every day from investors who are seeking people who have carried mortgages on properties they have sold. People who carry notes on properties want to sell them for a variety of reasons, but usually they want cash out of a long-term investment with property buyers.

The value of a note to the investor (and to the seller) depends on a number of things, such as

- Face value. How much was the note originally written for and what is the remaining balance?
- Interest rate. What monthly income is the note earning and are there built-in increases for late payments or nonpayment?
- Term. How long was the note written for, and how much longer will the investor have to wait before realizing the expected yield on the investment?

Generally, a longer term and a lower interest rate originally charged to the borrower translates to a lower offer from the investor to purchase that note. A note that will be paid off in one year with an interest rate of, say, 15% would not be discounted as severely as a note that still had ten years remaining and an 8% interest rate. All investors believe in the expression *time is money,* and the longer they have to wait to realize the return of their investment and the return on their investment, the more they take away from the face value of the note they are buying.

The return *of* the investment indicates how long it will take them to recover the amount of money they paid for the investment. The return *on* the investment indicates how long they have to wait to get their anticipated yield on the investment.

Most discounters expect to receive anywhere between 18–25% annual return on their investment. Therefore, if a note they were considering buying had been written at 6% interest over a ten-year period, that note would probably be discounted more than 50% from its face value for investors to realize their return on investment over such a long holding period.

As a real estate investor, you may be wondering how you can profit from discounted paper. Let's assume you are buying a property that has a $40,000 second mortgage held by the previous owner, along with a $100,000 first mortgage. The property has increased in value to $200,000 due to market appreciation. Your credit is in good shape, so you decide to refinance the property. You can get a decent thirty-year, fixed-rate mortgage that would reduce your monthly payments. So you arrange a new loan for 80% of the appraised value, or $160,000 ($200,000 appraised value times 80%).

Before completing the refinancing, you contact the holder of the second mortgage to see whether they would like to receive a lump sum in cash versus continuing to receive payments over time. They are remodeling their house and are in a bit of a jam and need $28,000 in cash right away. You suggest settling the outstanding debt and considering it paid in full if you can pay them $28,000 in the next two weeks rather than the entire $40,000 later. They agree and have the paperwork drawn up to cancel the second mortgage upon payment of the $28,000. Congratulations, you just made $12,000 on discounting the note!

The first mortgage holder is a tough nut to crack. He has no immediate need for cash and actually prefers receiving his payments over time. He knows what the property is worth and knows that you would never default on your payments. He knows that if he had to foreclose on the property, he would stand to make a lot of money when he resold it, so he isn't interested in discounting his note for immediate cash.

Fortunately, the note has no prepayment penalty, so nothing is stopping you from refinancing the first mortgage. You call your lender and give them the go-ahead. Here is the result:

- Refinance with a new thirty-year first mortgage
  ($200,000 appraised value x 80%) $160,000

- Pay off the $100,000 first mortgage
  $160,000 – $100,000 = $60,000

- Pay off the $40,000 second mortgage as negotiated with a discount
  $60,000 – $28,000 (the discounted cost) = $32,000

- Cash in your pocket after the refinance = $32,000

Congratulations! You just put $32,000 in your pocket. So now what are you going to do? That's right, you will use that money as your down payment on your next property purchase. I still consider this technique no money down because you will use the equity from this property to purchase another property.

CONCLUSION

As you can see, you can find money to invest in real estate in dozens of ways, from traditional loans to private lenders to leveraging your own assets. Don't let lack of money stop you from investing in real estate. The secret to real estate investing is to research a piece of property completely, determine the cycle you are in, and decide which strategy to use. Then it's all about mixing and matching the correct type of financing so you can purchase the property.

*The secret to real estate investing is to find a
way to make money from a piece of property
and then figure out how to buy that property.*

I hope you can put some of these creative financing techniques to use in completing successful real estate investments. Find the right property, use the right financing, and rent or sell for maximum profit.

CHAPTER 15

PROFITING FROM LEASE OPTIONS AND LOCKING UP DEALS

Landlords grow rich in their sleep.
—JOHN STUART MILL

If you can't afford to buy a house, what can you do? You can rent (also called lease) a house instead. Leasing property gives you the right to use the property and even make changes to it, within certain limits.

Leasing property doesn't give you ownership, so if you want to buy property, you can either pay for it through a loan or use something called a lease option. A *lease option* basically gives you the right to buy property with little or no money down, taking up to a year or two to decide whether to do so.

Real-Life Story

This strategy came in handy when a friend called me about a piece of property he wanted to buy. Unfortunately, he didn't have any money to buy it at the time, although he would be getting enough money for a down payment in several months.

I told him a lease option might be his ticket. He said, "I want to buy it, not rent it." I was in the middle of a meeting, so I said, "Let me e-mail you tonight." My e-mail went like this:

Doug,
   First, because a buyer's agent is not representing you, make the offer directly to the seller's agent and do not try to contact the seller. You can tell the agent that if the deal goes through, he can represent you as the buyer's agent as well and he will get all the commission. Although he will be looking out for his client, he will also have a huge incentive for you to get the property over anyone else because he will make twice the commission.
   I suggest that you make an offer as a lease option purchase. You told me you think the price is very fair, so I suggest you agree to full price—but only under these terms:

You lease the property for one year with an option on a second year.

The first year you pay $1800 a month and the second year you bump it to
$2000 (or whatever you think you can afford).

You set the sale price as the full amount and that price stays consistent for
the duration of the lease.

During the lease, you can purchase the property at anytime for the sale price.

If or when you activate your option to buy, 50% of the money you paid on your
lease goes towards the purchase price.

This gives you time to try to resell it or get your finances in order, while getting
the property with no money down.

The only downside is that if you don't do anything with the property and you
want to give it up after a year, you lose a year's rent. Best of luck,

This strategy gave my friend the opportunity to lock up the property with an option
to buy. Two weeks later he called and told me that he got the property.

WHAT IS A LEASE OPTION?

A *lease* lets you rent property for a fixed period of time and gives you (the
tenant) the option of purchasing the property within a given time period for
a fixed price agreed upon in advance. Usually, during this lease period, you
can exercise the option and buy the property (with a portion of your rent
applied towards the down payment), or you can choose not to exercise the
purchase option and the property stays in the hands of the original owner.
Lease options let you delay buying property (with no money down), while
locking up the property and preventing others from buying it.

Lease Contract + Option to Purchase Contract = Lease Option Contract

With a lease option, you pay a monthly rent plus an additional amount
that goes towards your down payment to purchase the property. This excess
payment is referred to as the *rent credit*. If you plan to get financing to buy
the property, make sure the contract or agreement meets two criteria before
signing:

- The total of the monthly rent plus the rent credit exceeds the current
  market rent in that area.
- A valid lease option contract is attached to the loan application.

If you fail to meet both of these criteria, an institutional lender, such as a bank, may not recognize your lease option and therefore may not grant you the loan to purchase the property.

I need to make an important clarification of terms between a lease option and a lease purchase. A *lease purchase* obligates the tenant to purchase the property at the end of the lease. With a *lease option,* you as the tenant have the right, but not the obligation, to purchase the property. You want to carefully review all documents so that the option to purchase is legally yours.

> *One possible obstacle with a lease option transaction is the real estate agent, because he or she will receive only a portion of the commission when the contract is signed and the balance if and when the option is exercised. Explain to the agent that he or she will get both the seller's and buyer's commissions.*

WHEN TO USE A LEASE OPTION

You can use a lease option in any market cycle. However, it is definitely useful during a down and bottom market because many people are stuck with homes they can't sell, leaving them with payments they can no longer afford. A simple lease agreement can allow some people to reduce their loss each month by leasing it to you, while you lock up a deal at a lower price with little or no money down.

After you lease the property, that property is essentially yours for the duration of the lease. During the lease, you have several options:

- Rent the property to someone else and use their rent to cover your monthly lease payments.
- Use the property yourself.

You can exercise your option to buy at any time. If you do not exercise your option to buy, the worst that happens is that you'll lose a year's worth of monthly payments (assuming a one-year lease). But if you re-rented the property to another person, that loss can be minimal to nothing. So structured correctly, lease options can be a great strategy.

As a further protection, I like using a lease option with an assignment clause. This means that the lessee (the person leasing the property from the owner) can assign the lease to another party. Even better, if the property appreciates quickly or is worth much more than you are renting or buying it for, you could assign the contract over to another party and make a profit—

sometimes a huge profit. (I talk more about locking up deals and assigning them to another person later in the chapter.)

The upside of a smart lease option is huge. But in case it does not go right, you can sell your lease option to someone else if you have a lease option with an assignment clause. For example, suppose you use a lease option to buy property for $300,000. Now you can assign (sell) your lease option to a new buyer. That new buyer takes over the monthly payments. If you've already made four months' worth of payments, the new buyer needs to make an additional eight months' worth of payments before that new buyer can exercise the option to buy or not (unless the contract allows you the right to exercise anytime during the lease period).

The new buyer gets the advantage of not having to wait a full year before exercising an option to buy, the seller still receives monthly payments under the lease option, and you (the original buyer) get out of the lease option early while collecting money for selling the lease option to the new buyer.

If I find property without an agent representing me, I also like to specify in the contract that the seller's current real estate agent works for both the buyer and seller. That means the real estate agent can earn a commission for selling the property (for the seller) and a second commission for buying the property (for you as the buyer). Normally, any commission is split between the seller's agent and the buyer's agent. By offering a real estate agent twice the normal commission, you'll motivate that agent to convince the seller to accept a lease option instead of a traditional lump sum payment. The agent gets twice as much commission as normal, the seller gets the asking price for the property along with the possibility of getting paid and still keeping the property, and the buyer gets a chance to buy the property with no money down. It's a win-win-win situation for everyone!

When creating a lease option, I recommend the following terms:

- Lease the property for one year with an option to rent for a second year as well. This gives you two years to decide whether to buy the property.
- Pay a monthly rent at a fixed rate (such as $1000 a month) for the first year, and if you exercise the option for the second year, offer to increase the rent a fixed amount (such as to $1200).
- Set a fixed price to buy the property.
- Try to extend the option period as long as you think you need to get your financing together. If you need five years, ask for it.
- Include a rent credit in the agreement. If and when you activate your option to purchase, a certain percentage of what you paid in rent goes toward the purchase price. Depending on how motivated the seller is, you can agree to a rent credit between 10% and 100%.
- Include an assignment provision that allows you to assign your interests

and obligations in the lease option to someone else, preferably with no preapproval by the seller.

A lease option structured this way gives you time to try to do one of the following:

- Find a buyer and resell the property, referred to as a *simultaneous close,* where you exercise your option to purchase the property and then re-sell it to the third party you found.
- Get organized and build to suit your needs.
- Use the assignment clause and assign the deal to another buyer and get paid a handsome fee for assigning this over to someone who wants the property.
- Get your finances in order so you can exercise your purchase option and get the best financing.

If you can afford the monthly payments, a lease option is a way to purchase property with no money down while giving you time to strategize.

Lease options can also be a great way to buy property that already has tenants. The seller may be tired of renting a house and dealing with tenants moving in and out. By offering a lease option, you give the seller guaranteed rental payments for a fixed period of time. If the market value of the property has increased and exceeds your option price (the price at which you agreed to buy the property), you are purchasing a house below its market value. Best of all, you can use the tenant's rent to pay your own monthly payments.

Here is an offer I made recently that I sent by fax to the owner of a ten-unit apartment house that I wanted to purchase.

Dear Bob,

It was a pleasure speaking with you over the phone. Here are my thoughts. This offer may be a bit different but in the end I try to make a win-win situation for everyone and I think I have accomplished that here.

After a more in-depth look at the place, it is in much poorer condition than I originally thought. That does not scare me but rather makes me think tactically. In its present condition, I am not sure a bank would give a mortgage on the place nor would it appraise for the amount needed. So here is a solution that could work well for all.

I offer to pay $500,000, structured as follows:

$10,000 nonrefundable to you upon signing.

A one-year lease option to buy.

$2500 per month to you.

I pay all expenses related to the property, including but not limited to taxes, insurance, and utilities.

I am responsible for renting, vacancies, and collecting rents.

I keep any rents.

I take the property in as-is condition.

After the lease option is signed, I would most likely vacate 50% of the apartments for immediate renovation. After those renovations were completed, I would move on to the other half of the house.

At the end of the lease, I will have the house in renovated condition with all apartments rented, allowing for a better appraisal and the ability to fund the property through a bank.

I will purchase the property at the end or before the end of the lease.

When I do initiate the buy option, 50% of all rent that I paid you until that point (rent only, not other expenses I paid) would go towards the purchase price, along with the $10,000 I paid you up front.

I provide you with any credit history, credit reports, banking information, and whatever else you need to feel secure.

Call me with your thoughts on my cell phone at XXX-XXX-XXXX.
Thank you.
Dean Graziosi

My reasoning for this type of offer was exactly what I said to him. I wanted to use my money to get the place in great shape before I went to the bank. Plus if I vacated even 25% of the units to remodel them, the income from the rest of the units would still cover the monthly expenses while I was doing this. Whenever you see a deal, try to think of all the different strategies that you have learned and are about to learn because there is no one way to make money.

Another time a lease option can be handy is when someone buys a house as an investment to sell later. If they can't sell the house, they're stuck with an empty house with a mortgage payment and no buyer. At this point, a seller may be motivated, and if he can cover his costs or at least cut his expenses, he might be interested in a lease option.

Occasionally, the seller asks for a small fee upfront to enter into a lease option. But this fee is much less than the costs of traditional financing. If your market is in a lull right now (a down or bottom market cycle), a lease option could be the perfect strategy to use.

I was presented with a lease option offer on a property I was selling in chart form, like the following. I loved the format because it enables you to present the advantages of a lease option in an objective, analytical way. Take a look at the table below and then I will explain.

By showing the property owner the benefits of a lease option, you can convince him that a lease option can be more profitable in the long term than

Market Cycle Strategy: *Using Lease Options just after a peak market cycle can be an effective way to "tie up" properties at today's price and allow you time to actually purchase the property in a few years no matter what the market cycle is.*

simply renting or selling the property. With this model, even though you are offering less monthly rent, the money is guaranteed. With all other factors, the seller stands to save $5900 over six years, with no hassle. This model

	Assumptions	Owner's Existing Option to Continue Monthly Rent	Proposed 6 Year Lease/Option with You
Monthly Rent		$1,250	$1,050
Average Stay of Tenants	18 months		6 years
Total Rent for 6 Years		$90,000	$75,600
Avg. Vacancy Length	6 weeks		
Re-Letting Costs:			
Commissions		$1,250	
Ads		$500	
Clean/Fix Up		$1,000	
Utilities		$450	
Lost Rent		$1,875	
Cost per Vacancy		$5,075	
Vacancies in 6 Years		4	0
Cost of Vacancies		$20,300	$0
6 Year Return		$69,700	$75,600
Net Improvement over the Option Period			$5,900

Market Cycle Strategy:
Consider using a lease option to turn your rental house into an investment. This strategy works well in up, down, and bottom markets.

---

doesn't account for market value appreciation, which is where you, the optionee, stand to make money.

During this time, you are building equity in the property. When the six years are up, or any time if the contract is worded correctly, you can activate your option to purchase the property for the agreed price. During those six years, you can rent the property to tenants who will cover your lease payment. This is a great way to purchase a property with no money and little risk while someone else is building your net worth. If the property has dropped in price during those six years, you can walk away after the first option period specified in the agreement. This is an incredible strategy during a down and bottom market.

BUYING YOUR FIRST HOUSE WITH A LEASE OPTION

Lease options aren't just a great investment strategy; you can also use them as a way to buy your first home with little or no money down. The advantages should be clear. If you just rent, you lose all your rental payments anyway after a period of time. But if you use a lease option, your rent payments give you the chance to buy property at a fixed price in the future, and you can arrange to get a rent credit for a portion or all of your rent payments.

To set up a lease option, the seller usually requires that you pay a nonrefundable deposit. This can be any amount, but it is usually one to three months' rent, which is almost what you would have to come up with anyway if you moved into a new apartment or rented a house. (The difference between the option payment and a security deposit and first and last months' rent requirement is that the seller does not have to maintain the option money in a trust account and can spend it immediately.)

If you don't have all the money the seller is requiring that you put up for the option fee, another excellent no-money-down technique is to ask the seller whether you can pay the fee in monthly payments over, say, twelve months. If this is agreeable, write it into the lease option agreement.

Also, make sure the property is located in an area that is likely to appreciate and that fits your lifestyle. Nothing is worse than moving into your new home and finding out that the neighbors party all night and work on their cars in the front yard. It's always a good idea to check the police reports on any neighborhood you are considering, whether you are using a lease option or any other method of purchase.

Let's assume you have found a property in a quiet neighborhood and home values have been on the upswing for several years, but this property needs some work to bring it up to the community's standard. This owner is a perfect candidate for your lease option techniques, because he or she is probably having a hard time keeping tenants in the house as a result of the lack of maintenance. If the owner lives out-of-town, a lease option technique is even better!

Suppose the owner wants $850 a month on a lease and has been trying to sell the property at $75,000 for quite a while. Your research indicates that the average rent for the area is $750, but nicer homes rent for $850 to $900 per month. The comparable sales for homes that have been fixed up are averaging $82,000.

You can have a rent survey prepared by a real estate agent or appraiser for around $100—and it may be the best $100 you'll ever spend. When you meet with the owner to negotiate the transaction, show him the rent survey and comparable sales report and make him the following offer.

You agree to pay $950 per month, with $200 counting towards the down payment at a later date. You offer a purchase price of $75,000, with the owner paying all your closing costs when the option is exercised. You agree to paint and fix up the property in lieu of any security or option payments. And you agree to five one-year option periods that you can renew solely at your option.

If the owner accepts this offer, you will have purchased a property for no money down—and your sweat equity will count for something because it will add to the value of the property and enable you to avoid paying additional money upfront to secure the option.

If you fix up the property and it appreciates at 7% annually, the property will be worth $115,000 in five years and you will have accumulated $12,000 toward the down payment ($200 x 60 months), which means you will be seeking financing for only $63,000 ($75,000 minus your $12,000 accumulated down payment). You have just created equity of $52,000!

Remember, you have fixed up the property over the years, so its appreciation value will be based on the same numbers that the nicer homes in the area were selling for when you wrote the option to purchase ($82,000). Even if you kept the home for only two years, the value would be $94,000 and you would have accumulated $4800 toward the down payment on a $75,000 purchase price.

In the five-year scenario, the seller receives his asking price, less the closing costs he pays for you and the $12,000 in the additional monthly amount, which is credited toward the down payment. And you now have $52,000 in equity built up in the home. Not bad for someone living in an apartment just a few years ago.

Benefits for buyers

Following are some of the benefits for the buyer in a lease option arrangement:

- You can purchase a property with little or no money down and part of the rent payments and any option fees go toward the down payment.
- Your equity (profit) accumulates during the option period because you locked in the purchase price when you signed the lease option contract.
- You can sell the property for profit simultaneously when you exercise the purchase option.
- You have control of the home and enjoy pride of ownership.
- You don't have to pay property taxes during the option period.
- You get the maximum use of leverage by controlling a property with little or no money down.

Benefits for sellers

As a seller in a lease option agreement, you offer attractive financing to help a future tenant buy your property. Such tenant-buyers tend to pay a higher price for properties and pay slightly higher rents if you make it attractive for them to get into the property.

In return, you can structure the deal so that you have no maintenance, lower closing costs, and a nonrefundable option fee. You also maintain ownership of the property until the tenant elects to buy the property for the option price, so you get the tax benefits right up until the option is exercised. If the tenant-buyer does not exercise the option to purchase the property, you are free to continue renting to the tenant or advertising the property again.

LOCKING UP DEALS WITH ASSIGNMENTS

Normally the way to make money with a lease option is to hold property until you can buy it later. But if you use a lease option with an assignment clause, you can make money in what I call my wholesaling strategy.

If someone does not want a lease option and would rather sell the place outright, you can try this wholesale strategy option without a lease being part of the contract. This can still make you a fortune without risking anything and help the seller get his or her property sold faster.

The basic idea is that I do my research and find a property that is gem. Then I lock up the deal on paper with a lease option or just a contract of sale that has a thirty- to ninety-day time frame to close with—the most important part—an assignment clause, so I can get the property under a contract with little or no out-of-pocket money or risk. Then I look for someone who I can assign the option to and get paid a fee for doing so. I have students who have made a few thousands dollars for a few hours' work and I know people who have made millions doing this.

Real-Life Story

Here is an example of how one of my students started his real estate investing career.

Brett was a twenty-two-year-old college student who wanted to get involved in real estate but did not have enough money for a down payment. Because he was a full-time college student, he had no income, so getting a loan was out of the question. But that didn't stop him. He spent $25 and signed up for an online service that provides information on foreclosure listings, similar to what I offer at www.deangraziosi.com, and began searching listings near San Diego State University. He found about ten properties that he was interested in, so he got their addresses from the foreclosure service and sent out a postcard to each owner who was in default:

Mortgage payment behind?
In jeopardy of losing your home and hurting your credit?
WE CAN HELP!
We buy homes! Any area or condition!
We could get that payment off your back immediately.
Call the Problem Solvers right now at
555-555-5555

Three days later, one of the owners contacted Brett and explained his situation. The owner owed around $450,000 for the house and was three weeks away from foreclosure. After doing a little work to find comparable houses in the neighborhood, Brett knew that the house was worth between $500,000 and $525,000, so the deal had a good amount of equity. Brett immediately called an investor he knew in the San Diego area and explained the situation, asking for a 2.5% finder's fee from the investor.

Brett sent over a spreadsheet showing the asking price as well as the comps for other houses in the area. The investor called Brett and agreed to his terms. Brett put the owner and the investor in contact and they closed the deal in two weeks. The owner was able to walk away with a few thousand dollars and his credit intact. The investor was able to get a great deal on a house and had to pay only 2.5% instead of the traditional 3% or 6% that a realtor charges. Brett profited more than $11,000 without using any of his own money and little of his time. It was a win-win-win situation.

What types of properties do I look for when wholesaling? All kinds, but especially ugly houses that need repair—fixer-uppers with unkempt and overgrown yards and other signs of neglect. This situation occurs for a reason, and chances are the owner has no idea how to correct the problem. Drive around neighborhoods you're interested in and write down addresses of homes that look like potential opportunities for problem solving.

If you can find a motivated seller when you research these addresses, the opportunities for profit improve greatly. Who are the motivated sellers you should look for? Out-of-town owners, estate sales, and financially distressed sellers.

Here is a summary of what to do if you want to wholesale a distressed property.

Find a property. Go online, call a title company, talk to the county assessor, and search for the owner's information. If I have a hard time locating the owner, I purchase a report for a small fee from www.SkipTracer.com and get a cell phone number and contact information.

Contact the owner and attempt to buy the property. If you can agree on a price, write up a purchase and sale agreement with a low earnest money amount, such as $100, an assignment clause (which gives you the right to assign the contract to another person or investor), and a sixty- or ninety-day closing date (which gives you time to find a new owner). You essentially have equitable title to the property.

Call everyone you know who may want that type of property. Run an ad in the local newspaper worded like the following: Handyman special. Cheap, cash. Call (123) 456-7890. When you get calls, qualify the potential buyers over the phone. Ask questions politely to find out what projects they have worked on, how extensive were the repairs, and how they financed the projects.

Finally, assign the sale agreement and collect an assignment fee of $1000, $5000, $20,000, or more. This strategy can give you the cash needed to facilitate other deals that require some money out of pocket.

Here is the script (adapted for this book) that one of my students uses when he calls owners to discuss buying their properties:

You: "Hello. My name is _____. I am interested in buying your house on Elm Street."

Owner: The owner will likely have a response indicating their level of interest and possibly say something like, "Tell me more" or "What did you have in mind?"

You: "If I pay cash and close quickly, what would be the least you could accept?"

The owner might ask what you are willing to pay, but don't be the first to mention a number.

Owner: "Is that the best you can do on this?"

You: "Are you saying that if I don't pay you $_____, we can't do business?"

If the price the owner states isn't quite what you were hoping for, you are still building a rapport with the owner, so make sure you end your conversation on a positive note. Then politely go back to looking for another property.

If you do agree on a price, you can try the two options that have assignment clauses attached to them. You can do a lease option if you think you can rent the property to pay a mortgage, or you can reimburse yourself if you have cash. Or you can do a basic purchase agreement that gives you enough time before closing on the property to find an interested buyer to assign it to.

I know a person in Salt Lake City who locks up deals on paper and assigns them to someone else on a huge scale. He has the vision to see where new areas are potentially going to develop. He contacts landowners when the demand for that property is low, and locks up the property on paper with a contract or a small nonrefundable deposit for the first right of refusal on the property. (A *first right of refusal* means you obtain the right to match any acceptable offer someone makes to buy the property.)

He's offering the owners more money than the property is currently worth but less than he feels it will be worth by the time his contract or option to buy runs out. He has made millions from this strategy.

You might know of a big old farm that seems like it is in the middle of nowhere, where property is selling for $5000 per acre. But from your research, you feel that the area near the farm will skyrocket in the next twenty-four months. You could approach the farmer and say, "I would like the opportunity or first right of refusal to purchase your land within the next two years for $7500 per acre. I will give you a $2500 nonrefundable deposit for this."

The farmer may think you are crazy for offering him 50% more for his property than it's worth, so he'll likely agree. You know from watching the real estate cycle that his land could be worth $30,000 or $40,000 per acre in less than two years and are ecstatic to lock it up at that $7500 per acre price. If you are correct and the area starts to boom twelve to eighteen months later, you can activate your option (and buy the land) or assign your option to a developer or buyer for what they're willing to pay.

Some of my students have locked up deals and made a quick $1000, and one locked up a deal that made him a quick $10,000 in four hours. I'm currently working on a deal right now using this strategy. I worked for a long time to get a parcel of property that I knew was very valuable. Because my contract to purchase is assignable (I have not closed on the property yet), I may never take ownership and instead just assign the contract to an eager buyer for a little more than $600,000. These types of deals happen every day. You just need to take action.

So locking up a deal basically means the following: Finding a good deal; signing a lease option or purchase agreement, along with an assignment clause, with thirty to ninety days to close; and either buying the property (and selling it later) or assigning the option to another buyer for a fee. Your risk is minimal but the rewards are huge.

CONCLUSION

Lease options and locking up deals are both amazing ways to generate significant profits from real estate without using a lot of your own money. Why not go out there in the next week or so and practice? Find a few pieces of property that may have been for sale for a while, and then determine whether the rent could cover your payments and whether the house will appreciate with a little work. Then write up an offer with a lease option.

Write up a few deals and make a few offers. I promise that you will be shocked by how receptive some people will be to an offer that seems like it is beneficial mostly to you. After you see how lease options and locking up deals work, you can use them as just more ways to make money on property you find.

CHAPTER 16

MAKING MONEY WITH FORECLOSURES

*It is on our failures that we base a new
and different and better success.*
—HAVELOCK ELLIS

Basically, *foreclosure* is a legal process in which a lender sells or seizes a person's property to recoup and repay the debt attached to that parcel. For whatever reason—such as the loss of a job, illness, a death in the family, a change in the interest rate—sometimes people cannot continue making their mortgage payments. If a homeowner can't keep up with the payments, the lender puts the property in foreclosure. None of us wish hard times on anyone, but when a foreclosure does happen, it creates an investment opportunity.

You can make money with foreclosures in any market cycle: down, bottom, peak, and even up. In peak and up markets, demand is higher than supply, so not only are lots of investors looking for foreclosures, but homeowners can usually sell their home before losing it to the bank. Down and bottom markets are the best times to find and make money with foreclosures because demand has shrunk and many people have no option but foreclosure.

In the past, foreclosures often occurred through unexpected tragedies, such as the death of a family member. Nowadays, foreclosures are more likely to happen due to the types of loans homeowners used to buy their properties.

In the early 2000s, low interest rates and liberal lending practices made it easier for people to qualify for loans that were actually more than they could afford. Unable to qualify for a traditional fixed-rate mortgage, many people chose a riskier adjustable-rate mortgage (ARM).

While interest rates remained low, making payments on an ARM was affordable. But when interest rates increased by even 1 or 2 percentage points, that was often the difference between someone being able to make a payment or not.

Another popular loan in recent years is the interest-only loan. This type of loan lets a homeowner pay only interest payments for a fixed number of years, and then pay both interest and principal payments later. Unfortunately, many people could barely afford the interest-only payments. When they had to start paying both interest and principal payments, their monthly mortgage payments increased by 25% and more. When this happens, people default on their loans. As I write this book in late 2006, the wave of foreclosures from this type of lending will likely be the largest in United States history.

Up until recently, most people who got a home loan put 20% down and financed the remaining 80% with a traditional thirty-year fixed-rate mortgage. But when people use 100% financing and take out adjustable-rate and interest-only mortgages, all it takes is something like the loss of a job, health problems, or a divorce combined with rising interest rates to create foreclosures at an unprecedented rate. This is unfortunate, but by understanding how people end up in foreclosure and how to read the current real estate cycle, you can always find opportunities.

At any given time, about 1% of all the residential property in the United States, or approximately 1 million homes, are in foreclosure or facing foreclosure. This makes investment opportunities with foreclosures readily available no matter where you live.

The key to successfully purchasing properties in foreclosure is doing your homework upfront. But after you find a foreclosure, you will want to learn how the house wound up in foreclosure and what condition it is in. In some cases, foreclosed properties may have been neglected for months or even years, so it is best to hire a home inspector before purchasing a foreclosure. Regardless of the real estate market cycle (up, peak, bottom, or down), I recommend offering to purchase the property at a discount, depending on its condition.

How do investors profit from foreclosures? They buy properties for substantially below the market value, fix them up as needed, and then rent or sell them. The banks, which own foreclosures, simply want to sell these properties to get them off their hands. Banks make money loaning money, not owning property; the sooner they can sell foreclosed properties, the faster they can cut their losses.

Now that you understand what foreclosures are and how they can happen, I want to teach you to think differently than everyone else and learn how to profit from foreclosures in any market.

THE FORECLOSURE PROCESS

A foreclosure occurs when someone borrows money to buy real estate but cannot pay the agreed-upon monthly payments. The first step toward foreclosure usually happens when the lending institution notifies the owners in writing that they are in default of payment.

In most cases, the lender will bring in an attorney to start the foreclosure process after three consecutive payments are missed. At this time, the attorney will send a letter informing the owners that if they do not pay what is owed, the lender will be forced to begin a foreclosure proceeding. The lender can also request a trustee's sale or a judicial foreclosure, where the property is sold at a public auction.

The homeowners can still avoid foreclosure at this time by making the loan payments current and paying all overdue amounts after the notice of the default has been recorded. This is called the *right of reinstatement*. The last date for the money owed to be brought up to date and paid is called the *cure date*. This is usually no later than a few days before the property's impending sale.

If the homeowner cannot make these overdue payments, the foreclosed property is often sold at a real estate auction or trustee sale, where it is sold to the highest bidder. If the property is worth less than the total amount owed to the lender (which can occur if property values have dipped since the homeowner took out the original loan), the lender could seek a deficiency judgment, and the homeowner would not only lose the home but owe additional debt (the difference between what the home sold for at auction and the balance of the loan).

Real-Life Story

John and Vickie are from the small town of Van Buren, Arkansas, where John worked as a pastor at the local church and Vickie worked for a collection agency. They began investing in real estate after purchasing my "Think a Little Different" real estate course. Before investing in their first deal, they had no money and limited income.

First, they found a partner who was willing to use his money and credit to help them begin investing. In return, John and Vickie agreed to find the property, do the renovations, and sell the property. They would receive 50% of the profit. After just two real estate deals, they made enough so that Vickie could quit her job and focus on real estate full-time. They made more on their first few deals than Vickie was making all year working a full-time job.

They had just finished reading and learning about foreclosures, so they started looking for a foreclosure they could fix up. Their realtor, who also brokered REOs for a local bank, found a foreclosed house for them to consider.

Although the house had been neglected for some time, they saw its potential. They made an offer and bought the home for $23,000. John and Vickie fixed up the house themselves and thought about selling it for a great profit.

However, their newly married son was looking for a home, so John and Vickie let him take over the house for what they owed on it. This was a great deal for their son because the house payment was half of the comparable rent in the area.

When John told me the story about this deal, he finished by saying, "We could have made a great profit on that house. But allowing my son and his new wife start their life with their own home was so rewarding. As parents, you can't put a price on that."

TYPES OF FORECLOSURES

This next short section won't exactly make you money, but it will teach you more about the different types of foreclosures and how a particular foreclosure might work.

Foreclosure is the legal process of the *mortgage holder* (the bank) taking the *collateral* (a home) for a *promissory note* (the loan) in default. The process is slightly different from state to state, but the two basic types of foreclosure are judicial and nonjudicial. In mortgage states, judicial foreclosure is used. In deed-of-trust states, nonjudicial foreclosure is used. Most states permit both types of proceedings, but commonly use only one method or the other.

Judicial foreclosures

Judicial foreclosure is a lawsuit that the lender (mortgagee) brings against the borrower (mortgagor) to get the property. About half the states use judicial foreclosure. Like all lawsuits, judicial foreclosure starts with a summons and complaint served upon the borrower. If the borrower has borrowed money from multiple sources, such as taking out a second mortgage, the foreclosure essentially wipes out the second mortgage and the bank holding that second mortgage will get what is left over after the bank holding the first mortgage recovers the loan amount and legal fees related to the foreclosure. In many cases, few funds are left for the lender holding the second mortgage.

If the borrower does not file an answer (respond) to the lawsuit, or simply pays all fees, the lender gets a judgment by default. A referee is then appointed by the court to compute the total amount (including interest and attorney's fees) due. The lender must then advertise a notice of sale in the newspaper for four to six weeks. If the total amount due is not paid, a public sale is conducted by the referee on the courthouse steps. The entire process can take three to twelve months, depending on the volume of court cases in your county.

The sale is conducted like an auction, with the property going to the highest bidder. Unless significant equity is in the property, the only bidder at the sale will be a representative of the lender (the bank). The lender can bid up to the amount it is owed to purchase the property. If the bank purchases the property, it becomes an REO property, which I'll discuss in Chapter 17.

If the proceeds from the sale are insufficient to satisfy the amount owed to the lender, the lender may be entitled to a deficiency judgment against the borrower and anyone else who guaranteed the loan. Some states prohibit a lender from obtaining a deficiency judgment against a borrower.

Nonjudicial foreclosures
Most states permit a lender to foreclose without a lawsuit, using what is commonly called a *power of sale.* Rather than a mortgage, the borrower (grantor) gives a deed of trust to a trustee to hold for the lender (beneficiary). Upon default, the lender simply files a notice of default and a notice of sale, which is published in the newspaper. The entire process takes about ninety days. The borrower usually has a right of redemption after the sale (described shortly).

Strict foreclosures
A few states permit a *strict foreclosure,* which does not require a sale. When the proceeding starts, the borrower has a certain amount of time to pay what is owed. After the date has passed, the title reverts to the lender. In many California and Oregon cases where the seller has sought forfeiture under a land contract, the court has ordered strict foreclosure.

Foreclosure laws
Although foreclosures work the same all over the country, each state has its own foreclosure laws. The following chart gives a state-by-state breakdown of foreclosure laws, current as of 2006.

Making Money with Foreclosures

State	Judicial/ Non-Judicial	Process Period (Days)	Sale Publication (Days)	Redemption Period (Days)	Sale
Alabama	Both	49-74	21	365	Trustee
Alaska	Both	105	65	365	Trustee
Arizona	Both	102	41	None	Trustee
Arkansas	Both	70	30	365	Trustee
California	Both	117	21	365	Trustee
Colorado	Both	91	14	75	Trustee
Connecticut	Judicial	62	NA	Court Decision	Court
Delaware	Judicial	170-210	60-90	None	Sheriff
District of Columbia	Non-Judicial	47	18	None	Trustee
Florida	Judicial	135	NA	None	Court

State	Judicial/ Non-Judicial	Process Period (Days)	Sale Publication (Days)	Redemption Period (Days)	Sale
Georgia	Both	37	32	None	Trustee
Hawaii	Both	220	60	None	Trustee
Idaho	Both	150	45	365	Trustee
Illinois	Judicial	300	NA	90	Court
Indiana	Judicial	261	120	None	Sheriff
Iowa	Both	160	30	20	Sheriff
Kansas	Judicial	130	21	365	Sheriff
Kentucky	Judicial	147	NA	365	Court
Louisiana	Judicial	180	NA	None	Sheriff
Maine	Judicial	240	30	90	Court
Maryland	Judicial	46	30	Court Decision	Court
Massachusetts	Judicial	75	41	None	Court
Michigan	Non-Judicial	60	30	30-365	Sheriff
Minnesota	Both	90-100	7	1825	Sheriff
Mississippi	Both	90	30	None	Trustee
Missouri	Both	60	10	365	Trustee
Montana	Both	150	50	None	Trustee
Nebraska	Both	142	NA	None	Sheriff
Nevada	Both	116	80	None	Trustee
New Hampshire	Non-Judicial	59	24	None	Trustee
New Jersey	Judicial	270	NA	10	Sheriff
New Mexico	Judicial	180	NA	30-270	Court
New York	Judicial	445	NA	None	Court
North Carolina	Both	110	25	None	Sheriff
North Dakota	Judicial	150	NA	180-365	Sheriff
Ohio	Judicial	217	NA	None	Sheriff
Oklahoma	Both	186	NA	None	Sheriff
Oregon	Both	150	30	180	Trustee
Pennsylvania	Judicial	270	NA	None	Sheriff
Rhode Island	Both	62	21	None	Trustee
South Carolina	Judicial	150	NA	None	Court
South Dakota	Both	150	23	30-365	Sheriff
Tennessee	Non-Judicial	40-45	20-25	730	Trustee
Texas	Both	27	NA	None	Trustee
Utah	Non-Judicial	142	NA	Court Decision	Trustee
Vermont	Judicial	95	NA	180-365	Court
Virginia	Both	45	14-28	None	Trustee
Washington	Both	135	90	None	Trustee
West Virginia	Non-Judicial	60-90	30-60	None	Trustee
Wisconsin	Both	290	NA	365	Sheriff
Wyoming	Both	60	25	90-365	Sheriff

Note: In states that use both judicial and non-judicial foreclosures, the lender determines which type of foreclosure to use, based on the conditions defined in the original loan.

FINDING FORECLOSURES

Now that you understand how foreclosures work and the different types of foreclosures, your next question might be how to find a foreclosure. To find foreclosed properties, you can use the following:

- Classified sections
- Legal newspapers
- Attorneys
- For sale by owners
- Realtors
- Auction companies
- REO departments at banks
- U.S. Marshall's service
- IRS auctions
- Bankruptcies
- Probate court
- Your own advertising
- County courthouse or town hall or registry of deeds: check for new cases and sale file
- Word of mouth
- By looking for physically distressed properties and contacting the owners
- Title companies
- Foreclosure Finder Service at www.deangraziosi.com

In addition to bank foreclosures, another way to find foreclosures is through Fannie Mae and Freddie Mac. These corporations buy mortgages from mortgage lenders soon after loans are made and then bundle them as securities and sell them on the New York Stock Exchange.

Fannie Mae and Freddie Mac are private, shareholder-owned companies that work to make sure mortgage money is available for home buyers. They do not lend money directly to home buyers. Instead, they work with lenders to make sure they don't run out of mortgage funds, so more people can achieve the dream of home ownership.

Fannie Mae was created by Congress in 1938 to bolster the housing industry during the Depression. At that time, Fannie Mae was part of the Federal Housing Administration (FHA) and authorized to buy only FHA-insured loans to replenish lenders' supply of money.

In 1968, Fannie Mae became a private company operating with private capital on a self-sustaining basis. Its role was expanded to buy mortgages beyond traditional government loan limits, reaching out to a broader cross sec-

tion of Americans. Likewise, Freddie Mac is a stockholder-owned corporation chartered by Congress in 1970 to increase the supply of funds that
mortgage lenders—such as commercial banks, mortgage bankers, savings
institutions, and credit unions—can make available to home buyers and
multifamily investors.

Today, both Fannie Mae and Freddie Mac operate under a Congressional
charter that directs them to channel their efforts into increasing the avail-
ability and affordability of home ownership for low, moderate, and middle-
income Americans. Neither corporation receives any government funding
or backing.

So why should you know this? These two companies own the vast major-
ity of mortgage loans made in this country, so they end up with a lot of foreclosure properties as well. Just like banks, Fannie Mae and Freddie Mac feel
pressure to get rid of inventoried properties. Their mandate is to provide
mortgage loans, not to own houses. Therefore, they are highly motivated to
sell.

Another great source of foreclosures in many markets is HUD (Housing
and Urban Development). FHA is a HUD mortgage financing program.
Anytime an FHA mortgage goes into foreclosure, HUD administers it and
sells the property at auction. The same applies to VA mortgages, funded by
the Department of Veteran Affairs.

You can go to a single source to gather information about all these auction opportunities. The Homes For Sale section at the HUD web site (www.
hud.gov) has links to a number of government agencies and secondary market companies that hold foreclosure properties.

As opposed to the bank foreclosure auctions, these auctions make it a lot
easier for new investors to purchase properties. They allow you time to obtain financing after you win the bid, and all bids are submitted in writing, so
you don't have the auction mentality forcing prices upward. I suggest that
you go to these various web sites and read their information on making bids.

Two of my students in Washington State successfully targeted HUD foreclosures as investment properties. First, they searched the HUD web site for
HUD foreclosures, which typically require repair work. Some required minor repairs while others had been damaged by the owners before they lost
their homes. For example, in a bedroom in one home, the former owner
had kicked in all the drywall between the studs. In another, the home required only a fresh coat of paint, new carpets, and new appliances.

My students narrowed their criteria to three-bedroom, one-bathroom
homes in their city. They were building a rental "farm" and felt that homes
with three or more bedrooms could be rented and resold better than those
with fewer than three. They knew that HUD would take into consideration

the repairs needed and adjust the listing price accordingly. Through experience (and numerous offers directly with HUD), they developed a formula where they would offer 90.8% of HUD's asking price.

They used a 100% temporary loan from the bank to make the purchase and a line of credit and credit cards to purchase materials and complete the repairs. They rented each property and then applied for a thirty-year fixed-rate loan, rolling the total of the purchase price plus improvements into the loan for a no-money-down transaction.

BUYING FORECLOSURES

The basic reason for foreclosure occurs when the owner no longer makes payments on a loan they have, which is secured by the property. Some of the ways to purchase foreclosures include the following:

- Real estate auction sales
- Bank-owned REO properties
- Short sales

Real estate auctions

In a real estate auction sale, the property is sold to the highest bidder. The money from the auction goes towards paying back the bank that holds the foreclosed property.

Most real estate auctions take place at the courthouse through a systematic and well-defined process at regular times. You can find out the times by simply calling the office and asking the clerk. You may have heard the statement that the property "was sold on the courthouse steps." Most often it actually happens in the lobby, foyer, or a specified location indoors out of the weather.

A typical sale involves the following:

1. A time is scheduled for properties to be sold.
2. A clerk makes an announcement of file case numbers and their status (solved, available, and so on)
3. A clerk lists the case description, or property description, or both and asks for bids.
4. The bidding starts and a winner emerges.
5. The property is bought and paid for at the courthouse.

The property usually has at least one bidder. The lender wants to ensure that the property is sold for at least what is owed on it, so the lender or their designate starts the bidding at the amount being foreclosed on. If that is the only bid, the auction is over. The lender then owns and takes possession of the property. (These properties are known as REO properties, which are explained in the next section.)

To become familiar with the auction process, visit the courthouse and watch several auctions. You may even try to get to know some of the other individuals at the foreclosure, who can be excellent resources later. Lawyers, agents, investors, title company representatives, and more are sometimes in attendance. Also review the bulletin boards and pick up any publications and notices in the courthouse offices.

In deed-of-trust states, the process is a little different. The trustee controlling the title of the property can control the location of the sale, which may be at the courthouse or at the trustee's (an attorney's) office. Usually the trustee publishes a notice of the sale's location.

REO properties

A bank-owned REO (real estate owned) property is owned by a bank, usually after the property has been put up for public auction and nobody bid on it. Now the bank must take ownership of the property and will likely be eager to sell it as soon as possible.

With REO properties, you negotiate directly with the bank, usually through a real estate agent. Chapter 17 covers investing in REO properties.

Short sales

A short sale strategy is used when the owner owes more money on the foreclosed property than it's worth. When most investors look at a piece of property with no equity—or even worse, negative equity—they want nothing to do with it. But short sales give you the opportunity to purchase property at a discount and limit the competition of investors trying to buy that same property.

To do a short sale, you must make a compelling offer directly to the bank. You must support your reason for offering a lower price and provide a reason why the bank can benefit by accepting your offer now. You'll learn more about short sales in Chapter 17.

REDEMPTION RIGHTS

Many states permit a borrower to reinstate, or cure, the loan before the date of sale. This simply requires paying the overdue amount, plus interest and attorney's fees. It is certainly more desirable for a defaulting borrower to reinstate a loan rather than pay off the entire principal balance.

Some states give a borrower the right to redeem the amount owed and get back title to the property before the auction or trustee's sale. The length of the redemption period depends on the state. The highest right of redemption is from the owner, borrower, or guarantor on note. Next are the junior lien holders, who are in danger of being wiped out by the foreclosing senior lien holder.

A *junior lien* is a second or third mortgage. The first mortgage is the original loan. If you borrow more, the other lenders are in line behind the first lender. You would buy the junior liens only if you wanted to pay off the ones ahead of the lien you bought and take back the property. This would make sense only if you felt that the property was worth significantly more than the total of all the liens you had to pay off.

In states with a long redemption period, investors often buy the junior liens on the property to have the right to redeem the property from foreclosure. The holder of the most junior lien has the last right to redeem the property by paying off all underlying liens. The owner, of course, has the highest right. Obtaining a quitclaim deed from the owner gives you the right to redeem the property yourself.

CONCLUSION

Foreclosures can be a profitable portion of your business. Go online and search your local government web site and see whether they post foreclosures online. If not, call or go to your local courthouse and ask about the easiest way to get foreclosure notices as they come in. Go to a few auctions and see for yourself how you can buy property at discounted prices.

When you find a property going through foreclosure, ask a realtor to compare the home's price relative to similar homes in the same neighborhood (also known as *getting a comp*). Another way to find and compare home prices in a particular neighborhood is to check the local tax records.

By buying foreclosures, you can get great properties at discounted prices, which you can either fix and sell (flip) or rent for steady cash flow. You'll find that foreclosures can be a great way to make a fortune in real estate. And there has never been a better time than now to start investing in foreclosures!

CHAPTER 17
BUYING PRE-FORECLOSURES, REOS, AND SHORT SALES

There is no security on this earth. Only opportunity.
—Douglas MacArthur

People hit unexpected financial problems—the loss of a job, health issues and mounting medical bills, divorce, overspending, or maybe an adjustable-rate mortgage that has gone up a few points. In some cases, homeowners will try to refinance. But this may be an impossible task if the home does not have enough equity or the owners cannot prove to the bank how they can make the payments even if they do refinance.

When homeowners can no longer make payments, the property goes through a preforeclosure process, in which the bank notifies the owners that the foreclosure process will start unless payment is made.

Owners may be so anxious to sell their home before it is foreclosed that they rush to put the property up for sale and price it too high or too low. If the property needs to be fixed up, it can be even harder to find a buyer for it, especially if the owners are in a hurry.

Unfortunately, some property owners are in denial—and maybe I would be as well. They can't believe this is happening to them, so they don't even try to do anything about it. Eventually, they lose their home to foreclosure and are forced to leave.

Few things are more traumatic than losing a home. But as investors, we need to realize that by buying a home before it is foreclosed, we could help these unfortunate owners and also have the opportunity to make money. Become their problem solver.

If owners can't save their homes during the pre-foreclosure process, they'll lose their home in foreclosure. The bank will then auction these foreclosed properties to get their money back. In many cases, people buy these auctioned homes, but in many more cases, no one buys these homes and the bank is stuck owning them. This type of property is known as an REO (real estate owned).

Banks are in the business of lending money, not owning properties, so they want to sell their REOs as quickly as possible. Essentially, the bank is the home owner, although they may know little about the property's history.

In this chapter, I'll teach you how to buy homes before they go through foreclosure (pre-foreclosures) and how to buy homes after they've already gone through foreclosure and become REOs. In both cases, you can often spot bargains and buy homes at much lower prices than their actual worth. (To learn about foreclosures, refer to Chapter 16.)

I'll also teach you one more technique called a short sale. A short sale is basically buying property in the foreclosure process that has more owed on the home than what it is worth. In other words, the home has negative equity. With what you learn in the main foreclosure chapter (Chapter 16) and in this chapter, you will have the opportunity to profit from foreclosures in a variety of ways.

FINDING PRE-FORECLOSURES

A foreclosure begins with a *notice of default,* which informs the owners that they are in default on their loan payments and that the lending institution will begin foreclosure proceedings if the payments are not brought up-to-date.

At this time, the owner can make all past due payments and the foreclosure process will stop. If they cannot pay their past due payments, the bank will foreclose on the property anywhere from forty-five days to six months from the time the bank first sent out the notice of default.

Finding notices of default
You can usually find information about notices of default as a public record in the county courthouse. Visit the courthouse and put together a list of homeowners who have received notices of default. You can find homes in pre-foreclosure status also by investigating the places I listed in the "Finding Foreclosures" section in Chapter 16.

Don't be afraid to talk to the owners, even if they are losing the house due to delinquent payments. Be polite, try to understand everyone's position, and be sympathetic to their situation—but don't be afraid to ask. If you hear someone is having a hard time and can't pay their mortgage, if you see a house that is not being taken care of the way it used to be, if you know of a friend of a friend who is having troubles or has received a notice of default, don't be afraid to ask.

Most people think it would be rude to ask or try to communicate with someone about their situation when he or she may be losing a home due to a foreclosure. But I look at it differently. After all, if people have hit an unexpected financial bind and their house is in jeopardy of being foreclosed, you may keep them from having their credit ruined for years simply by speaking out.

Why? Because you may be able to stop the foreclosure process by structuring a creative deal or purchasing the house. So your speaking to the owners may be a blessing to them and they may even thank you for taking the burden off their shoulders.

If I knew of a property that I thought was in jeopardy of being foreclosed on by the bank, I would have no problem calling the owners, stopping by to see them personally, writing them a letter, or if all that failed, leaving a letter attached to the front door. You may find out that the owners are doing fine. If so, you can wish them the best and move on. Or you may find out that they are in over their head. If so, you may be able to relieve them of an obligation that they simply can't handle anymore and make yourself money. Strive to be a problem solver, because you can make a fortune being one.

In general, it makes the most sense to work with pre-foreclosures when there is a good amount of equity in the home (although you can still consider a piece of property even if it has no equity—this is the short sale strategy I cover later in the chapter). Make sure you inspect the home. If the owners do not have the money for mortgage payments, they may not have the money for repairs and maintenance.

When I send a letter, I am polite, I get to the point, and I keep my heart open to understanding the difficult situation the owners may be experiencing. Following is an example of a letter I would send, but feel free to modify it in a way that makes sense to you. Remember to be considerate and always think of what may be going through the mind of the person to whom you are sending the letter.

Opportunity Seeker
1111 Opportunity St.
Visionary, AZ 22222

John Doe
222 Possible Sale St.
Anywhere, USA 88888
Regarding: your property

Dear John,
    My name is Dean Graziosi, and I purchase property for investment. It has come to my attention that your parcel of property, located at

222 Possible Sale St., may be in jeopardy of being foreclosed on by the bank.

If this is not the case, I apologize for the intrusion. If this is the case, I am sorry that you are having difficulties.

I am contacting you to let you know that there may be a way that you can avoid the foreclosure process and keep your credit from being tarnished with this unfortunate circumstance. Most of us fall on hard times at some point in our lives, but there may be a way I can help make your situation a little easier.

I would welcome the opportunity to discuss this with you further, in person or on the phone. I can be reached at 555-1212.

Best regards,

Dean Graziosi

When you have the opportunity to communicate with the owner in person or on the phone, have a list of questions ready. Remember to be delicate and polite; the person is obviously going through a tough time. Most of us have been there in some way; remember how that felt when you are communicating.

In the nicest way, you should try to get the following information:

- How much is still owed on the mortgage?
- How many payments are overdue?
- Does the payment include property taxes?
- If the payment does not include property taxes, are any tax payments overdue?
- Has a notice for a sheriff's sale been sent?
- What are the owner's chances of making up the payments and costs?
- Has the bank sent you a list of additional expenses owed to them for the foreclosure process?
- Are any second mortgages or other outstanding bills attached to the property?
- If you don't have the money to pay off the lender, would you be open to discussing opportunities that could relieve you of this burden?

Remember, equity in the home is a great asset. Asking the preceding questions will help you find out how much equity the home may have, and whether the owner is willing to work with you to stop a foreclosure.

Property owners who have a good chunk of equity in their home will want to try and save a portion of it and keep a good credit rating. For these reasons, these properties have a strong investment potential. Until the bank actually forecloses on the property, you have the opportunity to stop that process, purchase the property, and arrange a way to assume the mortgage, get a new mortgage from the same bank, or put together your own creative financing plan.

In addition to finding notices of default through the county courthouse, you can find properties in pre-foreclosure by advertising in local newspapers. Here's an example of a classified ad:

Mortgage Payment Behind?
In jeopardy of losing your home and hurting your credit?
WE CAN HELP!
We buy homes! Any area or condition!
We could get that payment off your back immediately.
Call the Problem Solvers
right now at
555-555-5555

Try running an ad like this—or different versions of it—for several weeks, and track your results. Make sure that whatever phone number you list in the add is answered by you, by someone who knows exactly what you are doing, or by a polite and nicely worded voice message similar to the letter I listed previously.

When you buy a home in the pre-foreclosure process, you're negotiating a deal directly with the owner. The owner generally wants to stop the foreclosure process by selling you the property and settling with the bank. As the buyer, you want to buy the home at a price that's low enough to make it worth purchasing but fair enough that the current owner can escape foreclosure.

Real-Life Story

Jackie from Indiana told everyone she knew that she was starting her real estate investing career and was looking for property. A friend told her about a couple who were losing their home (pre-foreclosure status) even though they owed only $10,000 on it. It was a great buy because homes in the area were selling for $30,000 to $40,000. This was Jackie's first experience in buying a pre-foreclosure home, and it fit her investing budget. She was nervous about approaching the owners—almost as much as the owners were nervous about getting bank letters.

She asked the right questions and found out that they would be happy if they could walk away from the home and not owe anybody anything. Jackie got the exact amount owed to the bank and then asked the bank whether they could help with some of the penalty costs because she was going to pay off the debt. They agreed and took a flat $10,000 for the home.

Jackie had just enough in savings to purchase the home. Now she can decide whether to refinance and pull out her cash to remodel the property, or do a quick fix-up and try to resell it.

This is just one example on how you can buy pre-foreclosure property. After you find such a property, you can then negotiate with the bank for a loan. Or you could draw up a contract with the current owner stating that you will make all past due payments and continue to make payments on the house until it sells. Then you can split the profit. After you understand the owner's circumstances, build a relationship and figure out whether this house can make you a profit. If so, get creative and make the deal happen.

Another way to profit from pre-foreclosures

The safest way to deal with people in pre-foreclosure is to buy the owners out and have them leave. Emotional attachment can lead to a bad deal if the previous owners stay in the home. If the homeowners insist on staying in the property, lease it to them without an option to purchase. You need to use caution because the previous owners may still be in serious financial trouble, which means you could end up with a messy eviction and court battle.

If the homeowners are not willing to be just tenants and have significant equity in the property, offer a partnership arrangement wherein the partnership owns the property. Your contribution to the partnership is the money to cure (pay) the back payments due on the loans. The partnership will lease the property to the former homeowners for market rent. If they default on the rent payments, the partnership evicts them. The former homeowners still have a partnership interest, but they do not have possession. At that point, you can buy them out of the partnership. As you can see, this structure has the potential to get messy. Therefore, the partnership approach should not be approached without the assistance of qualified legal counsel.

Always make sure you have an exit strategy for yourself in case the owners suddenly come across some money. In your agreement, state that if the previous owners pay back all money you laid out plus an additional amount for your time and trouble, you will sell the house back to them. This way, there is no confusion and your profit is in writing. In most cases, this will not happen, but you should always be prepared.

PURCHASING REOS

Before selling an REO, the bank will usually evict anyone who is living on the premises. After the property is vacant, the real estate agency will have someone appraise the property to help them estimate the cost of repairs and determine the value of the property.

The condition of an REO can range from great to run-down. When you buy an REO, you are buying it as is with no warranties or guarantees on its condition. Before you buy an REO, inspect the property or hire a home inspector so you know its condition and flaws.

After an REO property is vacant and an appraiser has estimated the value of the house, the bank will list the property with a real estate broker who specializes in REOs.

Remember, an REO is a foreclosure that has already happened. The bank auctioned the property but no one bid the amount they wanted, so the bank owns the property. Instead of negotiating with the previous owner, you are dealing with the bank as the owner, through their official REO broker.

Finding an REO broker

A good way to obtain a list of brokers in a particular state is to go to the REO Network's web site at www.reonetwork.com. After you have a list of brokers, call them and tell them that you are looking to purchase properties. Be honest about your price range and how fast you think you could close on a parcel.

As the property lists start coming in, look at the actual properties and the surrounding neighborhood. Make sure that you can afford the properties before you go any further. Of course, you can always make a low offer if you think it may be accepted, but don't waste the broker's time or yours! Remember, make an offer that is backed by reasoning, not just because you want to pay less.

When negotiating to buy an REO, you'll be negotiating with the bank's realtor. Ask the realtor questions such as, "Have you shown the property recently?" and "What kind of condition is the property in?" Let the real estate agent provide as much information as he or she is willing and able to offer. In other words, be polite and don't interrupt. Ask open-ended questions that might offer some insight as to how motivated the bank is to sell this property. If the answers are what you're looking for, your next question should be, "When can I see it?"

Don't forget that these properties are considered liabilities (REOs are actually assets on the banks' balance sheets but they feel like liabilities) and the bank wants to get rid of them quickly. The more you know about a property, the better equipped you'll be to come up with an offer the bank will accept. Although the bank will want to sell for as close to the list price as it can—usually at least 85–90%—they may accept a lower offer if a property has been on the market for some time.

Be sure to compare similar homes in the same neighborhood to determine whether property values are rising or declining. When purchasing REO properties, always pay substantially under the market value. Most of these properties will need cosmetic work—at a minimum. Allow for the costs to bring them up to saleable condition.

These strategies can work in any market because you are buying under value. In an up market, there may be more competition in acquiring this type of property, so be careful not to pay too much. In a down market, find out the values of other homes that have sold in the neighborhood.

Remember that in a down market, more REOs are available with less competition. So if you can buy a home at a 20% discount, that might be just enough for you to rent the home and pay your mortgage while still generating positive cash flow. Hold it as long as needed until the market takes an upswing, and then sell it for a profit.

Finding HUD and VA REO properties

Banks are not the only institutions that wind up with REOs. Two government agencies, HUD (Housing and Urban Development) and the VA (Veteran's Administration) are government agencies that help people buy homes. If owners default on their loans, both HUD and the VA may wind up with REOs.

HUD has two areas for finding homes. They are listed separately and are classified as owner-occupied listings (for people who want to purchase a home in which to live) and investor listings (for investors). If you sign up on their web site and list yourself as an investor, you will be able to bid only on the investor listings. The HUD web site is www.hud.gov.

Properties owned by the VA are sold in the same way as those owned by HUD, through a bidding process. VA properties rarely sell for less than 93% of the listed price. All VA listings can be purchased by an investor. The U.S. government lists VA homes, along with other federal government properties, at www.homesales.gov.

Purchasing VA and HUD homes is popular among investors, so expect a lot of competition. But the two agencies are excellent resources for finding affordable investment properties.

Finding REOs from other government agencies

Many other agencies also seize properties and sell them at lower prices. They include the following:

- Federal Deposit Insurance Corporation (FDIC)
- Internal Revenue Service (IRS)
- Treasury Department
- County Real Estate Tax Authority

Federal Deposit Insurance Corporation (FDIC)

When banks become insolvent, the FDIC has the responsibility of administering their business. This means they will try to sell the bank-owned REOs.

There are eight regional FDIC offices across the United States. You can find the closest one by accessing their Web site (www.fdic.gov) or by contacting their home office in Washington, D.C., at the following address:

Federal Deposit Insurance Corporation (FDIC)
550 Seventeenth Street N.W.
Washington, DC 20429
(202) 393-8400

Internal Revenue Service (IRS)

The Internal Revenue Service is the office of the Treasury Department charged with collecting taxes. When someone goes into delinquency on their taxes, the IRS may foreclose on their property and sell it to recover some or all of the taxes owed. To find out the location and time of the next tax sale, watch your local classified ads in the real estate section, contact your local IRS office, or contact the office in the area where you are looking for property. The IRS Web site is www.irs.gov.

Treasury Department

In addition to the tax sales conducted by the IRS, the Treasury Department also auctions seized property. You can access their web site (www.ustreas. gov) or look in the local newspaper to find out when the next auction will be held. The property sold at these auctions has been seized as a result of illegal activity.

The main Treasury office address is:

Department of the Treasury
1500 Pennsylvania Avenue N.W.
Washington, DC 20220
(202) 273-4800

Real-Life Story

To see how buying REOs can lead to wealth, here's one of many stories that two of my students shared with me about a property that had been foreclosed and was in the bank's REO portfolio.

"You've probably heard this before, but it's worth repeating: Banks don't like to own real estate. Banks make money by making loans on real estate, not by taking ownership and selling real estate. As soon as the bank has gone through the long and expensive process of foreclosing on a property, they want to get the property off the books as soon as possible.

"Fortunately, we had developed a good relationship with our bank and maintained a good credit report. So when our bank foreclosed on some property, our REO real estate agent, who was always on the lookout for foreclosures and fixer-uppers, notified us. After we looked at the property, we were excited. We could see that it fit our budget, was in a decent neighborhood for growth, and needed repairs that we could handle mostly ourselves. So through our broker, we contacted the bank and they sold us the property for the amount of their loan, which was $41,000.

"My wife and I were ecstatic. The previous owners had begun remodeling the house, but they lost their home to the bank before finishing. They had installed new double-pane, vinyl windows and permanent aluminum siding, which was in great condition. In addition, they had built a large garage/shop with a high ceiling. The only downside was that we had to haul away 20,000 pounds of greasy auto parts from the garage. But because of the profit we stood to make, we cleaned out the garage with a smile.

"We estimated that the costs to remodel the kitchen and upstairs, haul the debris from the garage, and clean up the yard would be $15,000. Included in this amount were our holding costs for the loan payments we would have to make to the bank while we remodeled the property.

"We found a fantastic handyman who helped us complete all the work in just two short months. We then interviewed a few realtors and were pleased when one of them suggested that we list the property for $89,950. We reviewed the comparable sales in the area and realized that this was on the high side, but we decided to give it a try.

"The kitchen remodel appealed to the female buyers and the large garage/shop appealed to the men. We had offers within two weeks and sold the house for close to full price.

"After paying closing costs and realtor commissions, we netted $80,000. After paying back $41,000 to the bank for the first mortgage and the $15,000 line of credit for the remodeling costs, we netted $24,000. It was an incredible experience and just one of the deals that help set the foundation for a lot more deals in our investing career. We are surely not done. I would suggest to anyone that REOs are not something that they should overlook."

SHORT SALES

In the previous story, my students talked about buying an REO from the bank for the price of the amount owed on the loan. Now I'm going to show you a way to get property not only less expensively but also before anyone else can buy it.

Short sales are another way to buy properties that are near foreclosure, in foreclosure, or already foreclosed. To find this type of property, get a list of pre-foreclosures and foreclosures from the courthouse, from title companies, online, at my web site (www.deangraziosi.com), or from a list provider that sells pre-foreclosure and foreclosure lists. (These are the same sources of foreclosures we listed in the "Finding Foreclosures" section in Chapter 16.)

The difference with a short sale strategy compared to a straight foreclosure or pre-foreclosure strategy is simple. When you are buying pre-foreclosures, you are looking for homes that have equity, which means there is less money owed on the home than what it is worth. With a short sale strategy, you work with homes in which people owe as much or more than the property is worth. This turns a lot of investors away. But with a little work, you can make a profit as you do with any of the foreclosure strategies.

After you have a list, get the name and address of each property owner. You might want to send each owner a simple letter or a postcard, as follows:

$ NO EQUITY, NO PROBLEM $

I am sure you have probably already fixed your financial situation or are working on selling your property, but if there is still a problem, I may be able to help. If your current solution does not work, I would love to share with you a backup option.

No closing costs
No commissions
Move when you are ready
Have your money in 48 hours
We clean the house
We are here to help

Private Investor, Not a Real Estate Agent! Call (Your Name) for help. 555-555-5555
Get Results Today
www.yourwebsitehere.com

The goal is to send these marketing pieces so that homeowners in foreclosure start to call you. When they call, let them know that you are there to help them and keep the foreclosure off their record. Let them know that you realize there is no equity in their home, but you still have a possible solution. When there is no equity, a short sale option may be the only strategy that could allow you to make money and possibly help them at the same time.

Here is an example of how I made more than $30,000 in only ten hours. I did a short sale before I knew what such a term meant. (I'm telling this story not just to teach you the process, but—more importantly—to teach you to keep an open mind, think outside the box, take a chance, and make things happen.)

A piece of property located in a little town in upstate New York bordered the local middle school. As in many areas, the school needed to expand. However, the only area where it could expand was on to the property I am talking about. This property had an abandoned house on it. The owners had moved out, the house was condemned, and the bank was going to foreclose on the property shortly.

I knew that the middle school needed the property, so I wanted to buy the property, tear down the condemned building, and sell the land to the school for a profit. Pretty innovative thinking, I thought. But several other people were thinking the same way.

Now, here is where my ability to think a little differently led to not only a huge profit but also to a new secret to add to my collection of strategies for making money with real estate. I knew a foreclosure sale date was set and that I wasn't the only one who knew about it. I also knew that the competition at an auction would be high. I thought to myself, "How can I use my ability to think differently from all the other people who are going to try to buy the foreclosure?" I found out the mortgage holder, I naively called the bank, and . . .

But wait! Before I go on, I want to teach you another important secret. When you make a call—in any situation—make sure you have the right person on the phone before you waste time and energy explaining yourself to an unqualified person. Get the decision maker on the phone, so you know where you stand right away. Also, be prepared.

When I called the bank this first time, I simply said, "Hi, this is Dean Graziosi, and I am interested in purchasing a piece of property that your bank has a lien on. It is located at XXX and it is presently in the name of

XXX. May I please speak to the person at your bank who would be the decision maker on that property?"

Well it worked; they connected me to the right person. Now I was on the phone with him and learning as I went. I was polite but not afraid to ask questions. I had nothing to lose and a lot to gain, so I went for it and asked, "How can I buy this piece of property before it goes into foreclosure?"

His reply was, "You can't buy the property, but we could sell you the lien." And that's when the lightbulb went off. I asked him what he meant and he answered that $145,000 was owed on the property. He told me that I could fax over an offer. Well to me, "fax over an offer" means that the bank will probably take less than what is owed.

This property taught me that you can buy a lien from the bank at a reduced rate and get to the property before anyone else has a chance to buy it from the bank. And that is the basis of doing a short sale.

When only a small amount is due on a piece of property, you may have an opportunity to get a bargain. However, most of the time the bank will take possession of the property outright or bid on it themselves so they can reap the benefits. But in many cases, as much or even more is owed on the property than it is worth. So where is the room for your profit? Well, here is the answer: a short sale or buying the lien from the bank.

A bank or note holder may write a distressed property off as bad debt. They already took the loss or are ready to take a loss to get it off their books. In this example, they are owed $145,000 on it, and wrote or will soon write most of that off as bad debt. They know the property is not worth what they are owed and are looking to recoup whatever they can, so they often will take a fair offer.

Now, back to the banker. He told me to fax an offer, so I hung up the phone and ran over to the property to get a better look and more ammunition for the offer I was about to send.

It is important to remember that I was not making an offer on the property. Rather, I was making an offer on the lien that was owed on the property. So I was negotiating the purchase of the $145,000 of debt tied to that property. This means that even if I bought the lien for less money, I would still be owed the full amount of the debt. When you buy a lien or a note at a discount, you are still buying it at full face value.

In summary, I was negotiating the purchase of the note, or lien, that the bank had on that property, not the property itself.

After looking at the property, I faxed an offer of $12,500. Within a few minutes, the bank officer called me and said, "Dean, I got your offer. But I think you made a mistake. Did you mean $125,000?"

Here comes another important lesson. At this point I could have been intimidated and said, "Oh no, I made a big mistake offering such a small amount of money." But because of my ability to think differently, I answered, "To me, that property has almost a negative value on it." I was prepared with all the negative aspects of the property.

My answer surprised the banker. He said, "What do you mean?" I responded by pointing out that the property had a building on it that was old and condemned, and I would have to take it down. That meant I'd need permits, fees, approvals—especially because the property was next to a school.

There could be asbestos on the old pipes, so I'd have to test for that as well. (I found out later that there wasn't any asbestos.) Plus, almost $5000 in taxes were owed on the property. For these reasons, I told him, the property had almost a negative value. So, in my opinion, $12,500 was a realistic offer; if he would like to accept that, I could come up with the money quickly. A day later, to my disbelief, the banker called me back and accepted my offer for $12,500.

So I wound up buying a $145,000 lien from the bank for $12,500. Now, I could just have gone to my attorney and told him to handle it from here and still made a lot of money, but I wanted to see whether I could think a little differently and make this process quicker, easier, and less expensive for everyone involved.

Now, who was involved? The owners of the property, who unfortunately could not pay their mortgage—and me. After asking my attorney to tell me about the foreclosure process (always seek legal advice when you are unsure of something), I knew the process, but I also knew it would be easier if the owners simply signed over the deed to me.

You see, the foreclosure process would cost them additional money, and they could be liable for any uncollected debt. Obviously, they were not in a position to spend more money. It's important to remember that this is not a case of "you against them." Circumstances can affect people in different ways at different times. So I called the owners, told them I had purchased the lien on their property, and simply said, "I am sorry that you had to let your house go. As you may or may not know, I could start the foreclosure process immediately, but I think I have a way to make it simple for all of us. Are you open to a suggestion?" And their answer was a big "Yes."

So I explained that if they simply signed over the deed to me, it would save us all a bunch of money and time and also relieve them from the debt and any further responsibility. They agreed. My attorney prepared the papers, we both signed, and the property was mine for the $12,500 and a few thousand dollars in back taxes.

When you are considering buying a foreclosure, always run a title search on the property to see all debts related to that parcel of property. You don't want to take on a piece of property that may have some additional hidden debt.

Because I had bought the property for so little money, I went ahead and sold it to the school district at a fair price to help out the town. I made about $30,000 in ten hours' work. Why? Because I learned about the possibility of purchasing a lien before it goes to foreclosure. And I was not afraid to think on my own and not afraid to ask. Other more experienced investors than I was at the time wanted to buy this property, but I found a way to buy it before them, and for less money.

So to summarize, if a short sale is your only option on a piece of property, you can start by getting permission from the owner to talk to the lender on the owner's behalf. You can get the permission with a letter or a three-way call. Now it is time to connect with the lender. This way you will know exactly where everything is and how much is owed so you can plan your strategy and how much you are willing to spend. If there is no way to work with the current owner, you can talk to the correct representative at the bank and possibly purchase the lien at a discount from them directly.

Negotiating a short sale with the lender can reap huge benefits. Although not always easy, the reward makes the effort worthwhile. The first step is finding a bank officer who has the authority to accept a discount. You will have to call around to locate the lender's loss mitigation department. More than likely, each lender you deal with will have a different name for this department, so be patient when calling. Expect the process to involve some waiting on hold and being bounced around a maze of automated voice mail systems. After you get in touch with the right person, the negotiating begins.

From the lender's perspective, a short sale saves many of the costs associated with the foreclosure process: attorney's fees, the eviction process, delays from borrower bankruptcy, damage to the property, costs associated with resale, and so on. A foreclosure can cost a lender more than $30,000 on average. In a short sale scenario, the lender can cut their losses. Your job as the investor is to convince the lender that they will fare better by accepting less money now.

After you have made contact with the lender and you know who the decision maker is, submit an offer in writing. This offer has to show why it is a good deal for them. Make it clear that the best option for the lender is to accept this offer and stop the foreclosure. So, lay it out for them and make it an easy decision to accept your offer.

The lender will want some information about the property, the borrower, and the deal he has made with you. Specifically, the lender wants to know what the property is worth. The lender will generally hire a local real estate broker or appraiser to evaluate the property (called a broker's price opinion, or BPO)—but not always, as in my example. You can also submit your own appraisal or comparable sales information.

In addition, you will want to offer as much specific negative information about the property as possible, such as the poor condition of any structures on the property. Also include relevant information about the neighborhood and the local economy if things are bad (copies of newspaper articles with bad news may help). Also submit a contractor's bid for repair estimates.

The lender will also ask for financial information about the borrower, sort of a backwards loan application. The borrower must prove that he or she is broke and unable to afford the payments and has no other source of income or assets to repay the loan. This process may involve as much, if not more, paperwork than an original mortgage application! The borrower should submit a hardship letter, which is basically a sob story about how much financial trouble the borrower is in. This may require a little literary creativity and some help on your part. Don't lie; just paint a picture that doesn't look good.

Finally, the lender generally wants to see a written contract between you and the seller. The lender wants to make sure the seller isn't walking away with any cash from the deal. Generally, the contract must be written so that the buyer pays all costs associated with the transaction and the net cash to the seller is the amount of the short pay to the lender. A preliminary HUD-1 settlement statement is often requested, which can be difficult because many title and escrow companies simply won't prepare one before closing. However, you can prepare your own HUD-1 and simply write *Preliminary* on the top. You can get a blank HUD-1 type document at www.deangraziosi. com. This preliminary HUD-1 shows the bank how much you are offering and where the proceeds from the sale are going.

Don't be surprised if your first short sale bid is rejected. Lenders aren't emotionally attached to their properties, but they want to get all they can for them.

Short sales can be a great way to purchase property. They allow you to create equity where it did not exist. This gives you the opportunity to profit from investments that other real estate investors never look at. It may seem like a difficult process, but after you get your system down, you can make huge profits.

CONCLUSION

Pre-foreclosures and REOs give you a chance to buy property at steeply discounted prices, and short sales give you a chance to buy property at an even greater discount when most investors turn away. The key is that banks don't want to own homes; they want to loan money for people to buy homes, so they are more than willing to negotiate just to get rid of their properties. Banks are smart with their negotiating, but now so are you. The longer the bank is stuck with the property, and this is especially true in a down market, the more anxious and willing they will be to negotiate a deal, and that means bargains for you!

When negotiating to buy pre-foreclosures or REOs, keep the following in mind:

- Take the initiative to research and seek out pre-foreclosure opportunities.
- Be polite when communicating with people who are experiencing financial difficulties and could potentially lose their homes.
- Think creatively about how you can solve someone else's problem. This will go a long way towards finding opportunities for you to build wealth in real estate pre-foreclosures.

CHAPTER 18

CASHING IN
ON TAX SALES
AND TAX LIENS

Taxes, after all, are dues that we pay for the privileges
of membership in an organized society.
—FRANKLIN D. ROOSEVELT

Every property owner must pay property taxes. If you fail to pay these taxes after a certain amount of time, the county can recoup their lost tax revenue by selling the property or attaching a tax lien. The tax lien basically forces you to pay the property taxes one way or another.

If you want to keep your property, you have to pay off the tax lien, which includes the property taxes owed plus interest for late payment. If you want to sell your property, any money earned from the sale must first go towards paying your taxes. If you don't pay your taxes within a certain period of time, you will lose your property.

People don't pay their property taxes for many reasons, such as loss of a job, divorce, or death in the family. But some people stop paying taxes for other circumstances. Perhaps the land appears worthless, or is landlocked (the only way to get to it is to cross someone else's property), or contains a building in such bad shape that it would cost more to fix it up than it's worth. Or maybe the property is inherited and the new owner simply can't afford to pay the taxes.

Whatever the reason, the county needs to collect property taxes. So if owners do not pay their taxes, it's inevitable that there will be opportunities to purchase this type of property and make substantial profits. Here are a few ways in which this happens:

- Buy a tax lien. To remove this lien from the property, the owner must pay you the cost of the lien along with interest set by the state, county, or region or by a bidding process. If the owner does not pay you back, you have the chance to own the property. If the original owner sells the property to another person, the new owner must pay you to remove the tax lien.

- Buy the property. If the owners have gone long enough without paying their taxes, their property will be auctioned to the highest bidder or foreclosed by the county and available for sale at a later date. The county is looking to recoup their lost taxes, so if a piece of property is worth $100,000 but taxes owed are $20,000, you have an opportunity to get a $100,000 property for $20,000.

Soon I will explain in more detail the difference between buying a tax lien and buying property because someone did not pay their taxes.

FINDING TAX SALES

To find a list of properties that will be sold at the next tax sale (auction), contact the tax collection office, clerk's office, or treasury department for the county. In larger counties, you can often find this information on the county's web site (such as www.sdcounty.ca.gov for San Diego county).

After you get a list of properties delinquent on their tax payments, get a copy of the tax map, which gives you information about who owns the property, its exact location, and more. Tax maps are available online or at the tax assessor's office. Then go and look at the properties. You'll be able to see whether anything is wrong with them or whether the owners just couldn't pay the taxes.

Unlike real estate sales through a licensed broker, there is absolutely no guarantee regarding the condition of property sold at a public auction. That's why you must research and understand the property, its history, and the extent of repairs necessary to bring the property to rentable or saleable condition.

Why is it important to understand the background or history of a property? Let's assume you are interested in purchasing a wonderful corner lot that was once a local gas station. The corner lot looks like an attractive property in a good neighborhood. This is where your research can help you spot potential problems.

Many local gas stations have underground leaky storage tanks. Part of the reason why these stations have closed is that the owners couldn't comply with environmental standards requiring the removal of the tanks and contaminated soil. By knowing this ahead of time, you can avoid buying the property and paying these hidden costs. Preparation is the key!

MY FIRST TAX SALE

This is how I bought my first tax property. After getting a list of properties that people were delinquent on paying their taxes, I found a property that I liked in an area where I wanted to invest. I discovered that the owner hadn't paid the taxes on it for many years. Also, even though it was being sold at auction, no one was going to pay the minimum amount due. I knew this because it had already gone through the auction block several times with no buyers. Too much was owed on the property compared to its value.

Approximately $50,000 was owed on this property, so when it came up for sale the first time, no one bid the $50,000 minimum. When it didn't sell, the county took possession of it. (This is similar to a bank REO, which you learned about in Chapter 17. The only difference is that the county, not a bank, owned the property.) Each time the county put the property up for auction, they set the minimum at the $50,000 that was owed in past taxes.

Well, this seemed like a great deal of money to invest, but I looked at the property and loved its potential. I say "potential" because, at first glance, the property had a major drawback.

The property itself was beautiful, spread over nine acres, with a stunning hilltop view of more than fifty miles in two directions. I thought that the property could be worth hundreds of thousands of dollars, but a good portion of that acreage sat on top of an extremely steep hill, and it didn't look like there was a way to get a useable driveway or road to the top. This is why the owner let it go and also why other investors were avoiding it. But again, I thought a little differently: "If I can get this property for a low enough amount, it will be worth the expense of putting in an access road."

I showed the property to a friend who owned an excavating business. He said he could build a driveway, but it would cost probably $50,000. That was all I needed to know. Paying $50,000 for a driveway might seem crazy, but once the driveway was built, I knew the property would be worth hundreds of thousands of dollars.

So I started making calls to find out how to buy this tax delinquent property from the county. After I got the right person on the phone, I told him who I was and what property I was interested in. Then I said—and remember these words because they saved me tons of money and made me a fortune—"Listen, that property is no longer on the tax roll and hasn't been for years, so you are not collecting money. Also, this property has very poor access, and that's why you've been unable to sell it. Because it did not sell in a previous tax auctions, can I make an offer? If you sell it at a discount, at least the property will get off the county's hands and back on the tax roll." He said that they would take an offer.

As I mentioned, approximately $50,000 was owed in taxes. But with all the negatives I pointed out, I took a shot and made an extremely low offer of just $5000. To my surprise, they came back and said they would take $6000. Imagine how I felt about buying tax sales at that point. I got the property for a very low price and they were able to turn a liability into an asset, so everybody was happy.

In New York, when you purchase a piece of property for taxes, you get what is known as a quitclaim deed. You have to keep possession of this deed for a certain length of time, such as eighteen months. Within that time, the original owner has the opportunity to pay the taxes owed to the county plus a penalty and interest. If they do not pay within the allocated time, your quitclaim deed becomes a regular deed that allows you to get title insurance and completely own the property. But lots of variations of this can make it much better for you with a little creative thinking and knowledge. Remember, it takes only a few hours online, making some phone calls, or visiting your local tax collector's office to know exactly how the process works in your area. We will learn more of that in just a few moments.

Because I was a novice in the tax purchasing arena, I did some investigating and asked a lot of questions. In doing so, I found out a few things. First, my attorney could do an article 15, which in New York is an action taken by the purchaser to "quit" anyone who may want claim to the property. This process is a notification that if anyone has a claim to the property, they have to show up in court to prove it. In most cases, the person who lost the property is not going to challenge the transfer of ownership. This typically costs $100 to $1500, reduces the time to take full ownership of the property to about three or four months, and allows you to get a transferable deed. So that was one option.

The second option was that if the previous owner signs off on the deed (meaning volunteering to sign ownership over to you), you can get a transferable deed that you could get title insurance on immediately. Basically no waiting, no costs!

(Title insurance makes sure that no liens are on the property, which would allow someone else to purchase the property instead of you. So getting title insurance "insures" that you can safely take possession of the property.)

So I found and called the previous owner of the property. I explained who I was and that I had purchased the property from the county. I further explained that I was aware that I could just wait eighteen months and then turn my quitclaim deed into a regular deed or I could have my attorney do an article 15. Then I told him that I would rather have the opportunity to meet him in person and bring the proper paperwork for him to sign off on. If he did that, the experience would be behind him.

(If I had just waited eighteen months, I wouldn't have been able to do anything with the property during that time and I could have missed out on a lot of opportunities. It's always in your best interest to buy property with no chance that the previous owner or the owner of a tax lien could possibly make you wait to do something with your property.)

Then I added, "I know it is not a big deal, but I'll bring you $100 and maybe you can use it to go to dinner somewhere special." As I always say, be polite, be sincere, and take into consideration that it may be a touchy situation for someone.

Don't forget, this man had already given up on the property. He could not afford it or just did not want it. So he said, "Son (I was younger at the time), bring the paper out here and let's get this over with."

So I called my attorney and told him what had happened. He drew up the proper paperwork and took a ride with me over to this gentleman's house. He signed the paperwork, and I owned the property free and clear of any debt. I gave him $100, we shook hands, and I now owned the property for $6100. What a great thing to learn by thinking a little differently and not being afraid to ask.

I took thinking outside the box one step further on this piece of property. I sold a portion of the property (presubdivided) for $85,000. I took some of that money and had a driveway cut to the top, where the property was absolutely breathtaking. The remaining property is literally worth hundreds of thousands of dollars. But because it is in my home town and one of the nicest properties I have ever owned, I'm keeping the remaining part in hopes of building a great summer home.

You have to remember I did this with no guidance, no mentor, and no book like this one. I was learning as I was going along. How much greater chance do you think you have of making money with tax sales and real estate having this book?

A few months later, I bought another parcel down the street the same way for $10,000 and later sold half the property for $40,000. This isn't luck. It's about understanding what is possible, knowing how to do it, and taking action.

BUYING TAX SALE PROPERTIES

When a property owner fails to pay taxes after a specified period of time, the county tries to recoup their lost tax revenue by taking possession of the property and selling it at a public auction. Depending on the state, bidding at a public auction may get you one of the following:

- The actual property deed, which gives possession and ownership of the property immediately
- A quitclaim deed, which gives the original owner a certain period of time to reclaim the property by paying the back taxes and buying the quitclaim deed from you (plus interest)
- A tax lien (certificate), which means no one can take ownership of the property without first paying you for the amount of the tax lien (plus interest)

Every state has its own peculiar rules for bidding. In Oklahoma, the winner is not the person who bids the most but the one who gets there first!

This first come, first served policy, combined with the low interest rate paid on tax liens (certificates) in Okalahoma, may not make tax sales there as appealing for investors at first glance. But because you are not in a competing open bid format, that could allow you to purchase property for pennies on the dollar, with no competition.

In a few states, tax sales are public oral bid sales. However, this is not the same as a public oral bid *foreclosure* auction. In a public oral bid state, if property taxes become delinquent, the taxing body (usually the state or county) can foreclose and gain title to the property. So the taxing agency becomes, in effect, the owner, and they can resell the property at a public auction sale.

The biggest difference between these two kinds of tax sales is the typical opening bid amount. The opening bid at the public oral bid foreclosure auction is usually the amount of the taxes owed. But the opening bid at a public oral bid sales auction is usually higher—closer to the property's actual value. This, of course, makes the investment lose much of its appeal.

When I want to bid on property at a tax sale, I first find out the process in the area. If it's a process I find attractive, I get a list of the properties that are going to be sold and follow the steps. It really is that simple.

Buying property deeds

When county auctions offer property deeds, they usually set the minimum bid to the amount of the taxes owed. So if a piece of property has $25,000 in back taxes, the minimum bid will be $25,000. If the property is worth $120,000, paying $25,000 would obviously be quite a bargain. (If the property is being auctioned in a public oral bid, as explained previously, the opening bid will likely be much higher.)

Because paying less than the actual value on property is a bargain, other investors are likely to make competing bids, so bids often creep up near the actual value of the property. The highest bidder gets the property and the county uses the money to pay the property's taxes.

Buying quitclaim deeds

A quitclaim deed lets you take possession of property but gives the original owner a fixed amount of time to pay back the taxes (and to pay you back for holding the quitclaim deed). Either way, you'll make a profit because if the owner pays back the taxes, they still have to buy the quitclaim deed (plus interest) from you. If they don't pay back the taxes, the property reverts to you.

Each state has different opportunities to minimize or eliminate the amount of time that the previous owner has any recourse on the property. In New York, you can get a clear title in a few months by having an attorney take action with an article 15 (part of the New York State Real Property Act) or, as I mentioned in my story, by getting the original owner to sign over the deed to you. I prefer to buy property only when I feel confident that I will gain complete and uncontested ownership of it.

When you're buying a property and getting a quitclaim deed, check the redemption period, which can range from as little as zero days to as much as five years. The longer you have to hold the property without getting the title (ownership), the more you'll have to pay in property taxes.

With quitclaim deeds, you can make money by either taking possession of the property for pennies on the dollar or by selling the quitclaim deed back to the original owner (plus interest).

Buying tax liens (certificates)

When the county auctions a tax lien, the amount of the tax lien equals the amount of taxes owed. By selling a tax lien, the county can recover the amount of taxes. So if a property owes $4000 in taxes, the amount of the tax lien will be $4000.

You don't actually bid on this amount. Instead, you bid on the interest rate that you will earn on the tax lien you pay the county. Everyone wants a high interest rate, so bidders submit progressively lower bids on the interest rate, and the low bidder wins.

The investor pays for a tax lien (certificate), which essentially pays the back taxes owed to the county. If the property owner does not pay off the tax lien (by paying the amount of back taxes plus interest) within a specified time, the investor who holds the tax lien (certificate) eventually has the opportunity to gain ownership of the property.

Unlike a quitclaim deed, a tax lien allows the original owner to sell the property to another person after the legal redemption period has expired. However, the money from the sale must first go towards paying off any new tax liens (plus interest) in case the property owner fails to pay taxes in a subsequent year. So in this situation, you'll still make a profit although you won't get possession of the property.

If you purchase a tax lien, you can earn interest on the amount of the lien for the period of time the property owner has to pay you back for the tax lien. Many times, property owners do not want to lose their homes or properties for a relatively small amount of money when compared to the first mortgage. So they generally will work hard to find the money to pay the tax lien and keep their properties. Until the lien is repaid, the owner of the tax lien is earning interest on his or her money. As part of the settlement of the tax lien, property owners must pay the tax lien plus interest legally allowed by the state.

For example, an investment in a tax lien in Arizona can result in a return of more than 15%. Wyoming also has a 15% return as well as a 3% guaranteed penalty return when the lien is paid off. If the lien is paid off after one year, for example, the interest received is 18%. What's more, with a penalty return, the investor receives the entire penalty amount, no matter when the lien is redeemed.

Texas and Florida have some of the best legislated interest rates for tax liens. You can earn a high rate of interest on your money, and if your principal and interest are not paid back in the allocated time, you can gain ownership of the property.

Tax liens have some drawbacks. First, you have to tie up your money in the tax lien until it is either redeemed (the owner pays you for it plus interest) or you own the property. If you end up owning the property, you may have to evict the occupants, which can be a painful and troublesome process. Finally, if you don't do your homework on the property, you could find out that the taxes were not paid because there is a major issue with the property, such as toxic waste contamination. Make sure you do your homework before buying any property.

TIPS ON CHECKING OUT PROPERTIES

Before you bid on any property, get the property's physical address and parcel number (the number the county assigns to specific property). Then do the following:

- Call or visit a local title company, and let them know you want to run a title search on the property you are considering. Provide them with both the address and parcel number as prepared on the list by the county. This process will allow you to check to see whether there are any material title discrepancies, such as bankruptcy filings, IRS liens, or Superfund Site designations.

- Call a trusted real estate agent in the area and ask whether he or she knows anything about the property or would be willing to drive by the property and give you an opinion of it (for example, the area is underwater twice a year, has a high crime rate, or has a major chemical plant).
- If there are any possible environmental problems, you could order a Level 1 or Phase 1 Environmental Site Assessment report from an authorized environmental service provider. Your realtor, the title company, or even the local yellow pages should enable you to find this type of company fairly easy because they are nationwide. This report costs money, but it tells you whether the property complies with local, state, and federal environmental regulations. The company reviews government records and has discussions with appropriate officials. This report is advisable only if you are serious about buying a piece of property.

The reason why this assessment is important is that you could eventually own this piece of property if the property owner does not pay you the tax lien plus interest during the redemption period. So it is critical you do your homework before buying a tax lien.

PRE-TAX SALES

Just like you learned in the pre-foreclosure chapter, there is an opportunity to buy pre-tax-sale properties. Pre-tax sales are often properties that have no mortgages or liens other than delinquent taxes. This can happen when someone is left a piece of property from a relative or the property is seemingly useless to them and they feel that paying the taxes is a waste of money. You have an opportunity to contact these people before the property goes to auction and negotiate a deal so they come out with a little bit of money instead of losing their property.

When people are in danger of losing their home due to not paying their taxes, contact them with a letter or a phone call. Let them know that once a property goes through the tax sale process, either the fees start to grow or they will lose their property completely. But by working with you, they may have the chance to get some money out of the deal.

Here's a quick example. When properties are about to go in a tax auction, the parcels are listed in the local papers as a public announcement for legal reasons. One day I saw that a parcel close to where I lived at the time was going to auction. I called the owners and found that the family had gone through a rough time. They had owned a few pieces of property and could not afford the taxes on this piece anymore. Because they also had some other debt attached to the property, they just figured it was easier to let the property go.

After talking to them, I agreed to buy the property before it was auctioned. We made a deal with the other people who had a lien against the property. I purchased the property for a great discount, the sellers paid off a significant amount of other debts they had, and the lien holders got their money. I turned around and sold the property a few months later for a hefty profit.

Always remember that you may have the chance to work with the owners before the property goes to auction. Tell them you may have a creative way to resolve the problems attached to the property. You may be able to put some money in their pocket or, as in the case just noted, pay off other debts for them while buying property at a steep discount.

GETTING STARTED

Now that you've seen the process I went through, I want you to get started. Get a list of properties from your local area that have back taxes owed, that are for sale due to tax defaults, or that are about to go to auction. Find out how much is owed on each property. At first glance, some properties may seem worthless, but with deeper investigation and thinking outside the box, you may find your diamond in the rough.

Suppose you notice a piece of property for sale that is landlocked. I have seen landlocked land sell for peanuts because it seems to be useless. But what if you looked up who the neighbors were and asked them if they would be willing to sell you a small access strip of their land or swap land so you could access the landlocked property? Think differently and you'll find answers, profitable ones at that.

Suppose the land has a swamp on it? What if it lies between the main road and a nice, dry piece of property? Can you build an access road? You could possibly find clean fill for free from a construction job site; in many cases, they'll also deliver it for free. Or locate someone who is excavating land nearby. They can bring some dirt they need to get rid of and dump it on your property, giving you dry, level land to use.

Sometimes, people don't know that an adjoining piece of property is up for tax sale. They might be interested in buying it. Contacting the neighbors of a property you are considering purchasing at a tax sale could be lucrative. You can tell them you're planning on buying the property and you would consider selling all or a piece of it to them if they were interested. Because they are unaware that an adjoining piece of property is available as a tax sale, you could purchase the property and quickly sell it to them for double, triple, or quadruple what you paid for it and still be giving them a great deal.

With these examples, I've shown you how I was able to be successful at buying properties for the taxes owed on them or, in most cases, much less. It was not just because I knew the process; a lot of people may be able to figure that out. I was successful because I looked at the most unlikely properties—the ones that had what appeared to be extreme problems—and I looked at them a little differently.

The last tax sale purchase I worked on was helping my dad buy a few parcels right in his neighborhood. He had been watching these properties for some time and saw that they were ready to go up for auction. In this case, the partners who did the original subdivision got overextended and could not afford to pay the taxes on three parcels of land.

My dad simply got the list from the country treasurer's office with the date of the tax sale and bought all three parcels at the auction. The first was 6.2 acres with a barn-type building on it, the second was a vacant 1.3 acre lot, and the third was a vacant 4.7 acre lot.

By knowing his local rules, he knew that he received a quitclaim deed on the property. Now in this county, he had two options. To get the property insured and be able to sell it, he could wait a few years for the title company to feel safe enough that the past owner would not try to redeem the property. Or he could pay an attorney for the article 15 I described earlier. He chose the second option. The process on all three properties took my dad and his attorney about four months and about $1500 per parcel.

After my dad got clear title, he was free to do what he wanted with the properties. Over the next year he sold all three. He bought the parcels for $13,000 (6.2 acres), $7000 (1.3 acres), and $11,450 (4.7 acres), and sold them for $70,000, $60,000, and $50,000, respectively.

CONCLUSION

You can take advantage of tax sales in any cycle. I've made money in up markets and down markets with tax sales, but in down and bottom markets more people will miss tax payments. Keep your eyes open and you'll be sure to find a great opportunity in your area.

CHAPTER 19

MANAGING RENTAL PROPERTY

Acquire properties now, rent them out and improve them later,
so you can sell them when the market surges again.
—MICHAEL SEXTON,
PRESIDENT OF TRUMP UNIVERSITY

The most common way to make money in real estate is to buy property, hold it for a few years, and then sell it for a profit later. To make money while you're holding onto a piece of property, you can rent it out and use the rental income to pay all or part of the mortgage, essentially letting your renters pay for your property.

When you rent property, you can manage it yourself or hire a property management company, which takes a certain percentage (such as 5–10%) of the rental income for their fee.

A property management company spares you the problem of dealing with tenants. They find tenants, collect the rent, and take care of general maintenance and problems. Whether you plan on managing your own properties or hiring a property management company, this chapter provides some helpful tips that can save you time and money.

GETTING ORGANIZED

Get organized and keep good records. If you purchase one property, you might be able to get by with stuffing receipts and cancelled checks in a shoe-box, but if you own multiple properties, you'll need a better way to organize your finances, such as using an accounting program or a spreadsheet. (We have some great free tools and tracking sheets at www.deangraziosi.com.)

Following are a few organizing tips to consider:

- No matter how little money you earn through rental income, you need to keep track of it for tax purposes. If you have only a handful of rental properties, you could probably track your rental income using a computer program. But if you have dozens of properties, you'll probably be better off hiring an accountant. An accountant can not only free your time but also advise you on the best way to save on taxes.

- Create a rent roll, listing the name of each tenant, the amount of rent paid, and the date when it was received. A rent roll enables you to track your monthly rental income.
- Set up a folder for each rental property (apartment or house) you have. In this folder, put leases, correspondence with your tenants, and a maintenance log that shows when repairs were made, how much they cost, and when they were completed. By keeping such a file, you can quickly track down documents as evidence in case you need to settle a dispute in court between you and a tenant.
- Set up a separate checking account strictly related to your rental properties. When you receive your rental checks, deposit them in this checking account. When you pay repair or maintenance bills related to the rental property, write a check from your rental checking account. When you pay yourself, write a check to yourself from this checking account. By using a separate checking account, you can easily track the cash coming in and expenses going out. Then you can see how much money you're making from your rental property. A separate checking account tracks your income and expenses for tax purposes too.

SELECTING YOUR RENTAL PROPERTY WITH CARE

Location is just as important with rental properties as it is with homes. Look for rental properties where people need to live, such as around colleges or within easy access to parking, highways, and public transportation.

Avoid areas with a high crime rate. Such areas not only reduce the value of your property but also scare away the better tenants, leaving you with less desirable tenants who are more likely to damage your property or skip out of paying rent.

When you're just getting started renting property, I recommend that you keep it simple. Start with single-family homes, duplexes, and four-unit apartment buildings because these properties provide the ideal combination of size and manageability. Larger apartment complexes might be more profitable, but they can be difficult to manage for someone just getting started in real estate investing.

Beware of buildings made up primarily of one-bedroom apartments. One-bedroom apartments attract single people, which generally translates into a much higher turnover rate. Every time someone moves out, you have to clean the unit, including the carpets. Sometimes you have to replace the carpeting and repair appliances.

One-bedroom apartments can also be more difficult to rent because people are generally willing to pay less by sharing a two-bedroom apartment. Vacancies are a cost that you don't pay for directly, but you lose whenever the unit stays vacant.

As I've mentioned, the key to real estate investing is to find out how you can make money before you buy. Following is a quick cash flow breakdown that you can copy and use now or in the future. If you go to my web site (www.deangraziosi.com), you can download this chart and modify it for your own needs.

CASH FLOW ANALYSIS

Income

Estimated Gross Income _____

Other Income _____

TOTAL INCOME _____

LESS VACANCY FACTOR _____

EFFECTIVE GROSS INCOME _____

Expenses

Taxes _____

Insurance _____

Water/Sewer _____

Garbage _____

Electricity _____

Licenses _____

Advertising _____

Supplies _____

Maintenance _____

Landscaping _____

Pest Control _____

Management _____

Accounting & Legal _____

Miscellaneous _____

TOTAL EXPENSES _____

NET OPERATING INCOME _____

Debt Service

First Mortgage _____

Second Mortgage _____

Third Mortgage _____

TOTAL DEBT SERVICE _____

NET CASH FLOW _____

With this chart, you can see at a quick glance whether a particular rental property will have a positive cash flow. Make copies of this form and keep them with you whenever you're looking at rental property.

FINDING AND KEEPING GOOD TENANTS

If you did your homework in purchasing rental property and determining how much you can collect in rent every month, you still need to fill your rental property with tenants.

I run ads in my local newspaper on Saturdays and Sundays. Generally, the weekends are the time when most people read the paper and look for apartments and houses for rent. I've run ads from Monday through Friday and had similar results to running ads just on the weekends.

In my ads, I list the number of bedrooms, the location, the rent, and the security deposit. I also like to include one or two benefits that the rental property offers, such as the following:

- Conveniently located
- Newly renovated
- Utilities included or not included
- Close to shopping or stores
- Private
- Safe
- Nice views

Screening potential tenants

After you've advertised and attracted potential tenants, your next step is to screen them. Make up a list of questions to ask ahead of time. For example, you wouldn't want to meet a tenant to show your one-bedroom unit, only to find that the tenant has four children and two dogs.

The whole point of asking questions is to find the right tenant for your property. Some example questions follow:

- How many people?
- Any pets? Decide in advance whether you are accepting pets and, if so, will be charging an extra security deposit.
- Job status?
- Currently renting or do they own?
- What is their reason for wanting to move to the area?

After you find potential tenants, screen them carefully. There's nothing worse than accepting a tenant who later fails to pay the rent and damages your property. Not only do you have the hassle of evicting the tenant and making repairs, but you'll lose rental income in the meantime.

To avoid an unpleasant situation, run a credit check and employment verification on every tenant before he or she moves in. Services will perform this for you, usually for a small fee ($25–$35, which you can charge your prospective tenant). I strongly recommend calling the previous landlords—preferably a few if possible—for references. Before handing over the keys, call the bank to make sure funds for the security deposit are available.

Why do I recommend that you call more than one previous landlord? The current landlord may want this tenant out of his place as soon as possible, so his reference may be rosier than the actual situation. The previous one or two landlords before the current landlord are really important because they have nothing to gain or lose from giving you the real story.

When you call the tenant's previous landlords, have a series of questions ready to ask to verify the accuracy of the information the potential tenant gave you. Some of my favorite questions to ask previous landlords follow:

- Were you the landlord for the apartment/house located at _____?
- I have received an application to rent an apartment/house from me. When did (applicant's name) rent from you? (You want to ask these detailed questions to make sure the person on the other end of the phone is legitimate and not a friend of the applicant posing as a former landlord. Believe me, it happens.)
- What was the rent per month during that period?

- Did he/she pay the rent on time every month?
- If not, how many months was he/she late? What was the reason?
- How did the apartment/house look when he/she was a tenant?
- How did he/she leave the apartment/house?
- And the key question: Would you rent to him/her again?

The answer to the last question and the way the person answers are criti-cal. If the person wouldn't rent to the applicant again, he or she may come right out and say "no" or the may hesitate before answering, which is a strong indicator that the landlord wouldn't rent to the applicant again. If you have developed a rapport during your conversation, the previous land-lord might explain why he or she wouldn't rent to the applicant.

You might consider using a tenant-screening service, which you can find online. These organizations offer national databases and can often find out whether an applicant has a criminal record or has ever been evicted. Fees are less than $30 per evaluation.

After you have tenants in place, it's a good idea to set up an incentive for timely rent checks, such as discounts for early payments or penalties for late payments—if your state allows it. You should also set up a system for han-dling complaints. Tenants who nitpick about problems they can fix can cost you as much time and money as those who neglect to tell you there's a leak in the roof that's damaging the ceiling. Landlords should specify in the lease what repairs and improvements are permissible, grounds for lease termina-tion, and penalties if the lease is broken.

In areas where demand is higher than supply, you may get bombarded with multiple potential tenants. Here are two little timesaving tricks I have used. First, send all calls to a voice mail that explains in detail what features the rental unit offers and what type of tenants you'll accept (such as no more than two people, no pets, and no smoking). Be specific, and by all means stay within the legal guidelines of your state. Then tell the caller to leave a message if he or she is still interested. (You can find inexpensive voice mail boxes locally and nationally in the yellow pages or online.) By using voice mail, you can answer most tenants' questions right away without wasting your time answering the same questions over and over again.

Second, instead of meeting lots of people at different times, arrange to meet all potential tenants at the unit at the same time or within an hour's time frame. This not only saves you time showing the unit but also causes a little competition among prospective renters.

Minimizing vacancies
Owning rental property is great, but having it vacant means you're losing money. After you have dependable tenants, you'll want to keep them, so

when a tenant's lease is nearing the end I recommend contacting them to find out their plans. Maybe they plan on staying and would like to sign up for another six months or a year. Or maybe they just want a larger place. If you own other rental property, you might be able to rent them a different unit; that way, you won't lose a good tenant and you'll avoid a vacancy in your other property.

Depending on the type of property (apartment or house), I have offered a $20–$50 bonus to existing tenants if they recommend an applicant who ends up renting a unit from me. Friends like to live around their friends, and if you keep a property in good condition, treat people fairly, and go just a little beyond the status quo (by remembering birthdays and so on), your current tenants will encourage decent applicants to apply (and get an easy bonus!). It is the least expensive referral system out there.

The point is to stay in touch with your tenants because they are your customers who pay your bills. Maybe the only reason why a tenant is considering leaving is some small repair or update, such as new paint in the living room. By knowing what your tenants want, you can take care of a small issue now in exchange for getting them to sign a new lease. Now you won't have to spend time and money finding a new tenant and cleaning up the rental property. I hope you can see the value of maintaining good (and continuous) communication with your tenants.

Collecting the rent

I write my leases so that rent is due on the first day of the month for all my properties. That way, I don't need to keep track of when each tenant should pay rent. Rent is always due on the first of the month with a grace period with no late fees if paid *in full* by the fifth day of the month. But if rent is not paid in full or is paid late, I charge a late fee of 10% of the rent, as stated in the lease.

If a tenant delays paying rent beyond the fifth day, I have written in my lease that I can charge an additional $10 per day until the rent is paid in full. I did this because some tenants would say, "I know I am late, so I might as well wait a little longer to pay my rent." I want to make sure that the rent payment is one of the top priorities for my tenants (after all, it is one of the most important basic needs in their lives).

Even with my best tenants, if their rent is not paid by the fifth day of the month (the grace period), I deliver them a notice to pay or vacate. I soften the blow by explaining that I need to cover my bases legally, and all will be forgiven if they come through with the rent and late fees. If I serve them with this notice in person, I explain what is going on in a nice manner. If I hire someone to serve them, I call them ahead of time to let them know that I had no choice due to the rent being late—I make it the rent's fault, not theirs.

When you can deliver these notices to tenants and the length of time the notices allow for payment or vacating the premises depends on the state. Some states allow three days and some allow five days. Check your landlord tenant laws. But remember, if tenants have trouble paying you by the fifth of the month, and they promise they will pay by the fifteenth of the month, how are they going to come up with next month's rent by the first of the following month? It isn't prudent to delay the inevitable, so face the problem head-on now and you might be able to salvage a rough spot for your tenant. I have made arrangements with tenants to pay me weekly, letting them know that if they miss one scheduled payment in full, the legal process will unfortunately begin and take its course (which would not be good for them because their record would be blotted with an eviction).

I am not shy about letting my tenants know that I have a bank loan and that I rely on their rent payment to help make my mortgage payment. I sometimes make the bank the "bad guy" and often say, "I have a mortgage payment due on the first, and the bank doesn't care whether I collect rent or not. They just care that I make the payment by the due date or they charge me late fees. If you are late, I am late." This approach has gone a long way towards getting the tenant on my side and painting their late fees in a light they understand.

Handling security deposits

I always make my security deposits an amount that's noticeably different than the monthly rent. That way, tenants don't confuse their security deposit as their last month's rent. For example, if rent for the apartment is $525 per month, I charge a security deposit of $500.

As a landlord, you have typically fourteen days (check your local landlord tenant laws) to mail a security deposit disposition form to your former tenants. This form outlines any deductions for cleaning or repairs that were required to bring the apartment or house back to the rental condition it was in when you turned the keys over to this tenant. Tenants are financially penalized for things beyond the realm of normal wear and tear and if they did not abide by stipulations in the original lease agreement. Do not miss the date for mailing this security deposit disposition form! State laws penalize landlords who are late, and the penalties can be stiff. In Arizona, for example, a landlord who is late mailing this form can be penalized one and one half times the security deposit. So understand your state laws and meet your deadlines.

Move-in requirements

I require that all new tenants pay one month's rent in advance plus a security deposit. If someone moves in and starts the lease on the tenth of the month, and the rent is $525 and the security deposit is $500, I require $1025 to move in. Then on the first of the following month, I prorate the next month's rent for the ten extra days that the tenant paid for the move-in. As an alternative, I might prorate the first month's rent (in this case, the prorated amount is $350) and collect the entire security deposit.

Never, ever let your tenants move into your properties without paying the entire amount of (prorated) rent and security deposit. I did this once and got burned. Don't let it happen to you.

Before your tenants move in, make them complete a move-in property condition form so they can note any damaged items. Preparing and reviewing this form carefully will help you avoid hassles when tenants move out. On occasion, tenants might claim that an item you list on the security deposit disposition form was already damaged when they moved in. If the item was properly noted on the move-in property condition form, you can quickly show the tenants that they did not note the item at the time of move-in. So their claim that you should refund them for this particular item can, and should, be eliminated.

With a camera phone or a high-quality digital camera, make it a habit of taking pictures of your units (all four walls and the flooring) while you complete a walk-through with a new tenant. They can see that you are paying attention to details. You can easily store these images on your computer in case you need to refer to them. If you don't have a computer, use a cheap disposable camera.

Landlord tenant laws and fair housing laws

Every state has landlord tenant laws to address the rules and regulations outlining the legal rights of tenants as well as those of the landlord or owner of the property. In addition, federal fair housing laws directly affect the landlord-tenant relationship. These federal laws are strict and carry heavy fines if violated.

I recently attended a local, one-hour federal and state fair housing seminar. I encourage you to do the same because many things affect all landlords, such as saying something that could be misconstrued as discriminatory.

For example, you can state that you will not allow only a few things, such as no smoking and no pets. But you can't legally discriminate against a qualified applicant who, for example, has children. The critical point here is that you must be knowledgeable about fair housing laws and treat everyone fairly. Violations are expensive and can result in fines of $10,000 to $50,000 per occurrence.

Whether you are managing your properties or hiring someone to do so, you must get a copy of the landlord tenant laws for the states in which you own property. Keep in mind that if something goes wrong with the management of your property, you (the owner) will be held responsible.

Insurance

It is critical that you purchase adequate insurance on your property. I had a tenant leave a burning candle in a room, and the house caught on fire. The damage was contained to the living room because a good neighbor noticed the smoke and called the fire department. However, the smoke and water damage was extensive, so I was glad I had adequate insurance on the property.

Accidents happen, so you need adequate coverage and a good, responsive agent who can quickly answer all your questions. If your property is located in an area that has hurricanes, make sure you have coverage for wind and flood damage.

Besides insurance to protect your property from accidents, I suggest that landlords protect themselves against lawsuits by purchasing liability coverage of $500,000—with an additional $1,000,000 umbrella for extra protection.

As much as you might dread doing it (I know I do), evaluate your coverage annually. Then make the appropriate adjustments to the policy to deal with liability and property damage risks.

Liability insurance can protect you from legitimate accidents along with problem tenants. For example, I once had an older apartment building that had apartments on the main floor and the second story. I rented an apartment on the second floor to a single man.

For the first few months, he was a good tenant and paid his rent on time. Then suddenly, I received a letter from a free legal service attorney, claiming that my tenant had tripped on the top step and fallen down the stairs. In the letter, my tenant claimed that the top step was faulty, causing him to trip and injure himself.

The attorney made a claim for $2000 in monetary damages, which was the real motivation behind the claim. The truth is that nothing was wrong with the stairs. The tenant was merely looking for an easy way to get free money, and he sought free legal services to do this.

Unfortunately, unscrupulous people do things like this. If I can avoid a claim on my insurance, I negotiate with the tenant. But in this case, he refused to negotiate, so I called my insurance agent, explained the situation, and asked him to negotiate hard and handle this for the lowest cost possible. I suggested he drag it out as long as he could because this tenant had moved out and was likely looking for a new landlord to scam. (There is a silver lining to this story. The tenant needed a reference about six months after this incident. Do you think I set the record straight? You bet!)

In your lease, make sure your tenants know that your insurance policy does not cover their personal property (I have a place in my lease for tenants to initial), and advise them that they should obtain renter's insurance to cover their personal property.

Dealing with problem tenants

Be particular about tenants because you are essentially handing over possession of your house or apartment to a stranger. Bad tenants pay late or not at all and can destroy your property. Even worse, their bad behavior can cause good tenants in the same building to leave.

If you're not using a management company to screen tenants, check the prospective tenants' credit and business references. If you use a management company, they can (and should) also run credit checks through the major credit bureaus. Many landlords won't rent to people who smoke or have pets. Prospective tenants who have children tend to stay longer than individuals or couples once they settle in and have their children in school.

To help prevent problems in the future, strictly enforce the late fee clause in your lease. In fact, enforce all the clauses in your lease. Otherwise, you could be asking for trouble down the road if you need to enforce the terms and evict a tenant for noncompliance.

A good rule is to treat all your tenants equally. Be professional and courteous. I characterize my method of managing as firm but fair. That way, tenants will feel that you're being fair with everyone and will be less likely to cause trouble later.

Dealing with good tenants

Fortunately, most tenants will be honest and cause no problems for you. That's why I like giving tenants gifts when they move in, for their birthdays, and on holidays. Such gifts show that you appreciate them and took the time to do something nice.

HANDLING REPAIRS AND MAINTENANCE

No matter how new your property is or how careful your tenants are, you will have to do occasional repairs and maintenance. The problems might be minor, such as a backed-up drain, or major, such as a leaking roof.

For your own protection, make sure that any repair or maintenance requests from the tenant are put in writing. This creates a record of the request, the nature of the problem, the date it occurred, the action taken, and confirmation of the tenant's satisfaction with the service.

Make sure you follow up with the tenants to confirm whether the contractor you hired to do the work showed up on time and was courteous, and whether the repair was completed to their satisfaction. This information will come in handy when deciding who to call for future repairs. Keep good maintenance records on each apartment or house.

I recommend that you give all your tenants a cell phone number so you can be reached at all times. However, ask that tenants only call during normal work hours unless it's an emergency.

If tenants have a problem, I like speaking to them myself. Not only does this give you a chance to understand the problem, but you may be able to tell the tenants how to fix minor problems themselves.

For example, a tenant called and said that no water was coming out of her bathroom sink faucet. Some landlords might have made a trip to the property or taken the easy (and expensive) way out and called a plumber. But if you ask a few commonsense questions to isolate the problem, you might save yourself both time and unnecessary expenses. I asked my tenant if water came out of the bathtub faucet. She said yes. I asked her whether any other faucets in the house were having problems. She said no. So I realized that the problem was isolated to this one faucet.

It turned out that the aerator (screen) was clogged with debris from the water supply. Over the phone, I was able to instruct her on how to clean the aerator. She was happy to get the problem solved right away and didn't mind helping in the process. I didn't have to drive over to the property or hire someone to go out there. Problem solved!

Here's a trick of the trade: If a tenant is past due on rent and calls in a maintenance request, you may not be obligated to make non-life-threatening normal repairs because your tenant is not in compliance with the terms of the lease. Check with your local laws before doing this, however. Tenants suddenly get motivated to catch up on their rent when they need something repaired.

Accounting for repairs and improvements

It's important to keep accurate records when you repair or improve your rental property because these are both tax deductions. A repair is deductible in the year paid. An improvement is deductible over its IRS depreciable life: 27.5 years for residential building improvements and 39 years for commercial building improvements). A *useful life* is merely the number of years that the lawyers who wrote the tax code in the United States deemed appropriate for the tax life of a building. This is the period of time that you can deduct 1/27.5 of the building cost as depreciation per year on your tax return if you own residential rental property. Although a complete discussion of what is a repair versus an improvement is beyond the scope of this book, here are some general guidelines.

A *repair* keeps property in good operating condition. Repainting, fixing floors and leaks, and replacing broken windows are repairs. An *improvement* adds value to your property or prolongs its useful life. Installing in new flooring, putting in extensive wiring or plumbing, adding a new roof, and repaving a driveway are improvements. If you make repairs as part of an extensive remodeling or restoration, the entire job is an improvement. If you claim large repair deductions and are audited, the IRS may question your repair deductions.

Maintaining a financial reserve

I recommend budgeting 10% of your annual gross income from the property to cover maintenance and repairs. The purpose of a financial reserve is to pay for unexpected repairs as soon as they arise.

For example, a failed heating system must be fixed immediately, or your building could be damaged (frozen pipes in the winter) and your tenants might leave if you don't fulfill your obligation of providing adequate heat in the winter. If you can't afford to maintain a financial reserve for repairs, establish a line of credit that will allow you to pay for unforeseen problems.

Preventative maintenance

The best time to fix a problem is before it even starts. Here are some tips I've learned for making maintenance easier and reduce the inevitable problems you'll face.

Expect the walls to get dirty and scraped through normal use. I use the same paint color for the interiors of all my rental properties. This makes it easy to touch up a wall, and there's never a problem of trying to match the right colors.

Many of my tenants have asked me whether they can paint a room. I usually politely refuse this request because in my experience, most tenants aren't good painters nor do they select the best colors. If the color turns out to be bad, I have to repaint the whole room again after the tenants vacate.

Use quality faucets that can be easily repaired. Leaky faucets can become an irritation to tenants. The faucets don't have to be fancy or expensive, just good quality. This will reduce the chance of leaky faucets and lower your repair bills in the long run.

Develop reliable contacts for repairs and maintenance. Maintenance companies can handle a broad range of services such as plumbing, electrical, and drywall repair. When a problem occurs, you want it fixed right away. Develop good sources for quality, low-priced floor covering. I have used 12-

inch-square vinyl tiles in kitchens and bathrooms. They are easy to install and cost only $1 apiece. This can save you big money in flooring costs.

Use the same brand of locks on all your doors. When one tenant moves out, you can switch locks from one property to another. The locks themselves last a long time, so you can keep them in rotation. But don't use the same locks at the same property after a tenant moves out because this is a potential liability issue. On occasion, tenants leave and don't return all the keys, or they might have made extra copies of the keys. You need to protect yourself and new tenants against someone coming back to the property and gaining entry to an apartment or house.

Label your keys with a code for each building and apartment. Just don't write the full name and address of the property in case someone you don't know finds the keys.

WORKING WITH A PROPERTY MANAGEMENT COMPANY

Property management companies can take the hassle out of renting. When you're first getting started renting property, however, I recommend that you manage your property yourself for several reasons.

First, doing it yourself saves you money that you would normally pay a property management company. You'll most likely get started renting one or two units, which are a manageable number of properties.

Second, and more importantly, managing your property yourself teaches you the ins and outs of property management. That way, you'll better understand what a property management company can offer in the future, if you choose to use one.

In most cases, managing property is really about having a list of people who do different tasks, such as plumbing, electrical work, and yard maintenance. When there's a problem, you simply call a repair person and make sure the problem gets fixed.

Although I prefer to manage properties myself, you might want to hire a property management company for several reasons.

First, property management companies get paid only when you get paid, so it's in their best interest to screen potential tenants and arrange for routine maintenance on the property. Property management companies want reliable tenants who plan to stay a long time, because that means more money for them and less time spent looking for new tenants and losing money through vacancies.

Second, a property management company provides a point of contact for your tenants at all times. If you manage properties yourself and go on vacation or travel frequently, you'll need to find someone to manage your properties in your absence. If you're going to be gone often, you might as well hire a property management company full-time instead.

If you don't want the hassle of dealing with tenants yourself, or you live too far away from your rental property to make it convenient for you to manage the property personally, consider hiring a property management company to screen prospective tenants, collect rent, and arrange for the maintenance of the property.

To find a good management company, check out similar properties that appear well run. Ask tenants whether they are satisfied. Call the owners and ask them how satisfied they are with the management company. Then ask for the name of the property manager.

Remember, having a dependable property manager can be nearly as important as having dependable tenants. A well-managed property will make money for everyone, which can free up your time to do something else, like invest in more real estate!

CONCLUSION

Whether you manage your properties yourself or hire a property management company, you still need to know other people who can help you. First, establish a relationship with an attorney who specializes in evictions in the city where you own your property. I have dealt with good attorneys and slow, inefficient ones. A fast and efficient attorney will save you tons of time, aggravation, and money.

Second, establish a relationship with a CPA (Certified Public Accountant) because you will likely use his or her services for tax return preparation and occasional tax questions when you buy and sell properties.

Finally, consider joining a local rental association. This type of organization can be a wealth of information and has all the forms you need for legally handling all the situations encountered by landlords, such as rent increases, security deposit dispositions, and pay or vacate notices. (Remember that www.deangraziosi.com is an entire resource center with hundreds of forms and documents that you can use.)

The fee to join a rental association is minimal and the benefits are huge! In addition, if you attend meetings, you will likely network with service providers that cater to investors, not to mention all the investors you might meet as well.

Knowing how to rent property is a crucial part of investing in real estate. No matter what the real estate market may be doing in your area, you'll likely rent your property to earn income while waiting to sell it later. Or you may just rent property to earn a steady source of income.

This chapter may be way ahead of where you are right now. But if and when you get to the point of managing your properties, don't forget these simple time-saving and money-saving tips.

CHAPTER 20

STARTING YOUR FIRST DEAL NOW

Do not be too timid or squeamish about your actions.
All life is an experiment.
—RALPH WALDO EMERSON

Now that you've read my book, you may be filled with excitement, knowledge, enthusiasm, and hope. If you're already a real estate investor, I hope I've given you a lot of new ideas to jump-start your investing into high gear. But if you're a first-time investor who has little or no money in savings, you might be asking yourself, "What do I do now?"

No matter how much money or experience you have, I want to suggest some steps for how you can get started. Take a moment to understand your current financial situation, goals, and dreams. Remember, if you don't know where you're starting from, it's hard to get to where you want to go. As part of this introspective look, please go through the steps that I discussed in the book.

First, I taught you that you could make money in any real estate cycle. All you have to do is identify the cycle your real estate market is in and then apply the proper investing strategies. It's literally that simple.

Second, I gave you the tools to help you take action. You may understand how to maximize your potential profits while minimizing your risks in real estate, but until you take action, all your knowledge about real estate is useless.

Finally, I gave you the specific real estate strategies you could apply in your own neighborhood. By applying the correct strategy at the right time, you can achieve massive success in real estate investing.

Keep in mind that these procedures aren't just a once-in-a-lifetime exercise but an ongoing process. Life changes all the time, so reevaluate your financial situation once a year. I know these steps may not sound glitzy or sexy, but they are practical advice that can be vital for succeeding in real estate and in life.

KNOW WHERE YOU ARE

The first step in starting any goal is knowing where you are. Climbing Mount Everest may seem impossible, but it's a lot easier if you know you're going to start ten feet from the top. Now that you've finished reading this book, I recommend you do the following:

1. Prepare a financial statement.
2. Prepare an income statement.
3. Write down your goals.

Prepare a financial statement

A *financial statement* shows your net worth, which is basically how much you're worth. To create a financial statement, take a sheet of paper and divide it into two columns.

In one column, list all your assets; in the other column, list all your debts. Total both columns. Then subtract your total debts from your total assets. This will give you your net worth. You have just prepared your first balance sheet.

For those who have completed this exercise before, it is a good review. Too many people focus solely on income, but it's just as important to build a balance sheet and understand your net worth. If you want to build and retain your wealth, you must focus on both. Believe me, it works!

Prepare an income statement

An *income statement* shows you how much money you have coming in. If your income exceeds your expenses, you have a positive cash flow. If your expenses exceed your income, you have a negative cash flow. Until you prepare an income statement, you may not know where your money is really going.

To prepare an income statement, get another sheet of paper and divide it into columns. Column one is (I hope) the fun one—sources of income. Column two is your list of expenses.

List income and expenses on a monthly basis. If some income or expense occurs on a quarterly or annual basis (such as a quarterly bonus or commission or semi-annual property taxes), you may want to prepare this statement on an annual basis as well as monthly. When you subtract the second column (expenses) from the first column (income), you get a realistic look at your net positive or negative cash flow for the period.

Define your goals

Now that you know where you are financially, you can set goals for where you want to be within a realistic time frame. Take another look at the goals you set in Chapter 11. Reevaluate them and create a plan to get you where you want to be one, three, five, and ten years from now.

You are creating a blueprint for your success, so you want to lay out your plans in as much detail as possible. For example, I have students who set (and surpassed!) a goal to create positive cash flow from purchasing ten properties—enough to make mortgage payments on their home. Other people may want to create a net worth totaling $1,000,000. This is an admirable goal and, with real estate investment, a realistic goal.

So be specific. How many properties at what price and of what type (homes or apartments) do you need to purchase to achieve this goal? As part of your written goals, build a quick schedule to make sure the numbers add up to the goals you set. Include this schedule with your written goals.

One of the most rewarding experiences is to look back on your goals five and ten years later, and see how many of them you achieved. I may not have achieved every single written goal within my specified deadline, but I was pleased to see that I made new achievements that far exceeded some of the goals in shorter time frames! It is amazing the power of written goals. Your subconscious mind immediately begins working on achieving these goals and influences your daily actions toward their success. If you ask most successful people, written goals are an essential part of their achievement personally and professionally.

DEVELOP YOUR REAL ESTATE FOUNDATION

Before you jump into real estate investing, it's important to set up your foundation. This means studying the real estate market in your area and finding people you will need to work with (real estate agents, mortgage brokers, loan officers, repairmen, and so on). Set a firm foundation so when you see a great real estate opportunity, you can jump on it right away. The following seven steps can get you started on your real estate investing career:

1. Fix your credit rating.
2. Decide where you want to invest.
3. Find the people you will need.
4. Get prequalified for the maximum amount of financing from a bank.
5. Apply for a home equity line of credit.
6. Identify other sources of possible financing you could access, including possible partnerships.
7. Study how promissory notes work.

Fix your credit rating
Your credit rating can directly affect your ability to borrow money, so it literally pays to have good credit. If you have a poor credit rating, you can still in-

vest in real estate. You just will have a much tougher time getting a loan than someone with a better credit rating.

The first step to fixing your credit rating is to pay off your credit card debts as much as possible. After banks see that you're making regular payments, they'll gradually boost your credit rating. Establish a record of lowering your debt each year, and within a few years, you'll have most or all your debt paid off and you'll have improved your credit rating at the same time.

Your credit rating can't stop you from investing in real estate, but a poor credit rating can definitely make borrowing much harder than it needs to be, so your first step should be to fix your credit rating as quickly as possible.

Decide where to invest

You know your neighborhood better than any outsider, so that's the best place to start investing. If your neighborhood is getting worse, choose a nearby area where you believe the opportunities are better. In fact, if you want to leave your neighborhood, your first investment can help you move to a better neighborhood and make money at the same time.

If it takes you an hour to get to an area, it's probably too far for you to understand the area with enough confidence to buy property there. As a beginner, start with the most promising area with real estate prices that you can comfortably afford.

After you find an area to invest in, study the real estate cycle for that area. If you choose a desirable neighborhood, it won't matter whether the real estate cycle is up, down, or at the bottom—you'll still find a way to make money!

Study the real estate listings for your chosen area and get a feel for the typical prices and how fast prices may be climbing or falling. Also pick up that area's local newspaper, which may have information that the city newspaper might ignore, such as stories of impending construction projects.

Build your investment team

To invest in real estate, you'll need the help of other people. You'll need an escrow officer or mortgage broker to help you apply for and process a loan. You'll need a real estate agent, who can often give you background information about a piece of property, such as how long it's been on the market or whether the price has dropped since being put on the market.

After you find property you may want to buy, you'll need the help of an appraiser to tell you the approximate value of the property. A home inspector can also help you spot potential problems, such as signs of water damage from a leaky roof or ancient electrical wiring that will need to be updated.

Finally, you'll need people to support your real estate investing business, such as an accountant (CPA) for taking care of your taxes. You'll need an insurance agent to insure any properties that you buy. To protect yourself, you should find an attorney who can advise you on legal matters involving real estate or help you deal with tenant problems if you rent your property.

To fix any problems with your property, you may need to know some handymen or home improvement contractors.

I recommend finding more than one person for each role, such as getting to know two or more real estate agents or two or more contractors. That way, if you need help but your first choice is unavailable, you can rely on the second (or third) one on your list.

The key is to build a solid, reliable network of people. Let everyone know exactly what you're doing as a real estate investor. This not only helps them understand what you may need but also increases the chances that you'll hear of the perfect real estate opportunity. So get ready!

Get prequalified for a loan

Nothing is more frustrating than finding the perfect real estate opportunity but not having the money available to take advantage of it. That's why you should get prequalified for a loan so you know the maximum amount of money you could borrow from a bank.

The earlier exercise in making financial and income statements wasn't just to show you how much money you have; you can also use them to show the bank your financial status. Keep your financial and income statements up-to-date and make extra copies of your Federal income tax returns for the past three years because a lender will ask for them before approving any loan.

The best opportunities tend to go to the person who is best prepared, so make that person you.

Apply for a home equity line of credit

If you own your own home, apply for a home equity line of credit. This will determine how much extra money you may have available (in addition to any loan you get). If you don't own a home, find someone who does and who would be willing to work with you in real estate investing. Then find out how much money they could borrow on their home equity.

Find other sources of money

After you've identified how much money you can borrow through traditional sources, it's time to discover how much money you can borrow through nontraditional sources, such as friends or relatives. The more money you can access right away, the faster you can move when you spot a real estate bargain.

Find at least three other people who may want to partner with you in real estate investing. If your partners have enough money, you can do all the work and they can put up all the money, and everyone can get an equal share of the investment and profits.

Study how promissory notes work

Promissory notes are legal documents that let you borrow from other people, so it's important that you know how they work and how to get one. You can use promissory notes when borrowing money from others or for creating seller financing so you can buy property with no money down.

A promissory note is no different than a traditional bank loan. One person (the borrower) promises to pay back a certain amount of money plus interest by a certain date, and the other person (the lender) lets the person (you) borrow a certain amount of money. If you default on the promissory note, the lender may be able to take possession of any collateral specified in the promissory note.

You'll need a lawyer to help you write a promissory note. It's a valuable tool that can help you borrow money quickly from sources other than banks. The more you understand how promissory notes work, the more they can work to your benefit.

DO YOUR HOMEWORK

After you've fixed your credit rating, lined up sources of money, and gathered a team of real estate agents, loan officers, and so on to help you, you're ready to study your target areas.

One of my favorite pastimes is driving through different neighborhoods until I find one that interests me. I love neighborhoods that are in demand or soon will be because of changing demographics (such as higher gas prices causing people to shorten their commute).

Some signs of a great neighborhood are ones located in a desirable school district, within an acceptable commute to significant employers in the area, or close to public transportation. I'll scour the classified ads in my target markets, call on the ads, and make appointments, looking for bargains such as run-down houses in nice neighborhoods.

I basically canvass an area, logging a lot of miles in my car and on the Internet, jotting down addresses, listing agents' names and numbers, and noting areas where I would like my real estate agent to run searches for me.

The more you look, the more opportunities you will find. Choose an area near you, study the market, and visit houses to see what's available. I don't expect you to make a killing on your first real estate deal; I just want you to get started and see exactly how you can make money.

RUN THE NUMBERS

For each property that you visit, look inside, estimate the work required to fix or improve it, and determine the maximum price you could pay for the property so that if you purchase and finance the property, you could rent it and cover your principal, interest, taxes, insurance, maintenance, and vacancy costs. Oh yes, and you want to have a little left over for positive cash flow!

Don't get discouraged. You might have to look at fifty properties before you find five opportunities. And maybe only one of the fifty properties you previewed works out for you. That's okay. The time you invest in studying different properties is worth it. The key to success in real estate is understanding how to make money from property before you buy. So make sure you identify how to make money with each property right from the start so you won't have to wait ten years (or more) to reap the rewards.

If you're a first-time investor, I recommend that you look around carefully and take your time until you find a property that you feel absolutely comfortable and confident buying. I want your first investment experience to be a positive and profitable one so you'll gain confidence to go out and keep buying more.

CONCLUSION

I had a lot of goals in writing this book, but my most important goal was to teach you as much as I could about the many resources that can help you make a fortune just by learning to think a little bit differently.

After you identify the current real estate cycle, you can find the right property at the right price using the right strategy. You may borrow money from a bank, friends, the seller, or a mixture of many of the creative financing opportunities you've learned. You can start with a lot of money or nothing at all. What is most important is to just get started.

Success in real estate has less to do with how much money you have than with how much creativity and desire you have. That's what this book is all about: helping you realize that you can make a difference in your own life— and the lives of those you care about—by thinking creatively and taking action.

Now that you have a basic understanding of some techniques used by me and others all over the country, you can see that buying property is more than just a transaction. In most cases it's about solving other people's problems.

After you know the seller's personality and their reasons for selling (their "magic buttons"), you'll know the available options that you can mix and match to make the deal work. These techniques and concepts aren't the only financing tools available. When faced with different situations, think outside the box and become creative in your approach to solving problems—for yourself and for others.

I have made a fortune by being creative and solving other people's problems, and you can too. All you need is the desire to move forward, to increase the quality of your life and the lives of those around you. It's that simple! However, you need to put your first step forward and start the process.

Now is the time to go out and achieve your goals, whatever they may be. You have the tools. Achieve or surpass the goals you have set. Take action, and bring those dreams to life! I wish you all the success in the world. And I look forward to hearing from you soon. Send me your stories. My staff and I are here to help as well. I wish you the best of luck—where opportunity meets preparedness. Live life to its fullest!

GLOSSARY

Addendum—An attachment to a real estate contract signed by both parties that covers additional items and agreements not addressed in the original agreement.

Adjustable-rate mortgage (ARM)—A loan with an interest rate that is subject to changes (adjustments) during the term of the loan and based on terms established at the time the loan is made.

Amortization—A reduction of debt on an installment basis over a fixed period of time.

Appraisal—An estimate of the current fair market value of real property.

Appreciation—The increase in value of an asset over time.

Asset—Any possession of value.

Assign or assignment—To legally transfer one's rights in a lease or mortgage to another party.

Assumable loan or mortgage—A mortgage that allows a new buyer to take over payments with the same terms given to the original buyer.

Assumption—Taking over responsibility for payments on a loan.

Balance sheet—A financial statement listing assets, liabilities, and net worth and is often provided to a banker or a mortgage broker when applying for a loan.

Broker—A state licensed agent who, for a fee, acts for property owners in real estate transactions in accordance with state laws and is also capable of managing other real estate agents.

Buyer's broker—A broker or agent who represents the buyer in a real estate transaction.

Buyer's (down) market—A real estate cycle where there are more sellers of properties than there are buyers. This situation can occasionally give buyers more opportunities to buy choice properties at lower prices.

Cash flow—Gross income minus operating expenses (for example, taxes, insurance, and maintenance) and debt service.

Closing costs—Expenses paid to complete a real estate transaction, such as title insurance, closing agent's fees, prorated property taxes, and commissions.

Collateral—The real or personal property pledged to secure a debt.

Commission—A percentage of the sales price paid to the real estate broker upon selling the property, oftentimes split between the buyer's broker and the seller's broker.

Contract—A legal agreement entered into by two or more parties.

Counter offer—A response to an offer that effectively rejects the original offer and introduces a new offer with different terms and conditions.

Deed—A legal instrument that transfers or conveys the property title from the seller to the buyer.

Deed of trust—An instrument by which a borrower transfers title to a third party (trustee) as security for a debt. The beneficiary of the trust is the lender.

Distressed property—Property in poor physical condition that is often priced substantially less than its present value or its future value when renovated.

Dual agent—An agent who represents both the buyer and the seller.

Earnest money—A deposit of money given by the buyer to bind the contract with an offer to purchase real property, usually credited toward the sale price.

Equity—The fair market value of a property less all debts associated with that property (such as any mortgages, loans, or liens secured by that property).

Fair market value—Estimated price in a sale that a property will bring from a willing buyer and willing seller.

Fannie Mae (FNMA)—Nickname for the Federal National Mortgage Association, whose primary function is to buy and sell FHA and VA mortgages in the secondary mortgage market.

Federal Housing Administration (FHA)—An agency of the federal government that insures private first mortgage loans for the financing of new and existing homes and home repairs.

Financing—The use of another party's funding (such as a loan from a financial institution) to purchase property.

Fix and flip—A money-making strategy in which you buy a house, fix it up, and then sell it a short time later for a profit.

Fixed rate—An interest rate that remains constant over the term of the loan, such as fifteen or thirty years.

Foreclosure—The process whereby property pledged as security on a note or loan is sold under court order because the borrower has defaulted on the note.

Home inspection—An examination of a home's construction, condition, and internal systems by an inspector or contractor before purchase.

Housing and Urban Development (HUD)—A department of the federal government responsible for the implementation and administration of the U.S. Government Housing and Urban Development programs, which include FNMA and FHA.

Income property—Property that produces a regular source of rental revenue.

Inflation—An economic occurrence in which real purchasing power decreases as prices of goods and services increase.

Lease—A contractual agreement between the landlord (lessor) and the tenant (lessee) that allows the tenant the use and occupancy of the property for a specified time period.

Lease option—An agreement between two parties in which the party who owns the property sells to the second party the right to purchase the property at a future date.

Leverage—The use of other people's money for investment.

Liability—A debt that is due and payable in the future or an obligation to pay or perform a particular duty.

Lien—A legal claim against property, which grants the holder of the lien the right to take and/or sell the property in the event of a default to satisfy the obligation of the debt.

Limited partnership—A legal organization consisting of two or more parties (a limited partner and a general partner) who own different percentages in the partnership. A limited partner contributes capital but cannot control or manage the partnership and is not liable for debts of the partnership.

Listing broker—A broker who has contracted with a seller to offer the property for sale at a specified price in exchange for a commission or some other consideration.

Loan-to-value (LTV) ratio—The ratio of a loan's value divided by the property's appraised value. Traditional lenders typically prefer to maintain an LTV of 80% or less for first mortgages.

Mortgage—A legal document that pledges property as security for repayment of a loan.

Mortgage broker—A company or individual who matches lenders with prospective borrowers to find the best loans for borrowers.

Mortgagee—The lender of money under the terms of a mortgage.

Mortgagor—The borrower who pledges his or her property to assure performance in repaying the loan.

Multiple Listing Service (MLS)—A regional service whereby members of the Board of Realtors display their listings, generally on a computer network.

Negative amortization—When a loan payment does not cover the entire monthly cost of borrowing, the excess is added to the principal mortgage.

Negative cash flow—When rental and other income does not cover the operating expenses and debt service of the property.

Net worth—Assets minus liabilities.

Note—The legal evidence of debt. *See Promissory note.*

PITI (principal, interest, taxes, and insurance)—Used when a buyer applies for a loan. The lender calculates the buyer's PITI to determine the borrower's actual monthly mortgage-related expenses.

Point—A percentage of the original balance of the loan that the lender charges for making the loan to the borrower. One point equals 1% of the original balance of the loan.

Positive cash flow—When rental and other income more than covers the operating expenses and debt service of the property.

Prime rate—The interest rate that banks charge their best corporate customers.

Principal—The amount borrowed.

Principal amortization—The reduction of the amount of the loan through periodic installment payments.

Private mortgage insurance (PMI)—A policy insuring a lender against a default on a mortgage loan issued by anyone other than the federal government.

Promissory note—A legal document that states a fixed amount of money to borrow, the interest rate, and the length of payment allowed to repay the loan.

Property management company—A company that finds and screens tenants, pays for routine maintenance, and collects rent from tenants for a percentage of the monthly rental income.

Quitclaim deed—A deed used to transfer whatever interest in the property, if any, the grantor may have.

Real estate agent—A person licensed in a particular state associated with a real estate broker who acts on behalf of the broker and has the legal authority to assist buyers and sellers in purchasing and selling real estate.

Real estate owned (REO)—A property that a financial institution owns as a result of a foreclosure.

Real estate tax lien—A lien that is the result of a real estate tax payment default and is generally always in first position above all other liens.

Realtor—A real estate broker or agent who is a member of the National Association of Realtors as well as state and local real estate boards.

Rent—Payments made to the owner for use of that property.

Sales contract—An agreement between a buyer and seller of real property to transfer title to that property at a future date for a specific sum of money.

Seller's market—A real estate cycle in which there are more buyers looking to purchase properties than there are sellers. In this situation, sellers can command higher prices or terms.

Tax lien—A lien imposed against real property for the nonpayment of both real estate and income taxes.

Title—A legal document showing evidence of the ownership rights and obligations of a property owner.

Title insurance—Insurance issued by a title company guaranteeing that the title is good and marketable. Title insurance policies can be issued to protect the mortgagee, the full interest of the buyer, or both.

Title insurance company—A company that performs a title search to make sure that the title of a property does not have any liens against it. The title company also insures the status of the title based on the coverage specified in the sales contract.

Title search—A review of recorded legal documents verifying the current ownership for a piece of property.

ACKNOWLEDGMENTS

They say it takes a village to raise a child and I can tell you it takes a team to create a book. I want to thank my students, my clients, and all from whom I have learned while developing my expertise as a real estate investor. I particularly want to acknowledge Keith and Peyton Bell, a wonderful couple, and perhaps the most meticulous real estate investors I know. They helped me refine the analytical aspects of the book and made certain that all real estate terms were used correctly and appropriately.

I am an expert on real estate but I am not an expert on writing. Just as I advise you to work with top professionals in all your real estate transactions I chose to work with the best people in the industry to ensure the best possible reading experience for my readers. Wallace Wang did much of the heavy lifting and worked as my personal editor and assistant. He was a pleasure to work with and was amazing and wonderful. I also want to thank my publisher Roger Cooper of Vanguard/Perseus. Roger was enthusiastic from the inception of this project and he and his staff were always available to answer questions and guide me throughout the publishing process. I believe in working with good real estate agents and it is no different in the literary world. My literary agent William Gladstone of Waterside Productions Inc. and his associate Ming Russell were simply extraordinary. Bill is responsible for dozens of bestselling books and hundreds of authors, yet he made me feel as if I were his only client. He and Ming were able to address any issue with clarity and vision.

The support of family and friends is vital in every life and mine is no exception. Without that support I would not have been able to take the additional time from normal business and family activities. I am lucky to have such a wonderful family and thank each of them for their understanding and many acts of kindness.

TAKE YOUR SUCCESS TO THE NEXT LEVEL

Visit www.deangraziosi.com and take advantage of the FREE downloads at my resource center where you can find additional tools and strategies to help you get to the level of real estate investing you desire. You will also get free access to my monthly newsletter filled with the latest strategies to help you profit in a changing real estate market.

FREE CONSULTATION

If you would like the opportunity to work with a mentor or get additional or advanced real estate training, please call my office toll free at 1-800-315-7782. Let them know you read my book and that you want additional guidance to achieving financial freedom through real estate investing.

HELP START A CHAIN REACTION

There are so many noble causes and charities out there, but there is one that has touched my heart deeply. Rachel Scott, the first child killed at the Columbine High School shootings in Colorado, has left us with so many incredible gifts that her father and entire family are spreading. They have already spoken in front of over 10 million children worldwide spreading Rachel's words of compassion in the hope that horrific events like Columbine will become only tragedies of the past. I would love if you could assist me in continuing the "chain reaction" of peace that Rachel Scott dreamed of. To learn more, go to www.deangraziosi.com and click on the Rachel's Challenge. Thanks in advance for taking a look.